The Christian Family
Practical Insight for Family Living

The Christian Family
Practical Insight for
Family Living

by
Frederick K.C. Price, Ph.D.

FAITH ONE
PUBLISHING
LOS ANGELES, CALIFORNIA

The Christian Family
ISBN 1-883798-17-5
Copyright © 1996 by
Frederick K.C. Price, Ph.D.
P.O. Box 90000
Los Angeles, CA 90009

Published by Faith One Publishing
7901 South Vermont Avenue
Los Angeles, California 90044

Contents

Part I
MARRIAGE

Chapter 1

MARRIAGE: A DIVINE ORDINANCE

And the Lord God said, It is not good that the man should be alone; I will make him an help meet for him.

And out of the ground the Lord God formed every beast of the field, and every fowl of the air; and brought them unto Adam to see what he would call them: and whatsoever Adam called every living creature, that was the name thereof.

And Adam gave names to all cattle, and to the fowl of the air, and to every beast of the field; but for Adam there was not found an help meet for him.

And the Lord God caused a deep sleep to fall upon Adam and he slept: and he took one of his ribs, and closed up the flesh instead thereof;

And the rib, which the Lord God had taken from man, made he a woman, and brought her unto the man.

And Adam said, This is now bone of my bones, and flesh of my flesh: she shall be called Woman, because she was taken out of Man.

> **Therefore shall a man leave his father and his**
> **mother, and shall cleave unto his wife: and they shall be**
> **one flesh.**
>
> **Genesis 2:18-24**

In this book, I want to discuss marriage and the family from the context of the Christian viewpoint.

I am not interested in what the world thinks or believes. I am only interested in what the heavenly Father thinks. I want to show from the standpoint of our "guidebook" — the Bible — how God created the institutions of marriage and the family.

I am not interested in "opinions," only in what the Word says. I want to bring to bear on the issues of life the things that will result in the greatest degree of blessing, the greatest degree of freedom in the Lord, the greatest degree of love, and the greatest degree of fulfillment.

Purposely, I am going to talk about these things on a street level, a very common level. I do not intend to be vulgar, but if some of this comes out sounding that way, it is not my intention. It is my intention to be understood by the people who really need it. It *is* my intention to say things so simply and clearly and on a down-to-earth level that there will be absolutely no way of misunderstanding.

The first thing I want to establish is that *marriage is a divine ordinance.*

If a couple is living outside a legal and sanctified relationship, their faith will not work, their prayer life will never work, and there will never be real harmony in that relationship.

Without marriage as a divine ordinance, you will not have a family. You may have a group of people all living in the same house, but you will not have a *family*. You will have a living arrangement but not godly relationships.

Of course, I am writing to Christians. Sinners living in today's society do not know any better. That is an entirely different situation. I am writing about people who claim to know Jesus

Christ as their personal Savior. Marriage is God-ordained. It is not a matter of society or custom or culture. It is God's principle.

Proverbs 18:22 says:

Whoso findeth a wife findeth a good thing, and obtaineth favour of the Lord.

You also could substitute *husband* for *wife* in that verse:

"Whoever finds a husband finds a good thing and obtains favor of the Lord."

God ordained that there be husbands and wives. Therefore, it is easy to see that anyone who promotes relationships between men and women outside of marriage is in total and direct opposition to the clearly revealed Word of God. Anything outside marriage is not right and will have to be answered for at the Judgment.

Marriage is honourable in all, and the bed undefiled: but whoremongers and adulterers God will judge.
Hebrews 13:4

Marriage Is Honorable

Some churches will not allow their ministers to marry. But the Word here says **marriage is honourable in all.** You may choose of your own volition not to marry. That is your privilege. No church or person can tell you marriage is not for you, however. The Word says it is honorable in everyone, and that certainly includes preachers, doesn't it? In Paul's letters to Timothy, he said:

Let the deacons be the husbands of one wife, ruling their children and their own houses well.
1 Timothy 3:12

I have heard it preached that Paul meant a man should never have been married but once, and you *could* read the verse like that.

"If a man has been married twice, or three times, or four times, he cannot be a deacon."

However, that is not what Paul was saying. At the time the first churches were being established, Christianity was in its infancy. About ninety-nine and one-half percent of the whole world was what today we would call "pagan." In pagan society, there was polytheism — the worship of many gods — and polygamy — the possession of many wives. In some few societies, there was even polyandry, which meant a woman took many husbands.

Changing Pagan Lifestyles

What the Holy Spirit inspired Paul to write as a guideline for deacons was also for the purpose of bringing born again people, who formerly were pagans, into a proper relationship with His original plan — one husband and one wife. Many pagans were getting saved as Paul and the other apostles came into an area and preached the Word. Then the apostles would establish a church and move on to the next area. They would have to set pastors or elders or deacons over the congregation.

Their choice of pastors, elders, and deacons had to be made from people who, in many cases, were still living according to the customs of the pagan cultures.

So Paul was saying, "Choose a man with only one wife at a time."

Paul was not saying "one wife in the man's total lifetime," but one wife at a time, because polygamy was rampant. In Gentile societies, it was the normal way of life. Jewish culture with its standard of monogamy was unusual for that day.

Paul and the other apostles had to re-educate many of the early Gentile Christians in God's moral laws that the Jewish Christians already knew. Therefore, Paul wrote, **Let the deacons be the husbands of one wife.** I believe that meant for them to have only one wife at a time.

In the 19th century, a group of people started a new "religion," called Mormonism. This group settled what is now the State of Utah, as is commonly known. But when Utah was attempting to be accepted as one of the states of the United States, polygamy became a big issue.

The concept behind the idea of polygamy with this group was that a man had to have more than one wife in order to populate the earth, or to populate the earth with their sect. If a man had more than one wife, he could have a lot of children.

Before becoming a state, the sect had to eliminate that practice from its official religious doctrine. However, there still are members of the group in Utah who practice polygamy. They do not publicize it, but a number of men have more than one wife. Many of them are wealthy. The wives do not simply have many children. Each wife usually is well-educated and makes good money, bringing all of it into one family.

Practiced as part of a religion or not, polygamy is not Scriptural. It may be the custom, but it goes against the teachings of the Bible. God does not hand down customs. He hands down decrees based upon His heavenly law, His character, and His design for the universe.

Then Paul went on to write:

> **I will therefore that the younger women marry, bear children, guide the house, give none occasion to the adversary to speak reproachfully.**
>
> **1 Timothy 5:14**

The point I want to make here is that it is all right for young women to marry if they want to. If you are a lady, do not begin to call me "a male chauvinist pig" and say that I am teaching marriage is the only way for you, or that I am saying you cannot have a job and be independent. But in Paul's day, there was no other course for women than marriage in order for them to have their own homes and be respected.

Sex Ordained Within Marriage Only

God's order is for male and female sexual activities to be carried out within marriage. That does not mean that you *have* to get married. You can live unmarried if you want to. That is your choice. But if you do not marry, then you must not participate in marriage activities. You *can*, of course, but you will not be operating within the blessing and sanction of God.

Also, that verse does not mean that older women cannot marry.

The phrase **that the younger women marry** implies that there will be a husband and a family, that God's plan for replenishing the earth is based on marriage. For a Christian, there is no other way for a male and a female to have an intimate relationship than within the bounds of marriage.

These are not all the scriptures we could look at that concern marriage. But these are representative and give a clear picture that marriage is ordained by God for men and women.

Marriage is a divine ordinance. It is right, sanctioned by God, and the blessing of God is upon it. God started mankind by putting a man and a woman together.

Also, we see that the male partner is usually referred to in Scripture as a husband, not as a "lover," or a "bosom buddy," or as a "companion." For the Christian, there is no other way to establish a morally right male/female intimate relationship than marriage.

The Purpose of Marriage

However, the Lord did not initiate marriage just so that Adam and Eve could begin to replenish the earth. If He could create the planet and everything on it, He could have arranged for babies to be born any way He wanted to. He could have made man able to have babies, if He so desired. That would be no big thing for God.

From Genesis 2:18, however, we see that God did not say He made woman to replenish the earth. He did not make woman just so she could have babies. He did not say woman was made as a plaything for man, or as a possession, a doormat, or a footstool. He did not say He made woman to be a "competitor" with man.

God said He made woman so that man would not be alone. He made Adam a help *meet* appropriate for him.

And I heartily agree with that! It is not good for man to be alone. It certainly would not be good for me to be alone. My wife, Betty, is an important and necessary part of my life. I am so grateful that God Himself said it was not good for man to be alone, because then no one can argue truthfully against that Word.

God did not take a bone out of Adam's foot to indicate that the woman should be under his feet. Nor did He take a bone out of Adam's head to show that woman should be above man. No, God took a rib out of Adam's side, indicating that woman was to walk beside man — not in front of him and not behind or beneath him.

God made man first. Therefore, it is clear that God made woman for man. The term "wife" indicates that there is a "husband," which means there is a family. Then the Lord said man was to *cleave* to his wife. God did not say man should cleave to his girlfriend or to his mistress, but to his *wife.*

Illicit Relationships
Lack the Divine Connection

Have you ever been talking on the telephone, and been cut off? You lost the "connection." That is what happens with relationships outside of marriage. The "connection" is not there. Christians indulging in illicit relationships are not making contact with God in their relationships. They are in the position of being a target for Satan, because they have stopped the angels of God from protecting them. They are outside the realm of safety, because they are operating outside the scope of God's divine order.

If you are living under the same roof with someone as if you were married, you need to get out of that relationship just as you would get off of a sinking ship. There is no protection for you. You have rendered your ministering spirit, your guardian angel, helpless because you are out of the will of God. You are living on dangerous ground and in a perverted situation. No blessings can come to you.

Marriage is the basis of the home, the basis of male and female relationship. Therefore, any relationship not functioning in line with the Word of God is sin. It is wrong and opens up those involved to the attacks of demons. There is nothing the heavenly Father can do, although He might, in His mercy, like to, but He will not protect the areas of your life where sin exists. He cannot protect sin, and if you are in sin, you are outside God's protection. His power operates within the framework of His revealed Word.

If the sanctity of marriage had been maintained in our society, we would not have so much lawlessness and crime. We would not have so many unwed mothers.

We live in a very permissive society. Almost anything goes. Anything that you can think up, you can pretty well do in today's society. I can remember not too many years ago when there were certain things you just did not do publicly. But morality is at a very low ebb today. But what I am talking about in this book is not what the world thinks. As Christians, we should not be interested in what the world thinks, only in what the Heavenly Father thinks. We want to find out from the standpoint of the Word as best we can understand it.

Marriage as a divine ordinance is the beginning of the family.

Chapter 2

THE WEDDING VOWS

Husbands, love your wives, even as Christ also loved the church, and gave himself for it;

That he might present it to himself a glorious church, not having spot, or wrinkle, or any such thing; but that it should be holy and without blemish.

So ought men to love their wives as their own bodies. He that loveth his wife loveth himself.

For no man ever yet hated his own flesh; but nourisheth and cherisheth it, even as the Lord the church:

For we are members of his body, of his flesh, and of his bones.

For this cause shall a man leave his father and mother, and shall be joined unto his wife, and they two shall be one flesh.

This is a great mystery: but I speak concerning Christ and the church.

> Nevertheless, let everyone of you in particular so love his wife even as himself; and the wife see that she reverence her husband.
>
> Ephesians 5:25,27-33

To the man, the scriptures say: "Love your wife as Jesus loved the church. Love your wife enough to give your life for her, if necessary."

To the woman, the scriptures say: "Be subject to your husband in everything, as the church is subject to Christ."

To both, the scriptures say: "Submit yourselves to one another in the reverence of God."

God has so united matrimony with human life that man's deepest interest revolves around this institution. When a man and a woman have chosen each other and come to that moment when they sincerely and publicly join in this covenant for life, they lay down on the altar a holy sacrifice to God, to each other, and to humanity. As they follow the Father's divine order, they find true and lasting happiness.

What Is Love?

The union into which a man and a woman enter with marriage is the closest and tenderest of any union possible between human beings. It is founded upon mutual experience and affection, and for believers, it is a union in the Lord. This union was initiated by God as a provision for the happiness and welfare of mankind. It is designed by God to perpetuate love — His love and His love through us for one another.

How can we know what is love? The Word gives us a clear description.

> If I speak in the tongues of men and of angels, but have not love, I am only a resounding gong or a clanging cymbal.
>
> If I have the gift of prophecy and can fathom all mysteries and all knowledge, and if I have a faith that can move mountains, but have not love, I am nothing.

If I give all I possess to the poor and surrender my body to the flames, but have not love, I gain nothing.

Love is patient, love is kind. It does not envy, it does not boast, it is not proud.

It is not rude, it is not self-seeking, it is not easily angered, it keeps no record of wrongs.

Love does not delight in evil but rejoices with the truth.

It always protects, always trusts, always hopes, always perseveres.

Love never fails. . . .

And now these three remain: faith, hope and love. But the greatest of these is love.

1 Corinthians 13:1-8a,13 NIV

Usually in a wedding covenant service, I have the man look into the eyes of his bride and say:

I take you to be my wedded wife, to love you with all my heart's affection, to endow you with all my earthly possessions, to give you all the honor of my name, and to share with you the grace of my God.

Then I have the woman repeat these words:

I take you to be my wedded husband. Where you go, I will go. Where you live, I will live. Your people shall be my people, and your God is my God.

Then the couple exchange wedding rings. The ring is an unbroken circle, an emblem of eternity. The gold is the symbol of that which is least tarnished and most enduring — the lasting and imperishable faith that is being pledged by the giving and receiving of the rings. With those symbols of purity and endless devotion, the man and woman are wed, and the marriage vows are sealed.

A Wedding Blessing

My desire and blessing for each couple truly married in God is this:

From this day forward, as you go down life's pathway together, may love be the charmed word in all of your relationship.

May the circles of your rings typify your unending happiness.

May Jesus truly be the head of your home, the unseen guest at every meal, the silent listener to every conversation.

May Heaven's constant benediction crown your union with ever increasing joy and blessedness and unite your hearts and lives by the grace and true affection of a happy marriage.

A Recommitment of Vows

However, many of you are like I was. As soon as the preacher said, "You may kiss the bride," I really did not hear anything else. All I wanted was for him to tell us it was over so that I could get out of that "monkey suit" and get out of that church. I was not saved at the time, and I did not hear anything else. All I wanted was *out!* That was more than thirty years ago, but I still remember how it was.

If your marriage was like that, and you feel a lack in the area of commitment; or if your wedding was not conducted by a minister, and since then, you and your mate have been saved or received fuller knowledge of the ordinance of marriage, perhaps you might consider going to your pastor and having him conduct the wedding ceremony all over again as a celebration or a memorial. Many people do this on certain anniversaries.

A Wedding Prayer

Heavenly Father, we praise You and thank You for these dear, precious people who stand in Your presence repeating their wedding vows.

I ask for them, Father, as they walk down the path of life together, that from this day forward their love for one another will grow more precious as each day comes and goes.

I ask You that, as they walk hand in hand with You, Your love will permeate their lives, and they will become a beacon light to others. And as others look upon their union, they shall know that surely these two walk with the living God.

*Father, I thank You that their life together will be as a **city set on a hill** (Matt. 5:14). I thank You that from this day forward, everything to which they put their hands will prosper. As they walk with You, allowing themselves to be led by Your Spirit, allowing Your word to be their marching orders, I thank You that they will prosper in everything they do.*

And, Father, I ask You to impress upon each of their hearts that the only "bill of divorcement" that should ever come between them should be the green grass upon one or the other's grave.

I commend this couple into Your care and into Your keeping, knowing that no demon in hell, no man or beast, can ever pluck them out of Your hand, for they are secure in You.

In the name that is above every name, the name of Jesus, we ask these things. Amen.

Chapter 3

LET NO MAN PUT ASUNDER

Mark 10:9, which I believe has been greatly misunderstood, is frequently used as part of wedding covenants.

> **What therefore God hath joined together, let not man put asunder.**

What *does* that verse mean?

Traditionally, what is understood by that verse is this:

If a man and woman get married, and someone comes between them causing them to split up — to get a divorce — then they have been **put asunder.**

However, I believe there is another aspect to that verse. I think there is another revelation involved.

If the traditional interpretation of that verse is true, then the implication is that *God joined together every couple that is married.* All of us know that is not true. Some people who are married had no business becoming involved with each other in the natural, much less in the spiritual sense which involves God.

If that verse is a blanket endorsement by God of every marriage, then it has to mean that God joins every couple together.

But the emphasis is on *what* God has joined, meaning man and woman in the institution of marriage! That is what I believe that verse is saying.

If every marriage is ordained by God, then free will is eliminated — and that is unscriptural. That would mean I had no choice in marrying Betty, and she had no choice in marrying me. That would mean our marriage was ordained by God, and our wills were *not* free to choose. If that were true, it would make God a liar!

He said, **Choose you this day whom ye will serve** (Josh. 24:15).

If we are allowed to choose in as eternally important a thing as serving God or serving the devil — in other words, to choose salvation — then surely we are allowed to choose whom to marry. God did not say that I had to marry Betty and she had to marry me.

This may shock some readers, but I believe I could have married someone else, and she could have married someone else. If that someone else was born again and got in agreement with me in the marriage, then God would have blessed our marriage just the same.

I do believe that, without question, God knows who is *best* for you and who you are best for, and He will let you know if you seek Him in that matter. But it is still your choice!

I was not even a Christian when Betty married me, and the Word says, **Be ye not unequally yoked together with unbelievers** (2 Cor. 6:14).

So God would not have made her marry me when I was not even saved. If the traditional interpretation of Mark 10:9 is right, then God would have violated His Word in 2 Corinthians 6:14.

Betty prayed, and she did not have full knowledge on how to pray as she does now. But out of the sincerity of her heart, she asked God for a Christian husband. That was the desire of her heart. And God's principles, or laws, work whether you know there is a law or not. Get in line with the principle of that law, and it will work for you. Come against that principle, and it will work against you, whether you are aware of the law or not.

The Word says:

> . . . **What things soever ye desire, when ye pray, believe that ye receive them, and ye shall have them.**
> **Mark 11:24**

She did not know that was in the Bible. She did not know how to "stand" on that promise in faith, but she did believe that she would receive what she asked for — and the law worked for her. God knew I would be the best person for her, and that she would be the best person for me — not the *only* person, but the best one, for each of us. I believe that God answered her prayer even when she did not really know how to pray.

Every Marriage Is Not "Made in Heaven"

Couples can marry for various reasons then come to just tolerate one another. You can live in toleration for a long time, but that does not mean that person is the best person for you. I know situations where folks stayed together because of the children. They really hated one another, and hated every moment of their association together after a certain point.

But they said, "We don't want the children to be without a mother or a father," and they stayed in that hellish situation for the "sake of the kids."

So everyone who is married is not necessarily married to the best one for them, or to the one whom God has chosen for them. I do believe, however, that once married, we should stay married. That is God's will in the situation. Even for Christians, it does not always work that way because they do not always have the spiritual knowledge necessary to make the situation work.

The only thing that made our marriage work in the beginning was the love in our hearts for Jesus and for God. She already had that when we married, and I had it after I became born again. Then we wanted to please Him more than we wanted to please ourselves. Betty's love for Jesus and her desire to do what was His perfect will was all that kept her with me in those early years of our marriage. I was not easy to live with. Not that I beat her, or went out and got drunk, or stayed out all night, and all that junk. But I was so immature and so ignorant of what life was all about that I made a lot of wrong decisions, and she had to suffer the consequences along with me.

It is not so bad when you have to suffer from the consequences of your decisions all by yourself, but when you drag yourself and your family into trouble as well, that is rough. So I made her existence hell on earth. It was only the grace of God in her that kept her from leaving me. Our relatives told her to leave me, but she didn't because she loved the Lord. Thank God for that, because we stayed together until I could grow up spiritually and get hold of the Word of God.

I do not know whether she could have a better husband, but I do know that I could not have a better wife. I do not know whether the average woman could stay married to me! That is not because I am a bad guy. I want to be, and try to be, an excellent husband. I work toward that goal. But I am a very honest person, very open and frank. Not everyone can handle that. Many people get their feelings hurt and just fall apart. My intention is never to hurt them, but I do tell the truth.

If you fix me some food that I do not like, I am going to tell you I do not like it! If it does not taste good to me, then it just does not taste good. I am sorry, but I am not going to tell you it does. I am not going to "string you along" to be polite. That would lead you into thinking you have cooked some great dinner for me. If I accepted it, then you would think you had "hit the mark" with me. The next thing I know, you would cook the same thing the next time I came to dinner. Then three months later, and six months later, and so forth, you are going to have that same meal.

All the time, having to be polite and eat that "special" food that I really do not like is going to gnaw away at my insides. The frustration will come out in some other activity or in some other area of life that we are involved in together. It is much more practical, as well as right, to deal from a truthful heart.

I am transparent. What you see is exactly what you get, and everyone cannot handle that. Not everyone is ready for Fred Price, but thank God, Betty is. In our marriage, we have a perfect fit, a "number nine foot in a number nine shoe." However, I still do not think God *ordained* that she marry me or that I marry her. It was our choice.

God Does Not Make Mistakes

I know people who are very happily married in the Lord, but this is not their first marriage. So if God ordains all marriages — causes them to happen — then He made a mistake the first time! Now God does not make mistakes, so why did you have to go through one or more husbands or wives to finally get the right one, if God is ordaining all marriages?

If you do not agree with me on this, just lay it aside until we can ask the Lord Himself. Because this point will not affect your salvation. Going to Heaven does not depend on whether you agree with my interpretation of this verse.

However, I do believe what this verse is talking about is the very thing we have seen played out in society over the years and becoming more and more prevalent: the demise and destruction of marriage as an institution. I believe that is what God was talking about. A lot of couples are living together who are not married. Society has come to the point where it does not have much respect for marriage.

I can remember the time when it was a disgrace for someone to get a divorce. It was considered disrespectful, and people frowned on it. Now it is no big deal. You can get married one year, get a divorce the next, and then go marry someone else immediately, and no one thinks anything about it. Nobody cares. In fact, society today does not even encourage marriage. Modern thinking and customs encourage living on a trial basis.

God ordained the institution of marriage. He ordained that a man and a woman be joined together in a union. And that is what the Holy Spirit was talking about in Mark 10:9, I believe. **Let no man put asunder.** Yet, that is what man is now doing. In general, in this country, educational, social, cultural, and even religious leaders are trying to put asunder the institution of marriage by treating it with very little respect.

Through ridiculing marriage openly in literature, films, and television, today's writers, actors, and directors let you know marriage is not necessary. You do not have to waste time getting a license. Just live together and do your own thing. Through infiltrating our society with the concept of "free love," Satan has attempted to put asunder marriage. That was what Jesus was talking about.

People get married for all kinds of reasons. Sometimes it is strictly convenience. Sometimes it is position. Sometimes it is the color of the skin. Among Caucasians, there is basically one color — white. But among blacks — and as a black man, I am free to say this — there are various shades of color from very light to so dark there is a bluish cast to the skin. And some light-skinned blacks look for others like themselves to marry, or they look for somebody very dark, unlike themselves. Then those very dark may look for those very light to marry.

Some people look for mates with curly hair or with straight hair, or men look for women with breasts of a certain size or shape. Women may look for men who are handsome or well-to-do. Then when you find the person who fits your fantasies and marry him, or her, you may find that person the absolute worst person on earth to live with!

You thought you could not live without "Mr. Tall, Dark, and Handsome" (or "Miss Pretty" or "Miss Perfect Shape"). Now that you have that person, you find you cannot live *with* him, or her.

People Get Married for Many Reasons

My point is that people get married for all kinds of reasons, and you cannot blame God for those reasons. So that is why I do not believe this verse was referring to an individual man and woman, but to an institution. Our society has been moving more and more toward "putting asunder" the institution that God ordained. That is what Jesus was talking about. Living together without marriage is a satanic concept.

I believe without a doubt that God knows the best person to fit your life and His purpose for you. If you learn to wait on God, I do not have any question but that He will show you the right woman, or the right man. But there is no way I can believe that God is putting together all the people that are together. Because if He is — He does not know what He is doing!

I have seen people who were miserable their entire lives. They were people who never grew up, never changed. They were the same at 80 years of age as they were at 8 years of age. And the people married to them were miserable because of their attitudes and behavior. God does not ordain that.

If God would put people together against their wills, then why would He not save people against their wills? That would be of much more importance in eternity. We would not even have to preach. We would not have to tell people of the Gospel of Jesus Christ. They would get saved or not get saved anyway. If God does not "ordain" your salvation, then He certainly is not going to "ordain" a certain person for you to marry.

Chapter 4

THE OBLIGATION OF MARRIAGE

We are moving into a very touchy area in this chapter, and I want to preface my remarks by saying that we want to find God's best on this subject:

Once you are married, how obligated are you to stay with a husband?

How obligated is a man to stay with a wife?

According to the Apostle John:

> **Then said Jesus to those Jews which believed on him, If ye continue in my word, then are ye my disciples indeed;**
>
> **And ye shall know the truth, and the truth shall make you free.**
>
> **John 8:31,32**

The point I am making is that God's Word is not going to put you in a box. The Word will not frustrate you, if you are willing to hear it and willing to obey it. It will not "blow you away." The Word will not put you under condemnation but set you free.

If you do not want to live right, there is nothing anyone can say that you will accept — unless they agree with you in your sin. But the Word of God brings freedom. It brings truth. It brings clarity, and it will help you to see situations clearly.

All pastors today have to deal with people from the society in which *we* live, just as the apostles had to deal with new Christians re-born out of the cultures of that day. We have to deal with people getting divorces, people already divorced, people who have been married four, five, and six times — and they want to get married again. But what do you tell them? How do you deal with them?

We need to realize that there is the "letter of the law" — legalism, Pharisaism — and there is the "spirit of the law." The Word very clearly says the letter kills, but the spirit brings life.

> **Who also hath made us able ministers of the new testament; not of the letter, but of the spirit: for *the letter killeth, but the spirit giveth life.***
>
> 2 Corinthians 3:6

In reading any scripture, what we need to find out are these questions:

What was God's intent? What is His purpose in saying whatever we are reading? What is the "bottom line," the final thing He is trying to get across to us?

Those are the things we need to be very careful about. Also, we must be careful not to take verses out of their setting, and we must try to understand the social setting in which the Holy Spirit was explaining any particular principle, law, or concept.

When Does Your Obligation End?

Looking again at Genesis 2:24, we see what kind of obligation a married person has and how God views the responsibilities of marriage.

> **Therefore shall a man leave his father and his mother, and shall cleave unto his wife: and they** [plural] **shall be one** [singular] **flesh.**

So it would seem to me that if I get rid of my wife, I am getting rid of myself because the Word says we are *one*. When we come together under God, we become *one*. We are no more *two*. Now keep that in mind. How obligated am I to stay with my wife, and how obligated is she to stay with me? We are married, but can she just drop me like a hot potato? Can I drop her and be in line with the Word of God?

This area needs to be dealt with, because today, it is unusual to find couples who have been married to each other for more than twenty-five years. It is not unusual to find Christians who have been partners in multiple marriages. Probably the majority of the members of my own church, Crenshaw Christian Center, have been married more than once. At this point, however, I am not addressing that fact. What I want to discuss, regardless of anyone's personal life or example, is exactly what the Word says about the obligation involved in the institution of marriage.

Even with counseling before marriage, most of the time, the same people will be back *after* marriage to discuss problems. Many times, very shortly after marriage, already they are considering divorce. We have counseled with people who have not been married three months, yet they are considering divorce!

But what does the Word say? If your wife burns your eggs, do you have a right to seek a divorce? That may sound funny, but most of the troubles in marriages and the reasons people have for seeking a divorce are just as foolish. Of course, there are some situations that become really terrible, really hellish in which to live. But a large percentage of the time, the reasons for divorces are so "Mickey Mouse" it is unreal.

The causes are ignorance or self-will. People just are unwilling to do what is right if it takes self-discipline and self-sacrifice. Each wants his own way. Each is going to *have* his own way, and if he does not get his own way, he is going to get a divorce.

God Is Not the Author of Confusion

In the book of Deuteronomy, we see the perimeters that God set for unregenerate mankind in obligations in marriage.

> When a man hath taken a wife, and married her, and it come to pass that she find no favour in his eyes, because he hath found some uncleanness in her: then let him write her a bill of divorcement, and give it in her hand, and send her out of his house.
>
> And when she is departed out of his house, she may go and be another man's wife.
>
> Deuteronomy 24:1,2

> It hath been said, Whosoever shall put away his wife, let him give her a writing of divorcement:
>
> But I say unto you, That whosoever shall put away his wife, saving for the cause of fornication, causeth her to commit adultery: and whosoever shall marry her that is divorced committeth adultery.
>
> Matthew 5:31,32

God is not the author of confusion, is He? But it almost seems as if some confusion is going on here. Here Moses was passing on God's will in the form of laws, and he says a wife who was divorced could marry someone else. Yet it sounds as if Jesus was saying you could not marry again without commiting adultery. But Jesus only said what He heard the Father say (John 5:19), so there has to be some confirmation between these two scriptures. There must be a correspondence there. There must be guidelines.

Without guidelines, there would be no morality, no reverence of life or other people. Look what is happening today when we still have some guidelines or standards operating. What would the world be like without any?

In Paul's first letter to the Corinthian church, he said.

> And unto the married I command, yet not I, but the Lord, Let not the wife depart from her husband.
>
> 1 Corinthians 7:10

That is the ideal way. That is the highest, or perfect, will of God. But then Paul goes on:

> But and if she depart, let her remain unmarried, or be reconciled to her husband: and let not the husband put away his wife.
>
> But to the rest *speak I, not the Lord:* If any brother hath a wife that believeth not, and she be pleased to dwell with him, let him not put her away.
>
> And the woman which hath an husband that believeth not, and if he be pleased to dwell with her, let her not leave him.
>
> For the unbelieving husband is sanctified by the wife, and the unbelieving wife is sanctified by the husband: else were your children unclean; but now are they holy.
>
> But if the unbelieving depart, let him depart. A brother or a sister is not under bondage or under obligation in such cases: but God hath called us to peace.
>
> 1 Corinthians 7:11-15

Now if divorce is categorically wrong, with no exceptions, why does the Word allow for exceptions? If divorce is wrong, it is always wrong. Yet obviously, from the Word, God allowed exceptions. Many people have been divorced and are remarried in the Lord, yet the guilt and condemnation of religious teachings keep them from being happy. They feel very guilty about their present marriages, and that takes away any possibility of joy. Their present marriages become shaky because of guilt.

Living an Abundant Life

Look at John 10:10:

> The thief cometh not, but for to steal, and to kill, and to destroy: I am come that they might have life, and that they might have it more abundantly.

Abundant life cannot be had by a mother trying to raise several children by herself and be both mother and father. Abundant life cannot be had by a woman married to a monster who beats her and abuses, or even violates, the children. I cannot believe God intends for one of His children to remain in a relationship with a child of the devil and be abused or perhaps even killed. I do not believe that pleases God, or that you have to stay there "come hell or high water." That is not *abundant living*.

In a case such as that, however, the person involved must make the decision in line with his or her conscience.

I have sat across my desk from many people caught in such situations and wanted to tell them, "Why don't you leave that person?"

That is what I *wanted* to say, but I would not dare say it, because the counselee would be certain to go out and say, "Pastor Price told me to divorce you."

Then two weeks later, here comes "Godzilla" hunting me down! Oh, no! Seriously, the choice to leave has to be made by the woman or man involved. No one else, not your pastor, parents, or children, should make that kind of choice for you.

What I do in these cases is let the person know what the options are. There always is more than one way. One way may cost you more than you are willing to pay, but there always are alternatives.

I remember the Nuremberg Trials held after World War II where accused Nazis were tried for alleged war crimes.

There were those who testified, "I had no choice. I had my orders. I could not help myself. There was nothing else I could do. I had to turn the ovens on with Jews inside. I had to shoot them down. I had my orders."

No, that person did not have to do the things he did. There *was* an alternative. But that alternative would have cost him a high price, probably his own life. Still, he had an alternative, and he made his choice. There always is a second or a third way out.

So what does a wife do in an abusive marriage. Does she stay and watch that man abuse her children? I know of situations where men were having forcible sexual relations with their daughters. Is that mother supposed to remain in that situation?

Make the Word Your "Bottom Line"

The bottom line must be this: Whatever you do, let it be from the standpoint of the Word of God to the best of your ability.

> **If it be possible, as much as lieth in you, live peaceably with all men.**
>
> **Romans 12:18**

All men would take in your husband or wife. But notice what Paul said: **If it be possible.** If you are in an impossible situation — and as a pastor I have seen some impossible situations — you had better think about the life you have chosen. Is there a better way? Whatever decision you make, I know God wants you to be happy.

If you really want to grow in the Lord, and if it is possible to be at peace, then the best way is to stick with the marriage. If you grow in God, you will have to grow somewhere, and the next situation might be worse! You can speak in tongues and quote all the scripture you want, but you are still going to have to mature. And it takes time to grow.

If you are really committed to the Word and committed to one another, you are going to stay there and work it out. There may be some rough edges which will take some time to smooth off or sand down until everything fits, but it will be worth it in your Christian life as well as your personal life.

Although it may seem at first glance as if these scriptures about marriage are inconsistent, God *is* consistent. It must be possible to reconcile the seeming inconsistencies between these scriptures. One key thing involved is whether you have a heart of flesh or a heart of stone.

After the New Covenant

After Jesus ascended to the Father, and the new covenant with man became effective, mankind was able to be born again. Those who accepted the only way back to God no longer had hard hearts. God had promised Israel through the prophets of old that the day was coming when He would give them new hearts. (Ezek. 11:19.) Finally, that day arrived.

So when Paul wrote to the Corinthians, he was writing to Christians who had been pagans and who still had to live in the middle of a pagan culture. When you read the New Testament, you need to remember that it was written for born again believers. It was not written for the world. The Bible is a book written for the people of God.

In fact, when Jesus told the Pharisees that Moses had allowed exceptions to the *one flesh* ideal of God because of their hardness of heart, He was saying they had *unregenerate* hearts. Israel, although called the "chosen people," were not yet children of God.

> **Now I say, That the heir, as long as he is a child, differeth nothing from a servant, though he be lord of all.**
>
> **Galatians 4:1**

The phrase *children of Israel* means *children of Jacob* because Jacob's name was changed to Israel. They were called "servants of Jehovah," but they were not the children of God. Those who receive Jesus and are adopted through Him into the family of God are the children of God, the *Israel of God*.

> **For in Christ Jesus neither circumcision availeth anything, nor uncircumcision, but a new creature.**
>
> **And as many as walk according to this rule, peace be on them, and mercy, and upon the *Israel of God* [those of** every race who are born again through Christ].
>
> **Galatians 6:15,16**

Jesus is the firstborn of God. Jesus is called **the firstborn among many brethren** (Rom. 8:29).

> **For as many as are led by the Spirit of God, they are the sons of God.**
>
> **For ye have not received the spirit of bondage again to fear; but ye have received the Spirit of adoption, whereby we cry, Abba, Father.**

> **The Spirit itself beareth witness with our spirit, that we are the *children of God:***
>
> **And if children, then heirs, heirs of God, and joint-heirs with Christ; if so be that we suffer with him, that we may be also glorified together.**
>
> **Romans 8:14-17**

The children of God are those who receive and accept Jesus Christ as Savior and Lord.

Jesus once told His disciples:

> **It is the Spirit that quickeneth; the flesh profiteth nothing: the words that I speak unto you, they are spirit, and they are life.**
>
> **John 6:63**

Did He mean that those words floating out of His mouth were little spirit beings, little entities that sort of floated along the ether waves? No, of course not. What He meant was that the words He was speaking to them were not addressed to the flesh, the ears or intellect of the natural man, but to the spirit man.

That is why the people had such a hard time understanding Him. His words were addressed to their spirits, even though the spirits were still "dead." Those who received His words and pondered them received life and received hearts of flesh.

God's Word and God's Works Are Consistent

We read the Bible and see laws and principles and examples, then we see God moving in the lives of people today in ways that seem to be contradictory. But experiences in God cannot be inconsistent with the Word. Ultimately, experience and the Word must agree. God will not tell us one thing in the Bible and then go and do something else in life.

1 Corinthians 2:11-14 tells us:

> **For what man knoweth the things of a man, save the spirit of man which is in him? even so the things of God knoweth no man, but the Spirit of God.**

> Now we have received, not the spirit of the world, but the Spirit which is of God; that we might know the things that are freely given to us of God.
>
> Which things also we speak, not in the words which man's wisdom teacheth, but which the Holy Ghost teacheth; comparing spiritual things with spiritual.
>
> But the natural man receiveth not the things of the Spirit of God: for they are foolishness unto him: neither can he know them, because they are spiritually discerned.

Those verses are a warning not to try to interpret things of God with the natural mind. If the Word and God's moving in people's lives *seem* contradictory, it means that we are not looking at one or the other with our spirits. Either we are reading the Word or judging experiences with our natural minds.

The main reason people are confused concerning the obligation of marriage today is that the Church has not done what God commissioned it to do. Jesus said to *feed* His sheep and His lambs, and if they had been fed properly with the Word down through the ages, the Body of Christ today would be strong and able to feed on the strong meat of the Word.

If people knew the perfect will of God from His Word and were able to walk in that, there would not be any divorces among Christians. There might be some before people were born again, but not after.

The obligation of marriage, then, in God's highest will is *to stay married*. New life (babies) should only be created in the crucible of marriage. Most people do not realize that by getting married and beginning a family, they have become workers with God. He is allowing you, in one sense, to become the "creators" of new life.

Therefore the real obligation of marriage would be to choose your mate spiritually, become one flesh, and then stay married for life. The ideal assumes, however, that both husband and wife are starting out as children of God, filled with the Spirit, knowing their covenant rights, and walking in the Word.

But not very often do people get married on that basis. They get married for all kinds of reasons and on all sorts of foundations. It is not very likely that they will be able to completely fulfill the obligation of marriage: to become one flesh and not be separated.

Marriage does not work by itself. Say both husband and wife marry at twenty years of age. They are combining forty years of walking alone. Suddenly, they are to amalgamate and change their own ways to accommodate another life. That takes time — plus the knowledge of what is required and the desire to submit to one another!

God's best is to have two people marry who love the Word enough to make whatever adjustment is necessary so that the Word has first place in their lives. If they do that, there is no way they cannot have a successful relationship.

In the next chapter, we are going to discuss some of the exceptions to the obligation of marriage, situations from the Bible that alter the traditional view of marriage and divorce.

Chapter 5

DIVORCE: ANOTHER VIEW

In this chapter, I want to share something that is very different about divorce. I believe it will be a blessing and a help to some people. I have never heard anyone else deal with the subject in exactly this way. And I believe this is a revelation given me by the Lord to help clear the air, to help some people that have been caught in situations of divorce.

Today, there are almost as many divorces as there are marriages. That situation needs to be dealt with, and those people need to have something from the Word besides condemnation. They need to be loved and not ostracized. They need to be set free.

This other-than-traditional view of divorce I am presenting is only to use the Word in order to help people who are hurting. You do not have to accept my interpretations. If you do not agree, let us just stay in love in Jesus. Views on divorce will not affect your salvation. If you disagree with me, I cannot do anything about it, because I am not going to argue. If this helps you, fine. If it does not, then there is nothing I can do about it, is there?

This view is, I believe, revelation from God as I studied these scriptures to feed the sheep placed under my care. I have not gotten my ideas from experience or from trying to justify my own actions. I have never been divorced and have had the same wife more than thirty years. We have a blessed and happy marriage, so I do not need this teaching for myself.

What About Divorce?

Many people who come to me for counseling have these questions:

If I get a divorce, can I get married again?

Will I be living in sin if I remarry?

Will God bless me after I am divorced?

Am I out of line with the Word of God?

These are legitimate, common situations with which pastors have to deal.

Look again at Matthew 5:31,32:

> **It hath been said, Whosoever shall put away his wife, let him give her a writing of divorcement:**
>
> **But I say unto you, That whosoever shall put away his wife, saving for the cause of fornication, causeth her to commit adultery: and whosoever shall marry her that is divorced committeth adultery.**

That is about as strong as it can be. But what was Jesus really saying here in the total context of the Word concerning the interpersonal relationship of a man and a woman?

We need to get all of the principles involved, or the devil will be able to put people in the bondage of condemnation. If you take these verses out of context and consider them singly, it looks as if a divorced person could never remarry — and some churches interpret the Word that way.

Those denominations and groups hold to their interpretations dogmatically and adamantly. They would not change to save their lives. A divorced person cannot be accepted totally in their midst. A divorced person cannot be a minister or even hold an office. And that person is doomed to live single the rest of his life, if he stays in that group.

But if their interpretation is right, an awful lot of Christians are living in adultery today. So it really behooves us to take a good look at the entire teaching about marriage and divorce in the Bible.

Mark 10:2-9 states:

And the Pharisees came to him, and asked him, Is it lawful for a man to put away his wife? tempting him.

And he answered and said unto them, What did Moses command you?

And they said, Moses suffered to write a bill of divorcement, and to put her away.

And Jesus answered and said unto them, For the hardness of your heart he wrote you this precept.

But from the beginning of the creation God made them male and female.

For this cause shall a man leave his father and mother, and cleave to his wife;

And they twain shall be one flesh: so then they are no more twain, but one flesh.

What therefore God hath joined together, let not man put asunder.

In Genesis, God said of a man and a woman, "They shall be one flesh." So what was Jesus saying in this passage from Mark? Was He contradicting the Father?

I believe He was saying the Father's intention in the beginning was for every man to have a wife, every woman to have a husband, and each couple to have children. Each man and woman who were joined would become one flesh and never, but never, be disjoined or separated.

However, we are talking about God's intent, His perfect plan.

His perfect plan would have been in operation if man had never sinned. But man did sin. Many things have happened in mankind that are the result, or consequence, of Adam and Eve's original sin. God's perfect plan has never yet been able to be set fully into operation.

God, who is omniscient (all wisdom and all knowledge), made His plan for mankind knowing that man was going to sin. However, God's foreknowledge does not mean that man *had* to sin. To sin or to obey God was still man's free choice, although God knew in advance what Adam and Eve would do. Because of His foreknowledge, however, God was able to have contingency measures ready to deal with events.

God's Best Plan

God's best, His primary plan, was that man not sin. But man did sin, and God's secondary plan came into operation.

God's primary plan was for man and woman to be one flesh and never to separate. *But that was based on mankind never sinning.*

That principle requires mankind to be innocent in heart. It requires the spirits of mankind to be just as they came from the hand of God. Through obedience to God, they would have moved from moral innocency into moral perfection. But they did not. Not only did Adam and Eve mess up creation, mankind, and the world, but they messed up the family relationship.

In Adam and Eve's descendants, their spirits were (and still are) not innocent. Jesus knew this when He pointed out to the Pharisees that Moses wrote them a precept of divorce because of the hardness of their hearts. In other words, something was wrong with man's heart. The hearts of mankind today are estranged, or alienated, from God — just as they have been ever since Adam and Eve.

Your spirit being, the real you, is separated and cut off from God, not functioning according to God's original design. So God's alternative, or permissive plan was to allow a writing of divorcement. That is not His perfect will, but He permits it just as He permitted animal sacrifices.

Why were the Israelites allowed to make animal sacrifices? They were given a way to deal with the fact that because of Adam's sin, redemption was required.

Why did God make all these adjustments?

He allowed these things because *He had made man with a free will,* which added a "risk factor" to God's plan.

The Risk Factor

The risk factor involved in creating a being with a free will is this: the being might do his own thing and not God's will. He might exercise the right to choose against, and not for, God.

Sure, God knew what Adam was going to do, but apparently the Lord felt the end result — a people who chose to love Him and voluntarily be His children — was worth the risk factor.

There are risk factors in anything we do today. Can you be sure how your own children will turn out? The alternative is not to have any children.

When you buy an automobile, there is a risk involved of flat tires, accidents, and breakdowns. The alternative is not to own a vehicle.

To achieve His purpose, God could create beings in His image, with all the risks of free will, or not have mankind at all. He chose the risk alternative. Then, knowing that many men and women would choose against Him and live with hardened hearts, God provided ways to minimize the risks.

Just think what would happen if God had said to Adam's imperfect descendants:

"You must be perfect. If any of you ever sin, you are doomed. If you commit one sin, you are finished."

There would not be a human race today if God had not made provision for our failures, our "hardness of heart." Thank God for His mercy. Thank God for His adjustments.

Because of man's unregenerate heart, God had no other choice than to allow standards in which man could operate. God's perfect standard was no longer possible for man to reach, and if He set a standard no one could reach, then His standard would not help man but hurt him. So He set an "allowable" standard that man could reach while a plan of redemption was being carried out to bring man back up to God's perfect standard.

A young lady and a man came to me some time ago. She wanted to get married, but he had been married before. He was a member of a church that is very legalistic. He felt that as long as his former wife was alive, he could not get married — and she might live to be ninety years old.

He was very adamant about it and said, "I do not believe that I can get married."

I read him some scriptures that to me seemed very clear on the subject, but he said, "No, I can't see it."

So I asked the young woman, "Why do you want to marry a guy like that? If he is not comfortable marrying you, then there is trouble before you even get in the starting gate."

I do not believe God wants someone to live the rest of his or her life alone until a former wife or husband dies. I do not believe that is God's intent. I have seen Him bless too many relationships where the man or woman, or both, came out of bad, tragic backgrounds. Yet, when they gave their lives to God and began to live for Him, He blessed their relationship. That tells me there is more to all of this than the *letter* of the words on the page. The *spirit*, the intent, behind the words is what is important.

Two Kinds of Principles

There are two types of principles or laws in the Word: one type never allows an exception, and the other allows for extenuating circumstances. Some things are revealed in the Word that are absolute. They are fixed laws. For example, when Jesus talked to Nicodemus about salvation, He said:

> . . . Verily, verily, I say unto thee, Except a man be born again, he cannot see the kingdom of God.
>
> John 3:3

This is a *fixed* Word, confirmed by other verses.

> For God so loved the world, that he gave his only begotten Son, that whosoever believeth in him should not perish, but have everlasting life.
>
> John 3:16

> Neither is there salvation in any other: for there is none other name under heaven given among men, whereby we must be saved.
>
> Acts 4:12

There is only one way to be saved. There are no exceptions. That is a fixed law.

Here is the key to the difference between fixed and mutable laws: *With a fixed law, you will find no other scripture in the Bible that allows an exception.* There are no Biblical illustrations or examples that provide exceptions.

With salvation, there are no exceptions listed in the Word. Any man who gets to God *must* come through Jesus, the only Way. That is "cut and dried." Salvation is fixed. There is no scriptural precedent for exceptions.

But the guidelines for marriage and divorce do not seem to be fixed. There are Biblical precedents for exceptions. Some of the patriarchs of Israel had more than one wife at a time, men such as Abraham, Jacob, and Jacob's sons. But as we read the Old Testament, we can see God down through the years working to bring the permissive standard back up to His ideal, or perfect, principle.

God never told Abraham or Jacob not to take other wives. He blessed them exceedingly in spite of their marital situations not being up to His perfect standard. They were still His men, His servants. But by the time of Solomon, God was telling Israel not to take more than one wife. However, even then, His reason was not to bring them back to monogamy, but to prevent the nation from falling into spiritual adultery by worshipping the gods of pagan women. (1 Kings 11:1-8.)

The Lord became angry with Solomon, not because of taking many wives, but because his wives had **turned away his heart after other gods** (1 Kings 11:4).

We need to be careful, however, not to get off on the other extreme. We are teaching people how to live right, how to live in the power of God, and how to be free in Jesus, but some may misunderstand.

No Excuse for Sin

I want to make it clear that this teaching on marriage and the family is not an "excuse" to go out and sin. I am *not* saying you can do as you please and excuse it by saying, "God will forgive me."

The fact that God allows exceptions to His ideal of one man and one woman cleaving together for an entire lifetime does not mean you can do whatever you feel like with no consequences. If you think all you have to do is say, "Father, I'm sorry," then you are using the truth of the Word as a license to sin. That is not what I am saying, and it is not what the Word says. You *cannot* keep making the same mistakes, or sinning the same sin, over and over. God loves us unconditionally, but He does not give us unconditional permissiveness to sin.

If you have gotten that idea, you have missed the point of what I am saying by forty-nine million miles!

I am not advocating divorce, and I do not advocate sanctioning it. But neither do I see any Biblical reason to condemn those who *honestly* felt they could not continue in a relationship, got a divorce, and then remarried. However, if a Christian *keeps* doing this, then that person is in trouble and in sin.

The Word makes it clear that despite His allowances of divorce for man's hardness of heart, God does not approve of it. He hates divorce.

> For the Lord, the God of Israel, saith that he hateth
> putting away:
>
> Malachi 2:16a

However, I am not trying to make a case for, or against, divorce. I am simply trying to show what the Bible really says about it, so that people can be free in their relationships — *not free to sin.*

An Exception to the Rule: Fornication

One exception God allowed to His ideal marriage plan was *fornication.* Jesus said:

> But I say unto you, that whosoever shall put away his
> wife, saving [except] for the cause of fornication, causeth
> her to commit adultery: and whosoever shall marry her that
> is divorced committeth adultery.
>
> Matthew 5:32

It looks as if Jesus was saying that unless your former husband or wife was caught in adultery and you got a divorce, you would be causing that spouse to commit adultery if he, or she, remarried. But is that the intent of that verse? If no fornication is involved, but the husband comes home drunk and abuses his wife and children, is she supposed to stay with him? Is that what Jesus was saying?

Keep all of the different verses relating to divorce in mind as we consider this question:

God said for a man to leave mother and father and cleave to his wife and the two should be one.

Then Jesus said, **It hath been said** (that means someone said it before Him) that a man could give his wife a writing of divorcement (Matt. 5:31).

He also said, **But I say** that if you divorce her for any other cause than fornication (an illicit sexual relationship), you are committing adultery.

However, notice that He did give an exception to the Law of One Flesh, and that was *fornication*. Therefore, if the law was cut and dry — once married always married, no matter whether one partner is not a believer, or whether there was adultery involved — then there would be no exceptions made whatsoever.

Another Biblical precedent of an exception is recorded in John, chapter 8.

> **Jesus went unto the mount of Olives.**
>
> **And early in the morning he came again into the temple, and all the people came unto him; and he sat down, and taught them.**
>
> **And the scribes and Pharisees brought unto him a woman taken in adultery; and when they had set her in the midst,**
>
> **They say unto him, Master, this woman was taken in adultery, in the very act.**
>
> **Now Moses in the law commanded us, that such should be stoned: but what sayest thou?**
>
> **John 8:1-5**

It would have been enough to say, "This woman was taken in adultery," but they added, "in the very act." To catch someone "in the act," the Pharisees were not just walking down the street when they happened to look into the back seat of a car and see something. No, those rascals were out looking for something in order to entrap Jesus. And for them to accuse her of committing adultery, either she or the man had to have been married.

Apparently, they had interrupted this couple in the act of committing adultery, grabbed her right out of the bed, and dragged her down the street and into the temple compound.

There they threw her down in front of Jesus and said, "Moses said she should be stoned, but what do *you* say about it?"

Then they stood back, folded their arms, and thought, "We've got him, now! There is no way he is going to get out of this one."

But He stooped down and wrote on the ground with his finger as if He did not even hear them. (John 8:6.) When they kept on asking him, He raised up and said, **He that is without sin among you, let him first cast a stone at her** (John 8:7b).

In other words, "Any of you that are free from sin, you throw the first rock. You 'perfect' people, you 'holier-than-thou' people who have never made a mistake, you throw the first rock."

> **And they which heard it, being convicted by their own conscience, went out one by one, beginning at the eldest, even unto the last: and Jesus was left alone, and the woman standing in the midst.**
>
> **John 8:9**

In the face of the law of Moses that said anyone taken in adultery should be stoned, Jesus let the woman go, telling her to sin no more. If that is not grace, I do not know what is. He forgave someone caught *in the very act* — not looking like it or thinking about it, but caught in the act. He made an *exception* to the law of stoning one caught in adultery, which shows it was not a *fixed* law, either.

A Second Exception: Unsaved Mates

In 1 Corinthians, the Apostle Paul discussed another *exception* to the no-divorce law.

> **And unto the married I command, yet not I, but the Lord, Let not the wife depart from her husband:** [That is the most perfect way, and the "law."]
>
> *But and if she depart* [here comes the exception] **let her remain unmarried, or be reconciled to her husband: and let not the husband put away his wife.**
>
> **But to the rest, speak I, not the Lord: if any brother hath a wife that believeth not, and she be pleased to dwell with him, let him not put her away.**
>
> **And the woman which hath an husband that believeth not, and if he be pleased to dwell with her, let her not leave him.**

> **For the unbelieving husband is sanctified by the wife, and the unbelieving wife is sanctified by the husband: else were your children unclean; but now are they holy.**
>
> **But if the unbelieving depart, let him depart. A brother or a sister is not under bondage [or obligation] in such cases: but God hath called us to peace.**
>
> 1 Corinthians 7:10-15

It sounds to me as if Paul was making an exception there. For example, a couple marries, and neither one is saved. Then one of them becomes born again and tries to help the other one, but that one refuses to receive it, and the relationship gets into terrible shape.

Finally, the unsaved one walks out saying, "I'm not going to church, and I'm not going to have anything to do with Christians."

Paul said, "If they go ahead and divorce you because you are a brother in Christ, then *you are not under obligation* to your marriage vows."

Fornication is not involved, yet Paul said the person left behind is not under bondage. Apparently, that meant they could marry again.

Also, there is another aspect of this question, and that is the state of the heart.

Jesus' disciples even had difficulty understanding His teaching on divorce, just as people do today, for later they asked Him about what He had said to the Pharisees.

> **And in the house His disciples asked him again of the same matter.**
>
> **And he saith unto them, Whosoever shall put away his wife, and marry another, committeth adultery against her.**
>
> **And if a woman shall put away her husband, and be married to another, she committeth adultery.**
>
> Mark 10:10-12

That seems very cut and dried. There seems no way to get around that. In other words, it seems you cannot get a divorce and remarry and not be living in sin. Yet out of the mouth of the same Jesus had come these words quoted in verse 5: **For the hardness of your heart** Moses allowed exceptions.

Natural Man Has a Hard Heart

Remember your heart is the real you, the inner man or woman. When the Bible talks about the heart, it does not mean the organ in your chest that pumps blood. So Jesus said that God permitted them through Moses to get divorces. Why? **Because of the hardness of their hearts.** What does a "hard heart" mean? It means an unyielding, unbending heart, a heart with no pliability to it.

The natural man, outside of Jesus, has a hard heart. His spirit is hardened because he is cut off, separated, from God. His spirit is alienated from God and unresponsive to Him. When your natural heart is alive, it is soft, wet, and pliable. It moves. But if it stopped and died, that same heart would become hard and rigid as a rock. No blood could move through it.

Natural circumstances make a picture of the spiritual. So if your spiritual heart is dead to God, it is hard and rigid. The "lifeblood" of living waters cannot flow through it, until you accept Jesus and He gives you a heart of flesh.

Jesus was using figurative language when He said **for the hardness of your heart.** Because of sin, God knew that the hearts of men and women were hard and rigid, spiritually dead in trespasses and sins. God knew that no man could really live right, the way he was created to live. Therefore, God made some exceptions.

He told Israel, "Thou shalt not sin," yet He turned around and provided a way for them to bring sacrifices and offerings in order to wipe out their sins! His perfect will was that they not sin. Yet because of the hardness of their hearts, He knew that they would. There was nothing else possible with their dead, hardened

55

hearts than for them to end up sinning. So He gave them a way out, an exception to the rule.

He said, "Sin not," *but if they did,* He made them a way out. They could come to God with a sacrifice, and He would acquit them. He would cover their sin. He would atone for it by the sacrifice made. Then that gave them them a clean slate, as it were.

Without Guidelines, There Is Chaos

Remember that the *letter of the law* kills, but the *spirit of the law* brings life. Laws of behavior, if strictly adhered to without mercy, bring bondage. But society without law becomes chaos, so there must be laws.

God's laws that govern man's behavior in the natural world are guidelines, not bondage, and are mutable or pliable. In other words, He allows exceptions in the letter of the law. *But He allows no exceptions in the spirit of His laws.* God's *fixed* laws, such as having only one way — Jesus — for man to return to Him, govern the spiritual world. Those laws already are *spirit* and have no *letter,* or bondage, for which man's hardness of heart needs an exception.

Even with the law of God and man, many people today are "doing their own thing." Now suppose you remove the law, what do you think you are going to have? Complete and absolute chaos. So there must be standards and guidelines, laws that allow exceptions because of man's present condition, and spiritual (fixed) laws that reflect God's immutable character.

Looking at Deuteronomy 24:1-4 again we find:

When a man hath taken a wife, and married her, and it come to pass that she find no favour in his eyes, because he hath found some uncleanness in her: then let him write her a bill of divorcement, and give it in her hand, and send her out of his house.

And when she has departed out of his house, *she may go and be another man's wife* [a second marriage].

And if the latter husband hate her, and write her a bill of divorcement, and giveth it in her hand, and sendeth

her out of his house; or if the latter husband die, which took her to be his wife; [Notice, this is the second divorce with no adultery involved.]

Her former husband, which sent her away, may not take her again to be his wife . . . .

Moses said her "former husband" could not take her again as his wife, but that implies that she could be *somebody else's wife.* Otherwise, Moses would have said "no man" could take her as wife. But that would mean three marriages for that woman.

Look at the Whole Picture

To see the whole picture, all of these scriptures must be put together. If you take just one of these verses scattered throughout the Bible, you could show that divorce aside from fornication is absolutely forbidden — and some people and denominations do just that. On the other hand, we can look at Deuteronomy 24 and see that it is allowable for a person to be married at least three times *with no fornication involved.* At least, that is the implication.

Is that what God is trying to tell us? Are these scriptures laying down fixed laws? If so, there is confusion, because in one place a woman could have three marriages simply because her husbands did not like her, but in another, no divorce is allowed unless one party commits adultery.

However, God does not contradict Himself or create confusion. The reality is that He was not trying to give us hard and fast rules where marriage is concerned. He was trying to get across to mankind a *principle:* His highest way is to have one man and one woman become one flesh.

The Problem Lies With the Church

Most Christians started out in churches that either killed them with the letter of the law (like the church at Galatia) or went to the other extreme and led them to believe that, because this is the "Age of Grace," anything goes (like the church at Corinth). Most churches have not even told the sheep how to be filled with the Holy Spirit in order to be endued with power to do the commissions of God. (Acts 1:8.)

In recent years, I have seen a number of Christians who have been married several times. They did not know how to walk in line with the Word of God. They did not know how to live in Christ, how to walk in Him, or how to be victorious in Him. They had never had any spiritual instructions on how to live.

They did not know their enemy was the devil. They thought it was their husband or wife. The problem was not their mates but the devil working through both husband and wife to break up the relationship.

I have seen the same people come into the light and learn how to live and walk in line with the Word. I have seen them learn how to exercise faith and stand on the Word of God. Then I have seen God take a relationship like that of the woman at the well who had been married five times and bless the sixth marriage. God would bless the efforts if both husband and wife turned to him and set themselves to become "one flesh" in their present marriage.

You cannot tell me the devil was doing that for them. All of those people have said, "Praise the Lord. Thank You, Jesus." The devil is not going to do something for you that will bring glory to Jesus. There is no way the devil would put a man and woman together after messing up several different marriages for them, then bless them in the next one! The people I am talking about are being blessed and are being a blessing to the Body.

If their union is wrong, it would be completely out from under God's hand, protection, and blessings completely. To bless them in a wrong relationship would be for God to aid and abet their sin. That would make God an "accessory." And I do not believe that is possible. Therefore the couples being blessed by God after being divorced and remarried must now be walking in the will of the Lord. They have been forgiven and are now becoming "one flesh."

Suppose you told a lie, would God forgive you? Suppose you told a second lie, would you still be forgiven, if you repented? The Word says **the wages of *sin* is death** (Rom. 6:23). It does not say the wages of telling a lie, or the wages of adultery, or the wages of stealing, but the **wages of sin.** Therefore, *sin* must be *sin.* And if you can be forgiven of telling a lie or stealing or adultery, then you can be forgiven for getting a divorce.

A Summary

What God was saying through all of the scriptures about marriage is that *there is an ideal, a perfect, way* for relationships between men and women. That way is to become one flesh. He wants man to raise his sights, to stop living in the permissive way allowed because of the hardness of hearts, and to begin to live according to the way of the Lord. He wants us to elevate our sights to His level.

However, thank God, if you have messed up, made a mistake, and failed in marriage, you do not have to stay in the muck and mire. You do not have to be guilt ridden and condemned and live lonely and alone the rest of your life.

Traditional religious doctrine is trying to say that Jesus forgave the woman taken *in* adultery, but He will not forgive you your mistake! Even if He did not stone her, why did Jesus not condemn the woman and tell her she could not marry again?

Why did He not say, "You dirty thing, you. You have messed up right in the face of the law. Just suffer the rest of your life, and always remember that you committed this act of adultery."

That is what many ministers and many churches are saying you have to do because you messed up a relationship when maybe you were not even saved yet. Now you are trying to "sin no more" and make your life right. But you cannot do it, because God is not going to forgive a divorce. He forgave a woman taken in adultery, but He will not forgive a divorce.

God's best is that you marry and stay married. But that is assuming that you know the Word, are committed to the Word, and love the Word enough to make whatever adjustment necessary for the Word to have first place in your life. If both people in a marriage do that, there is no way they cannot have a successful relationship.

Chapter 6

THE DUTIES OF A HUSBAND: HEAD OF THE HOUSE

But I would have you know, that the head of every man is Christ; and the head of the woman is the man; and the head of Christ is God.

1 Corinthians 11:3

God placed the man as head of the house. That does not mean that he is the *god* of the house, or the *lord* of the house. That simply means that, relative to rank, man is the caretaker and protector of his wife and children. And just as God placed Jesus over His children, the Church, as custodian, He has ordained that man be the custodian over the family.

There has been a lot of distorted understanding about that, and a lot of men are taking undue and unfair advantage of their mates. They are distorting the idea of being head of the family and making a mockery out of what God intended. They are lording it over their wives and making them run around like little robots at their commands. Being head of the house does not mean that at all.

The Principle of Rank

The verse at the beginning of this chapter is taken from *The King James Version* of the Bible, but there needs to be some clarification here. What it appears to be saying is that every man is head of every woman — and some people and some denominations have interpreted this verse that way. But no way in the world could that be correct. That would mean that I was over every other man's wife, and every other man would be over my wife! That would bring confusion and a lot of trouble, and I know God is not the author of confusion.

If some other husband began to tell my wife what to do, I would be very upset. And if I began to tell some other man's wife what to do as her "head," I am certain he would be upset!

As I am dealing with the duties of a husband in this chapter, I am only using this one verse. However, in order to understand the principle involved, we need to understand the context of Paul's statement.

The principle is *the principle of rank,* a general principle. This verse is not meant to cover individual situations as a rule of life. Take the military services as an example. Each level of authority has a different rank, from private on up to general. Each officer, however, has his own troops under his authority. He is not set over the troops of a different company or battalion.

So what Paul was discussing here is *rank.* And he was showing God's divine order. Anything that supersedes God's divine order is *out of order.* And if you are out of order with divine order, you are courting disaster fast. You are out of balance, and it will not work for long. It certainly will not work as it is supposed to work.

God Is Not Every Man's Father

If you take the phrase **that the head of every man is Christ** literally, then it would mean that Christ is the head of every man on earth, including the sinner. But Christ is not the head of the non-Christian man. He is only *head of His family*. He is not the head of Satan's family. Satan, spiritually speaking, is the father — or head — of every person who has not been born again. God is not anybody's father who has not been adopted through Jesus. Then and only then does God become your legal guardian.

The liberal doctrine of "the fatherhood of God and the brotherhood of man" is a lie of Satan, spawned in the pit of hell itself. God is *not* every person's father, and Christians are not brothers to non-Christians.

Yes, God is the Creator of everything and of mankind originally. But He is not your father, if you are not His child. And you cannot be His child until you are adopted into His family. The only way you can be adopted is to go through the "Adoption Agency" — Jesus — and go through the proper procedures. Those procedures are: **Ye must be born again** (John 3:7).

> **But as many as received him, to them gave he power to become the sons of God, even to them that believe on his name.**
>
> **John 1:12**

The point is that Jesus is not the head of *every* man, only those of His own family. When you read the Bible, you need to remember to whom it is written. It is a book written to the family of God, not to the world at large. It is not a general treatise of human history. It is not a book to be studied in some university as just another "religious" book. If you are not in the family, you cannot even begin to understand it.

Corinthian Christians Formerly Pagans

What we read at the beginning of this chapter was written to a part of God's family living in a place called Corinth in the first century. It is the first letter we have any record of that the Apostle Paul wrote to the church established at Corinth. Ultimately, through the inspiration of the Holy Spirit, the letter was written also for all Christians throughout all time and history. It is not written to the world, but to the children of God.

Another thing to consider is that the letter originally was written in the Greek language, because that was the common language of most of the civilized world of that day, just as English is the common language today. In Greek, the same word for *wife* is the word for *woman*. It is translated into English according to the translators' understanding of the original context. The persons who translated the Bible you use had to decide how Paul meant each word he used.

Now all wives are women, but not all women are wives. So when you see that word in the Bible, how do you make a distinction between its definitions? You look at the context, at what else is being discussed. If you read the entire 11th chapter of 1 Corinthians, you will see that Paul was making a clear comparison between *husbands and wives* and *Christ and the Church*. He was not talking about women as *women*, but about women who were wives. It becomes clear when you read it this way:

> **But I would have you know, that the head of every (Christian) man is Christ; and the head of (every Christian wife) is her (husband); and the head of Christ is God.**

God is over all. Jesus is under God, and of course the Holy Spirit in terms of rank is under Christ, but here Paul is only using the examples of God and Jesus. Under Jesus, he places the husband, under the husband comes the wife, and under the wife, the children — as far as rank is concerned.

The purpose of his discussion was to show the responsibilities involved. You may have a rank, but with that rank goes certain responsibilities. If you do not discharge your duty in your rank, you can mess up a lot of people.

Now, when Paul said a husband ranked over his wife, he meant that a husband is *responsible* for his wife. God is holding us husbands responsible for our wives. We are responsible for loving them, taking care of them, providing for them, and protecting them in the domestic environment. That is an important point: *The husband's rank is only valid in the natural environment.*

Only Jesus Is the Spiritual Head

I realize this may be a revelation or a revolutionary idea to you, but the husband is *not* the spiritual head of the wife. A lot of people talk about the man being the high priest of the family, the priest of the house, and so forth. But the husband is not the priest of the house! How is he going to be a priest? He has no anointing as a priest. *Every* born again person is a priest and a king, regardless of sex, race, or class. (1 Pet. 2:5,9; Rev. 1:6.)

The only spiritual head in any home is Jesus. Jesus is the head. He is the only High Priest. We are corporately kings and priests, because we are the Body of Christ. Otherwise, you are saying that Jesus is the man's priest, but the man is the woman's priest! And that puts a human being between women and Jesus, just as in the Old Testament when a priest had to intercede between the Israelites and God. That was all done away with at the cross.

Jesus is the High Priest of each born again person. No man can usurp the authority of the Priest of all the ages. If men do not need a human priest over them, then neither do women!

This point is where a lot of people get into trouble, particularly Christian women married to non-Christian men. They are told to submit to their husbands. How can a spiritually alive person submit to a spiritually dead person? An unsaved husband does not even qualify as a *head*. He has no rank as yet, according to God's order. You mean to tell me that God is going to take His blood-bought, blood-washed, spirit-filled child and put that child under the domination of a satanically inspired, controlled, and directed person? You have to be joking.

The only person Who has any business telling a woman when to read the Bible, when not to read the Bible, when to go to Church, when not to go to Church, or whether she can tithe or not is Jesus. Your husband did not redeem you or die for you, therefore he has no right to tell you what to do spiritually.

A Christian husband *does* have the responsibility to live as an example in his home. He is the natural head of the house, and

65

he ought to act like a leader in terms of being an example to his wife and children. But he has no right to *force* her to submit to him.

Forced Submission Is Not Love

Submitting yourselves one to another in the fear of God.

Ephesians 5:21

Some little while ago, there was a heavy emphasis in some circles on *submission*. It seems Christians always have to come up with some new trend, just as the world does. We have to have a new hobby, a new fad in spiritual matters. They cannot just stay on the straight and narrow way. There always has to be some new thing.

At any rate, there were men and women going around teaching that women were to submit to their husbands no matter what he did, who he is, or how he acts. And that was so dumb! Do you think God wants you to submit to the devil? I cannot even believe the so-called intelligence of some people who call themselves Christian. To think that your loving Father would want you to knuckle down to some beast who would treat his dog better than you.

Men, the Word does not say that you are to love your wife the way Tarzan loved Jane. It does not say you need to beat your chest and proclaim that you are "the head of the house."

I do not recall that I have ever told my wife I was the head of the house. I have never told my children that. I just live in such a way that earns respect. I carry myself as the head of the house, I do not proclaim it. My wife should only submit to me to the extent that I treat her the way Jesus treats the Church.

If a husband does not treat his wife that way, she does not have to submit to him. Some husbands try to compel their wives to do all sorts of crazy things.

Love Is An Action, Not a Word

For God so loved the world that he *gave* (John 3:16a). Love is always expressed in giving, in doing something. The word *love* in itself does not mean anything. It is just a word. What means something is that it is a label for an action. Love really is doing something, not just saying something. Anybody can say, "I love you." But not everybody acts like it.

Movie stars are paid a million dollars a picture to say, "I love you." That is no big thing. God loved us and gave us His very best. We men need to give our best to our wives. If you begin to treat your wife right, she will begin to treat you right. There is something odd about human nature. It responds in kind. There is some kind of defense mechanism built into our flesh for self-preservation. You come at me, and I will automatically defend myself. Your wife is the same way.

Has it occurred to you that the only way your wife is able to get your attention is by hassling, complaining, and griping? Maybe nagging is the only way she can get your attention.

A lot of people have the erroneous idea that it is only women that are supposed to submit to men. But that is not the Biblical pattern at all. There is a mutual submitting. You might not understand exactly what that means. To explain it in modern terms: When you come to an intersection where there is no traffic light or no stop sign, there may be a *yield* sign. That means "let the other person go first." Well, that is what submit means.

A lot of marriages are like an intersection with two yield signs, but neither party is observing them. And at an intersection, if one car is going one direction and another going the cross direction, what happens if neither one yields? You have a crack-up.

And that is what is happening in many people's lives. A wreck occurs because neither is willing to yield. They are having confrontations and crack-ups in the intersections of their married lives. It is unfortunate and unnecessary. If they would adopt the Biblical principle of submitting, and each yield to the other, they would never run into one another. There would never be a confrontation. Each would always be giving deference to the other. There would be no instances of husbands beating wives.

Love Means No Violence

I have never seen Jesus slap down the Church, either physically or verbally. I have never seen Jesus lay His hand on the Church other than in healing or to set apart in sanctification to the Father. Yet I have heard of Christian men who beat their wives. If you are a Christian, you have no business beating your wife for several reasons in addition to the obvious one, that it is not right:

1. If she is a Christian, and basically I am speaking to Christians, she is a member of the Body of Christ. When you lay hands on your wife, you are laying hands in anger on Jesus. You would never slap Jesus, would you? Then why would you slap or beat your wife? Jesus does not strike the Church, no matter what we do.

2. Not treating your wife right will hinder your prayers. It also means you are not discerning the Body of Christ rightly, and as mentioned in 1 Corinthians 11:29-31, not discerning the Lord's Body is the open door for sickness, disease, and premature death.

Anybody can hit out. But even if Jesus got upset at us, and I am sure that many times we have upset Him with our way of life, He never strikes us down. He never blackens our eyes. A man who hits a Christian woman may not know it, but he just hit Jesus.

If you cannot talk to your wife, you have a bad situation anyway. If the only way you can get one another's attention is to hit one another, you have a bad relationship anyway. Your whole understanding is warped and twisted. Something is badly wrong in your house.

> **For we are members of his body, of his flesh, and of his bones.**
>
> **Ephesians 5:30**

How can you beat the members of His Body?

For this cause shall a man [Here we see it again. We have seen this verse before concerning marriage as a divine ordinance. Here we read it again in a different context.] **leave his father and mother, and shall be joined unto his wife, and they two shall be one flesh.**

This is a great mystery: but I speak concerning Christ and the Church.

Nevertheless let every one of you in particular so love his wife even as himself; and the wife see that she reverence her husband.

Ephesians 5:31-33

So we are admonished to love our wives, and *to love* means "to cherish," "to take care of," "to treat sweetly and kindly," even as Jesus and the Father treat us. Is that the way you are treating your wife?

Do you work all day, talk to everyone on the job and on the way home, then get home and do not say anything to your wife? Do you just run in, kick your shoes off, and sit in front of the television set? Do you expect her to fix your dinner, and still say nothing of any consequence to her, then expect her to jump in bed and have sex with you? Then you wonder why she turns away and wants nothing to do with you.

And you get mad and say, "What's the matter with her?"

She could say, "What's the matter with you? Why do you want to talk now? I was not good enough to talk to over the dinner table. Why do you want to talk over the bed?"

We would be in some kind of trouble if Jesus stopped talking to us. Suppose we talked to the Father, and there was no answer?

Love Is an "Even Deal"

Another passage about husbands and wives in 1 Corinthians tells us:

> **Let the husband render unto the wife due benevolence; and likewise also the wife unto the husband.**
>
> 1 Corinthians 7:3

That verse tells me that it is an even deal. Both husband and wife are supposed to be giving reverence to one another equally. Not just the woman to the man, or just the man to the woman, but each to the other.

> **The wife hath not power of her own body, but the husband: and likewise also the husband hath not power of his own body, but the wife.**
>
> 1 Corinthians 7:4

That is strong, strong language. It means my body belongs to my wife, and her body belongs to me, because we are one. Many men treat their wives as if they were a love machine. Your bodies belong to each other. You do not have any more right over your wife's body than she does over yours. And you should not misuse her. You should see to it that she is an equal partner in the relationship.

We are looking at things from the standpoint of the Bible, not from what society says. Many things are going on in society that are not sanctioned by God. People do a lot of things simply because they have been doing them so long, they believe those things are right or normal. But "it ain't necessarily so," as the song goes.

You need to understand, however, that there has to be some agreement between the two of you as to what is proper and normal in the marital relationship. Naturally, you do not give your body to your wife to satisfy sexual fantasies inconsistent with the Word of God. (I will discuss sex within marriage in a later chapter.)

But your body belongs to your wife. What are you giving her? Are you giving her your very best? You need to be bathed and smelling good. You need to make sure your breath smells good. Who wants bad breath in their face! You think she is falling out and swooning over your great love, and really you have asphyxiated her with your breath!

You Need God in the Relationship

We want to see what God says and base all our actions on the Word of God. That way, we will stay on safe ground and always have God involved in our circumstances. When we depart from the Word, we have departed from God. And you need God in your relationship. You need the architect while you are trying to build the house. You need to constantly refer to the plans to be sure you are building properly.

A lot of people start building "marriage houses" without the Architect, which is why there are so many "Leaning Towers of Pisa." Their lives are leaning over like that building in Italy because they never consult the Grand Architect of all the ages. They do not look at the plans to see if they are building correctly. They just go on how they "feel."

"Well, I'm just going to do what comes naturally."

You are naturally going to mess up, that is what you are going to naturally do!

A person with no knowledge of the Word is not going to be able to love his wife as Christ loved the Church. He is not going to know how Christ treats the Church. So what he does then is gather his game plan from television soap operas or the movies or the world and tries that mess out on his wife.

What we have to find out is how Jesus loves the Church. We already have seen that He does not abuse us.

Dwell With Them According to Knowledge

> **Likewise, ye husbands, dwell with them according to knowledge, giving honour unto the wife, as unto the weaker vessel, and as being heirs together of the grace of life; that your prayers be not hindered.**
>
> **1 Peter 3:7**

There are two kinds of basic knowledge: *revelation knowledge* that comes from God through His Word and by divine inspiration of the Holy Spirit and the *world's knowledge*. The Apostle Peter was talking in this verse about *revelation knowledge*, not about the knowledge that comes from the world's systems. That is mixing oil and water, and it does not work.

As children of God, we have been trying to mix oil and water, trying to pattern our home lives after the world while still living by the Word. And it will not work! God is not involved in that mixture. He will only be involved in His patterns and principles.

Out in the world, every time you turn around, some couple you thought was getting along pretty good is getting a divorce. I was watching a television program not long ago, and a person who had been married several different times was giving advice on how to have a good sexual relationship! Whatever he knew did not seem to be working too well for him, yet he was trying to advise other people. That is the same thing as someone who has never had children writing books on how to rear children.

But Christians have been following people like that, people with no successful track record, and no substance or consistency in their lives.

Peter also said for husbands to treat their wives as the *weaker vessels*. He did not say they *were* weaker, he just said to treat them *as if* they were. Treat your wife like a delicate, fragile, precious jewel, instead of like an old shoe. He said that if I do not treat my wife that way, if I do not share the grace of life with her, it could hinder my prayers. So, if you do not want your prayers hindered, treat your wife with love and respect.

You should be complimenting your wife, giving her honor. Some of you compliment other women almost to the embarrassment of your wife, or look at other women so obviously it is noticeable. That is a shame. You should not do that. If you want your wife to look good, then do what is necessary for her to look good.

Show your wife you appreciate the things she does for you by giving her a "tip," a little gift now and then unexpectedly. Sure, a lot of those things are part of her responsibility as a housewife, but it is the waitress's duty to bring food to your table in a restaurant, and you still tip her, don't you? If she smiles and gives extra service, you tip her more. You would feel like a dog not to do that. Give her a good tip, and she is going to remember you. Right?

Well, make your wife remember you, also. Compliment her as a "tip" when her hair looks nice, or when she has on a new dress or a new lipstick. Now, do not lie to her! If she does not look good, do not tell her she does. She knows the difference, and she will know you are being phony, not sincere. Just do not take your wife for granted.

Do not always expect to receive from her and never give. Give of yourself to your wife. Keep her in mind when you are away from home and look for the things she likes. Listen and pay attention to her conversation to hear what she likes and wants. Remember her birthday and your anniversary. If you cannot remember, write those special dates down. Buy her something when it is not Christmas. Take time to give.

Chapter 7

THE DUTIES OF A HUSBAND: LOVE YOUR WIFE AS YOURSELF

I am a firm believer in the scriptural admonition that the **truth will make you free** (John 8:32). The first truth I want to talk about here is found in Ephesians 5:25:

> **Husbands, love your wives, even as ....**

That term, **even as** is a prelude showing you how to do it. If you do not know how to love your wife, the Apostle Paul is getting ready to show you how. He is getting ready to give you an object lesson, one that you have to be deaf, dumb, blind, or dishonest not to see. He said:

> **Husbands, love your wives, even as Christ also loved the church, and gave himself for it.**

So we see that the relationship of Jesus to the Church is the example for the relationship of the husband to the wife.

If we want to learn how to treat our wives, all we have to do is examine how Jesus treats the Church. There are Christian men,

men filled with the Spirit, who do not know how to treat their wives. They are not treating their wives in a way or a manner that reflects love. They are surely not treating their wives as Christ treats the Church.

Love Means Giving

Notice that Paul said, **even as Christ also loved the church, and gave himself for it.**

So love is a giving of oneself to another. And in this context, it is the husband giving himself for his wife. That means *to* his wife and *for* his wife, because that is exactly what Jesus did. If you do give, obviously there will be some times of receiving. But your giving should not be based upon receiving. Giving should be a motive of the heart.

I am well persuaded that there are many Christian men who do not love their wives, because if they did, they would not treat them the way they do. The Word says **faith without works is dead** (James 2:20), and I have news for you: Love without works also is dead and meaningless. *Works* means "actions." I say many men do not love their wives, because the way they treat them is certainly not the way Christ treats us.

Love Means Communication

Some husbands spend time talking to every woman on the job, then come home and will not talk to their wives. Anything Jesus had to say to the Church, He said in the Word. He instructed us. He told us that which would help and that which would be good. He did not hold it back from us.

I do not find where Jesus ever went off somewhere without telling the Church He was going, leaving us to wonder where He went and if He was coming back.

He said, "I am going, but I am coming again. You can count on it." (John 14:3.)

Jesus never mistreats the Church in any way. He sacrificed Himself for the Church. Jesus gave everything for us. He said:

> **Greater love hath no man than this, that a man lay down his life for his friends.**

> **Ye are my friends, if ye do whatsoever I command you.**
>
>

John 15:13,14

He gave Himself for us, as His "friends," and He still is giving Himself for us as High Priest for the Church.

An awful lot of Christian men are not giving anything to their wives — no time, no love, and no respect. They treat them like cattle. They treat them like a machine in the home, a machine to provide sex, wash dirty clothes, clean the house, take care of the children, and fix the meals. But that is about it. There is no real respect, no bringing her into the conversation.

Even the Lord said, **Come now, and let us reason together** (Is. 1:18). Many husbands do not discuss things with their wives. They just decide to do something and go ahead and do it.

"Well, I am the man, the head of the house, and I have always wanted a red Cadillac with a white interior, so I'm going to go get one."

But the Word said that you and your wife are one. (Gen. 2:24.) Suppose she does not like a Cadillac? Especially a red one with a white interior. Does she not have a choice in the matter? She should, if she is one with you. Jesus never did that to the Church.

The Apostle Paul told us why Jesus gave Himself for the Church:

> **That he might sanctify and cleanse it with the washing of water by the word.**

> **That he might present it to himself a glorious church, not having spot, or wrinkle, or any such thing; but that it should be holy and without blemish.**

> **So ought men to love their wives as their own bodies. He that loveth his wife loveth himself.**
>
>

Ephesians 5:26-28

Paul is saying that Jesus loved the Body and gave Himself for it. Then He relates the love of Jesus to how men should act and feel toward their wives. **So ought men to love their wives** (v. 28a). Men ought to love their wives in a self-sacrificing way, as they love their own bodies. That is how Jesus loves us, as His Body.

The opposite would be true, as well. If a man does not love himself, he cannot love his wife. Probably this is one reason why some people have such a difficult time loving other people. They really do not like themselves. Many people do not like themselves because they do not have a good self-image, although they put up a big smoke screen. Then they only like other people to the point that they can use them or get where they want to go.

Communication is a two-way street. It does not just mean telling her what you think. It means listening to what she thinks. It does not mean coming home and giving her a blow-by-blow description of your day, then picking up the paper or turning on the TV when she begins to tell you about hers.

Also, husbands who cannot receive revelation knowledge from their wives are in trouble! God can give you wisdom through anyone or anything He chooses. If you refuse to receive spiritual revelation, you are refusing God, not just your wife.

You are in this thing together, and whatever one gets is going to affect both of you. If you have a good wife who is willing to share what she gets in study and prayer with you, then you are crazy not to receive it. You do not have to feel less than a man because your wife came up with it. Be glad she did. Be glad somebody came up with it, because you surely had not! You should not feel inadequate. Perhaps she has a little more time during the day. I am glad when my wife comes up with good ideas, because I am affected in a positive way.

Love Means Self-Sacrifice

Most men love themselves. I did not say *worship*. Nor did I say *idolize*. But I did say *love*. There is a difference.

The Pharisees (the religious leaders) were continually trying to entrap Jesus, and they came to Him one day and said, "What is the greatest commandment of all?" And He answered them this way:

> **... Thou shalt love the Lord thy God with all thy heart, and with all thy soul, and with all thy mind.**
>
> **This is the first and great commandment.**
>
> **And the second is like unto it, Thou shalt love thy neighbour as thyself.**
>
> **On these two commandments hang all the law and the prophets.**
>
> Matthew 22:37-40

If you do not love yourself, you certainly cannot love your neighbor. Your neighbor is not just the person who lives next door to you. Your *neighbor* is everyone else in the world but you.

Paul said it very clearly, He who does not love his wife does not love himself. He who does not love himself does not love his wife.

Most men take care of themselves. Most men spend time on themselves.

Let me say it this way: I surely take care of me. I found out that "me" is somebody. Jesus made me somebody. He told me that I was a priest and a king, a member of a royal priesthood. He told me I was the head and not the tail, above and not beneath. He told me that Father God loved me so much He sent His only begotten Son to redeem me. I must be worth something. In the sight of God, I am. I bathe myself, shave, and put on cologne. I comb my hair. I buy good stuff to put on me, because I love myself and God loves me.

If that is true, then I cannot love my wife less than I love me. Yet some men never buy anything for their wives, never do anything for them.

79

Paul said in Ephesians 5:29:

> **For no man ever yet hated his own flesh; but nourisheth and cherisheth it, even as the Lord the church.**

Do you hate your own flesh? I have never seen a man ball up his fist, hit himself, and give himself a black eye. I have never seen that. But I have known of Christian men who gave their wives black eyes. Now, what kind of man is that? What kind of love is that? That is not the way Jesus does. I do not even have words in my vocabulary to describe a man who beats a woman.

(That does not mean that some of them do not need chastising, because some of them do! I can see how a man would feel. Some women are something else, there is no doubt about it! But a Christian man needs to deal with that kind of situation without violence.)

Love Your Wife With Your Money

This verse is saying the same thing: We are to love our wives as our own flesh. That means to take care of them. Some men spend more money on their cars than their wives. Some spend more on bowling balls or golf clubs than they do their wives. Some spend more on fishing equipment than wives.

I know some wives who do not even know where their husbands work. They do not know how much money they make. The husbands just come in and hand them some money, maybe enough to buy groceries or pay a couple of bills. That really gives those wives a sense of security, you know!

Betty knows every nickel and dime I get. If I find a dime on the sidewalk, she knows about it. Not because I have to let her know or because somebody has a gun at my head making me tell her. She is my *wife*. She is equal partner in this relationship. Whatever I go through, she has to go through. If the congregation blesses me or praises me, she gets blessed too. On the other hand, if the next day, the congregation says, "Crucify him! Away with him!" she is in on that too.

It is not fair for a man to treat his wife like she was a piece of furniture. In fact, some men have more respect for their furniture than their wives.

Men, you should treat your wives like queens. Then maybe they would begin to act like queens and begin to live like that. You know, if you get stepped on every day, it is hard not to act like a rug. As you relate to your wife, that is really the way you relate to Christ. Tell her that you love her and just talk things over with her. You know she is a part of you. She is *one* with you. She should be involved in everything you are involved with.

If you think she will not understand the kind of work you do, perhaps that is because you have never taken the time to explain it. Talk about the part that she can understand. Of course, some women would not be interested or would not understand, but we will discuss that when we get to the duties of wives. In the meantime, I am talking about general situations and general principles.

Betty and I talk about everything at the dinner table. Usually, we have not seen each other all day and perhaps have not had time to talk on the phone, so when I get home, I begin sharing my day with her. She is a part of my life. She is a part of the ministry.

And I always ask her what happened with her day. We talk and share. We keep one another posted on what is going on, because whatever affects one of us is going to affect the other. We take time to talk. She is bone of my bone and flesh of my flesh.

In this book, there is not space to discuss all the areas of interpersonal relationships, so I am just going to talk about a few. The main emphasis I want to make in this chapter is how the Bible tells men to treat their wives.

One lady who had been married to the same man for thirty-two years wrote me a letter. She had always worked and helped her husband. Then in 1981, he closed out their checking accounts and refused to give her any money. He claimed their house and their money. She does not know where his savings account is. When his job requires him to go out of town, she does not know where he is; he does not call home. He will not buy any food or pay any utility bills. He will not go to church.

She said, "I work, and God supplies all my needs," but she wanted to know what to do. I had an answer for her. Boy, did I have an answer! But I thought I had better not give it. All I could do was tell her to pray. What do you tell somebody like that?

That is a classic example of a husband who is not carrying out the obligation of his marriage, nor is he providing for his own, nor is he walking in any of the responsibilities of a husband. I doubt if he is even saved.

Love Means Telling the Truth

Would Christ tell us the truth or lie to us? Then you ought to tell your wife the truth. Instead of looking at other women, tell your wife when she lets herself get out of shape. Have the decency and honesty to tell her. Then be an example yourself of what you expect from her. You cannot expect her to stay looking good if you are fat, sloppy, and out of shape. After all, when she married you, she did not marry the great white whale. It takes work and is a lifelong job, but it is worth it for your health as well as for your marriage.

Some of you do not like the way your wife dresses. Go and buy her the kind of clothes you do like. I want my wife to look the best, and I know what looks best on her better than anybody else.

Take the time and go shopping with her even if your feet do hurt. You find some sales people who will tell you the truth, but most of them will say anything to make a sale. Go with your wife and tell her what looks good. Sure it costs time. But it will cost you more if you do not go with her, because she has spent your money, and you may not like the dress. Ninety-nine percent of the time, I go with Betty to choose her clothes. I know what looks best on her. I want her to look good.

Of course, you need to use good sense. Don't go out and get yourself in debt buying clothes.

Love Means Cherishing Your Wife

Paul said no man ever hates his own body but cherishes it **even as the Lord the church** (Eph. 5:29). That is how God treats us. He cherishes the Church. He takes care of us. He is always looking out for our welfare. He is always seeking for us to have the best.

Jesus said, "I came that you might have life," and that would have been enough, but he added *more,* and as if that were not enough, he added a superlative — *abundantly.* (John 10:10.) Life more abundantly is what He came for us to have. He cherished us.

So, husbands, we should cherish our wives. You have no right to wait until she acts right in order for you to treat her right. Your responsibility is to treat her right, no matter what she is doing. That is what the Word tells you to do. If she gets ugly, she must give account of that. You must give account if you do not treat her right. Your cherishing her should not be based on her doing all the things you want her to do. Nor should it be based on her agreeing with all of your idiosyncrasies. Your cherishing her and nourishing her should be based on the fact that the Word tells you to.

That is what Jesus does. Think about it. What if He treated us the way we treat Him? Thank God, He does not treat us in kind. He cherishes us out of a heart of love and puts up with all our mess. Because of that, we should be able to put up with one another.

Love Has No Room for Bitterness

Paul tells us in Colossians 3:19:

Husbands, love your wives, and be not bitter against them.

A lot of men hold grudges against their wives for something they did years ago. They are bitter about it. Or a husband could be bitter at his wife for something his first wife, or some other woman in his life did. Because she was a woman, he has that attitude toward all women. If that is your case, then you need to forgive the one involved and turn loose of that bitterness. Suppose God held things against you? If anyone should be bitter about anything we do, it should be God.

If anyone has a right to be bitter, it is Jesus. After all, He is the One Who died for you, and you have just kicked up your heels and acted like a donkey with long ears. You acted ugly with God, and He just kept right on blessing you because you are in His family, and you are His child. He did not pull the carpet out from under you and leave you destitute.

How many times have you told the Lord, "Just let me get out of this, and I will serve you the balance of my days?"

Then when you got out of it, you forgot all about God. You might have meant it at the time, but you forgot, and it became a lie. So if anyone has a right to be bitter and hold something against us, it is God. So how dare we, as husbands, hold something against our wives?

You will have a right to hold something against her when you reach perfection. You can throw the first stone when you are without sin. But if you have not arrived at perfection yet, you had better forgive her as Christ has forgiven you.

Bitterness is not worth it, at any rate. Bitterness is from the devil. It will kill you. It will sour the sweetness in your spirit man. Bitterness does not come from the Spirit of God. I do not care what anyone has done to you or against you. It is not worth what bitterness will cost you.

Cleave *Only* to Your Wife

Genesis 2:24 says a man shall leave his parents and **shall cleave unto his wife: and they shall be one flesh.**

God did not say that husband and wife were to be one with mother, father, sisters, cousins, brothers, aunts, Grandma and Grandpa, and the parakeet! When your wife married you, she did not marry your family.

It is not right for you to bring your relatives into the house or to siphon money off to them — with one exception that I will get into later. Generally, it is w-r-o-n-g, wrong to have relatives living with you. Certainly it is wrong to take their side against your wife.

Your first obligation is to your wife. Your second is to your children by the wife you are presently married to. Your energies, your money, everything else belongs to the woman you marry.

Some men may weigh two hundred and sixty pounds and be six-feet-two and still be "Mama's little boy." I have heard of situations where the husband just suddenly told his wife, "Mama is coming to live with us."

That lady married you, Bud. She did not marry your mother, and you have no right to bring home any relatives against your wife's will. If you wanted to take care of your mother, you should have gotten a house and moved into it with her and never married.

The Bible did not say, "A man shall bring his mother and his father into his marriage with him."

God said to *leave* them. Do you know what *leave* means? He said you and the lady you marry are to be one flesh, not you and her parents and your parents. Your mother had her chance at bat. If she struck out, that is tough. I am sorry, but there is nothing I can do about it. You are not supposed to destroy or jeopardize your own family because your mother or father struck out in their own lives. They had their time at bat. That may sound hard, but it is the truth. Anything else is unfair.

Now let's talk about the exception to this truth. The exception is that you have a responsibility to do anything to help relatives that you can do *with your wife's agreement.* Your first duty is to her. If she does not go along with helping your family, then you have a challenge. You will need to do some praying! But you cannot give them money or bring them into the house without your wife's consent and be doing right.

Just because you are the head of the house, you have no right to take money from your wife and children to give to members of your family. Unless it is your *own* money. For example, if you and your wife have budgeted an allowance each, then in agreement, one or the other of you could use that money to give family members in need. But you should not take your paycheck and go pay your mama's rent, if your wife disagrees. That really amounts to stealing from your family.

Hopefully, if you and your wife both are saved, filled with the Spirit, and walking in the Word, you could sit down and come up with a plan to help them without hurting your own family. Usually, it is better not to move them into your own house — unless you have some unusual relatives, people who can live in your house and not interfere.

I know of one case where a man was living with his mother and taking care of her when he got married. He took his bride-to-be over to meet Mama, and everything was fine. Mama was real sweet and real nice until after that little girl became a part of the family. Then Mama started letting her hair down! Mama seemed like such a darling, then afterwards, she wanted to run the house.

If the husband loved his wife and wanted his marriage to work, he would have been foolish to answer his wife's complaints with, "Yeah, but you said it was all right for Mama to come and live with us."

Mama was tearing up his relationship. Things had changed. And Mama had to go. He had to lose a good wife or keep a no-good mother. Just because someone is a mother does not make them a nice person or of good character. We have institutionalized the word *mother* until it seems like *God.* We think mothers automatically are angels, when some mothers are devils.

Just to clear the air, let me tell you how my wife and I handled this situation in both our families.

Agree on Exceptions to the Rule

Betty's mother was afflicted with a very severe case of arthritis more than twenty years ago. We attempted to help her spiritually, because we knew what God could do. For some reason, however, we never were able to get her to a point where she could receive healing. So she suffered. My wife felt an obligation to spend certain days of the week with her mother and help out in the home.

I could have been selfish and said, "No, you can't go over there. I married *you*. Your mother has her husband and other relatives. You stay home and take care of me."

But I did not do that. I knew how much it meant to her, so we *agreed* that she should help on a limited basis. Then we went one step farther as time went on. Betty and some of her brothers and sisters went together and paid for someone to come in and do the house cleaning.

I said, "All right. That is fine. That's the least we can do." We stayed in agreement over this.

Then a little later, one of the other relatives quit a job and moved into the house full time. Betty and the others went together and supported that person, so they all knew their parents had someone looking after them who really cared.

Then another situation arose on my side. My mother had been alone for a long time, because my father had died years ago. For various reasons, the house they lived in meant a lot to my mother. So she was going to hold on to that house, I figured, until the day she died. It was her security.

But when she was seventy-five years old, we began to discuss her situation. It was a shame for her to live by herself. One of our daughters had married, and we had an extra room. So Betty and I talked it over and decided to ask Mama to move in with us, to let her last days be her best days. Then she would not have to be concerned about living alone. She was still trying to earn a little extra money to help herself out. I felt she had already "paid her dues" in life — but I did not think she would move.

But when I asked her, she surprised me. Really, I was shocked! She was ready to leave. Now I did not just bring her in and say, "Mama is coming to live with us." My wife and I talked about it, worked things out, and got in agreement on it.

We told my mother she could sell her house and buy a new car, bank the rest of it, and live happily ever after. She would never have to buy any more groceries, pay another utility bill, or pay property taxes. She would have no responsibilities in the house, because I already have someone helping out.

She comes and goes as she pleases and does not have to lift a finger. It has turned out very well, because my mother is the kind of person who you do not even know is in the house. She does not try to tell us how to run our home, our marriage, or our family. It has been a beautiful situation.

But the only reason we had no trouble over the situation with her family or with my mother is that we communicated our thoughts and plans, and *we got in agreement with each other.*

If your wife is not in agreement, then you need to figure out what else can be done. Once you marry her, you become one flesh, and she has to come first.

Children From Other Marriages

What about children from another marriage or out of wedlock? Husband, how responsible are you where they are concerned? (This question comes up quite frequently.) The same general guideline is true here. The wife you are now cleaving to before God and are one flesh with must come first. I know that Paul wrote not providing for your own made you worse than an infidel, but he said *those of your own household.*

> **But if any provide not for his own, and specially for those of his own house, he hath denied the faith, and is worse than an infidel.**
>
> 1 Timothy 5:8

Children by another wife or another woman are not now *of your own house.* As a Christian, you should do everything you can to see those children have all the possible advantages, especially spiritual advantages. You can still be a spiritual role model for that child even though you have another family. But, again, it has to be with the understanding, cooperation, and consent of your present wife. She is now your primary responsibility — not anything in the past, unless you made an agreement with her concerning those children before the two of you were married.

It certainly is not right to keep quiet about past children, then after you are married, to introduce them out of a clear, blue sky. Whatever you can do, and whatever your wife is in agreement with, is what you should do. Of course, the person caring for the children must also be in agreement. If that person is very bitter toward you, then you have another problem.

You can always pray and bind the powers of darkness that would hinder. You can pray the Lord of the Harvest to send someone to that child, who needs salvation just like you did.

The best thing to do when you get ready to marry is take your wife through the house of your life and open up all those closets. Let her see what is in your past. It is better that she knows now than later. If she loves you, it will make no difference.

The worst thing to do is keep her in the dark, then suddenly spring things on her.

Here come your twins, and she says, "Who is that?"

And you nonchalantly say, "Oh, those are my children from my third marriage."

Better not do that. That should all have been discussed beforehand.

If you are under a court order to support those children, you are a robber if you do not. You are being dishonest. If you tell your wife before you are married, and the child support is figured in the budget, then you are less likely to have problems.

Time Out With the Boys Is Out

Any man who has to go off somewhere and be alone should never have married. That also applies to men who have to have time out "with the boys." You go somewhere for an hour, then do not come back for three. That is not right. You would be upset if she did that. Why do you have to be alone or out with the boys? Why did you get married? Just to have a sex machine or a maid? Those days are over.

When you said, "I do," to that lady, it was the end of the boys and beginning of the girl, singular. Now, again, this is the same situation as the money: If you and your wife come to an agreement before marriage, there is no problem. If you want to set some time to go fishing or hunting, or something like that, and it is with your wife's agreement and consent, then it is okay.

But to just go off talking a bunch of junk with the guys and leave your wife at home by herself is not right.

If you belong to a club which has set times to meet, it ought to be with the understanding and cooperation of your spouse. That is all I am saying. There needs to be unity and togetherness on everything each of you does. That way she does not feel left out, or wonder where you are or what you are doing.

If you are not in agreement on these things, you have left a big hole for the devil to work through. Suppose you go off for an hour and three hours later come back, and your wife picks a long blonde hair off your jacket. Now you could be completely innocent. You could have been getting on an elevator and brushed close to some woman with long hair. But the devil is going to feed ideas into your wife's mind. You do not need those kinds of doors open.

There are things Betty and I do apart from one another, but always with the complete knowledge and understanding of the other. Most of the time, where she goes, I go, and where I go, she goes. If I go somewhere and get tied up longer than I expected, I call her.

One lady in our church who wrote me about her husband said he went out with the boys and stayed gone all night sometimes. This had been going on for eight years. He was supposed to be saved and filled with the Spirit, too. That man had deaf ears.

His conscience had been seared, apparently. He mistreated his wife by making her spend a lot of lonely nights at home while he was out there playing foot loose and fancy free.

My advice to her was to give him some of his own medicine. I did not advise divorce, but neither did I believe it was her duty to stay home and be mistreated. She should not do anything wrong, but she could go out with girl friends. For one thing, it would help her to find out where she is in that relationship. If he really cares about her, he will get a jolt that may make him look at his own attitude and behavior.

Men, if you want to be alone, then do not get married. The Bible says you are supposed to be *one.*

Chapter 8

THE DUTIES OF A WIFE: SUBMISSION AND RELATED MATTERS

> Wives, submit yourselves unto your own husbands, as
> unto the Lord.
>
> **Ephesians 5:22**

Wives, notice the term **your own husbands.** That is the only man you are supposed to submit to, your *own* husband. Nobody else.

> For the husband is the head of the wife, even as
> Christ is the head of the church: and he is the saviour of the
> body.
>
> Therefore as the church is subject unto Christ, so let
> the wives be to their own husbands in every thing.
>
> **Ephesians 5:23,24**

If the husband is carrying himself as Christ does relative to the Church, it is an easy thing for a wife to submit to her husband.

Remember: this book is written to Christians. I am not talking to unequally yoked couples — one believer and one unbeliever — nor am I talking to unsaved people. Also, I am talking about God's best. I would rather shoot for one hundred percent and only make fifty, than to shoot for nothing and make all of it. You have to have some goals.

If you have a husband who is a non-believer, you are dealing with an entirely different situation than I am outlining in this book. You will have to use the wisdom of God, the faith of God, and the power of God. You will have to pray and make the best out of the deal that you can. But I am talking to husbands and wives who are both Christians.

So if the husband is acting toward his wife as Christ behaves toward the Church, the wife will not have any problem submitting. Her responsibility is to submit. The husband should be the head. If he is not, the wife should help him to become the head. It will make her life what it ought to be.

I realize there are some strong women who will become the head if given half an inch. But I am convinced that deep down inside, they really do not want to be like that. Underneath all the outward strength, they really are not happy, because being the "head" is not natural for women. It is not built into them. Just like it is not built into me to have a baby! When you try to do something you are not really created to do, you never will be truly happy. You may have some degree of what the world calls "success," but you will be miserable, and everyone around you will be miserable.

If your husband is not the head he ought to be, and you are a strong woman, help him. You may have a diamond in the rough. With a little coaxing and a little tender loving care, he could be the man of your dreams. He could be just the kind of man you want, the one who will allow you to take the role you are designed to take.

When God made wives, He did not make them inferior. Having a lesser rank has nothing to do with equality. A private is as good as a general. He just does not have the general's rank and authority. Rank has nothing to do with intrinsic value or worth.

In the program of God, in terms of rank, the major responsibility is upon the husband. I believe that is why we do not find a lot in the Bible concerning the role of wives. But a lot of the things written to husbands can be flip-flopped or turned in reverse.

Your Body Belongs to Your Husband

You need to remember, once again, that I am talking about God's best. I am not talking about being married to some monster. We are looking at things from the standpoint of a Christian husband and a Christian wife. We are talking about people who have made a commitment to the Word of God.

In that sense, your body belongs to your husband just as his body belongs to you. If both of you are living in line with the Word, neither of you will abuse that privilege. And you will not deny or deprive your spouse of what belongs to him.

In 1 Corinthians 7:4,5, Paul was saying, "The wife does not have power or authority over her own body, but the husband does. Do not defraud each other."

Of course, we are talking about things within reason. We are not talking about perversions or obsessions. We are talking about what might be termed "normal" — the opposite of "abnormal."

Some wives defraud their husbands. They cheat their husbands out of their bodies, or use their bodies as a weapon of control. Some wives do not want to be bothered, so they stay in the kitchen half the night, fooling around with things and hoping their husbands will go to sleep before they get to bed. That is not right.

> ... **Except it be with consent for a time, that ye may give yourselves to fasting and prayer; and come together again, that Satan tempt you not for your incontinency.**
> **1 Corinthians 7:5**

As far as I can tell from this scripture, the only legitimate reason my wife has for denying her body to me would be if we agree to go into fasting and prayer. And I do not have any right to deny her. I am not supposed to defraud her, and she is not supposed to defraud me, unless we consent, and then only for a time.

Here is where the communication comes in that we talked about in the last chapter. If you do not know how to talk to one another, how are you going to be able to get into consent? How are you going to agree together to fast and pray if you are not communicating? Then you end up being miserable. But lady, you belong to your husband, so you should make yourself available to him.

If you are so busy that you are tired all the time, you need to cut out some extra-curricular activities and get yourself together. If you are too tired, you are too busy.

Be in Subjection to Your Own Husband

Let us look at subjection from the viewpoint of another apostle. First Peter, chapter 3, says:

> Likewise, ye wives, be in subjection to your own husbands; that, if any obey not the word, they also may without the word be won by the conversation of the wives;
>
> While they behold your chaste conversation coupled with fear.
>
> Whose adorning let it not be that outward adorning of plaiting the hair, and of wearing of gold, or of putting on of apparel;
>
> But let it be the hidden man of the heart, in that which is not corruptible, even the ornament of a meek and quiet spirit, which is in the sight of God of great price.
>
> For after this manner in the old time the holy women also, who trusted in God, adorned themselves, being in subjection unto their own husbands:

Even as Sara obeyed Abraham, calling him Lord: whose daughters ye are, as long as ye do well, and are not afraid with any amazement.

Likewise, ye husbands, dwell with them according to knowledge, giving honour unto the wife, as unto the weaker vessel, and as being heirs together of the grace of life; that your prayers be not hindered.

Finally, be ye all of one mind, having compassion one of another, love as brethren, be pitiful, be courteous.

1 Peter 3:1-8

That first verse is often used as a "proof text" to show how a Christian wife should handle herself in order to win a non-Christian husband to God. But I submit to you that the Bible is not written to non-Christians. It is written to Christians. It is a book for God's people. It is His directive as to how we should order our lives in order to experience the greatest degree of happiness, pleasure, and fulfillment. That is what He wants for us. But we cannot and will not have that unless we play the game by His rules. Only a few things in the Word relate to unbelievers, things such as how to get saved and what their destination is if they are not adopted into the family of God.

A non-Christian would not be reading the Word anyway and certainly not seeking to obey it. The very fact that Peter wrote **that if any obey not the word** shows that he was talking to Christians, not about unsaved husbands. These verses apply to husbands who are born again but not yet walking in the Word. And there are many like that. They are saved and even filled with the Holy Spirit, but they never read the Bible, go to church, pay tithes and offerings, and so forth. They sit and watch television all of the time they are home.

They are saved, but not doing anything with it. They are not being examples or letting their lights shine. So Peter is saying that the way to get a husband like that on course is *not* to nag him, hound him, or bug him. He is saying not to go on and on at him about what he ought to be doing.

Another clue to the fact that he was writing about saved husbands is that he told the women to "submit," and as I pointed out before, there is no way God is going to tell His children to knuckle under to a spouse whose father is Satan. The only person you are to be in submission to is a child of God.

The Apostle Peter was telling the wives in verse one how to win their husbands to being doers of the Word and not hearers only. Also in verse one, the word *conversation* in the Greek means "manner of life." It does not mean verbalizing or words of the mouth, as it does in English today. It covers the entire lifestyle, including the words of your mouth.

So what Peter was telling the wives was to shape up their own lifestyles and let their lights shine so their husbands would be made jealous for the Word. Every time your husband sees you singing praises to God, every time he sees you praying, every time he sees you studying the Bible, it will bring conviction to his heart. It will bring more conviction than if you nag him.

If you realize that you have a responsibility before God to live your life in the Word whether you are married or single, or whether your husband does or not, it will make your choices easier. In other words, deal with your own life in the Lord, not your husband's.

Whether your husband is saved or unsaved, until he comes in line with Jesus, why not take this position:

"I am going to fulfill my obligation as a Christian first, then as a wife, second. So that whatever this man does or does not do, he will never be able to point a finger of accusation at me and say, "Well, I would have become a Christian, but my wife was so wishy-washy, so sometimes up and sometimes down, so inconsistent in her Christian life that I did not want to be like her.'"

Even if you got a divorce, sooner or later, probably you would marry again, and the devil will always have that to condemn you with: You bailed out of that other relationship. You did not have victory. You did not succeed. Then you think, "Maybe I could have been a better wife."

I see that at funerals. The casket is sitting up at the front, and people come up, look in, and cry out of condemnation.

Inside, something is telling them, "You didn't do all you could have. You weren't the best parent you could have been. You weren't the best husband. You weren't the best wife."

Then they end up spending $50,000 for an expensive coffin to put in the ground out of guilt, when that money could have been spent on a lot of other things to greater benefit.

A husband may not have bought his wife any flowers while she was alive. Now that she is dead and cannot smell them, he buys all those expensive flowers to sit by the coffin. He is trying to make up for his shortcomings, but it is too late. The smartest thing is to do the right thing now.

Verse two talks about your **chaste conversation,** your modest lifestyle. The old adage, "Actions speak louder than words," is very true. That is why Jesus said:

> **Let your light so shine before men, that they may see your good works, and glorify your Father which is in heaven.**
>
> **Matthew 5:16**

Some have taken that third verse of 1 Peter 3 and made a sort of unwritten spiritual law that women are not supposed to get their hair done or wear jewelry and cosmetics. But the subject under discussion is not the appearance of women. The subject under discussion is *conversation,* or "lifestyle." All Peter was saying is not to let all of your time be taken up fixing up the outward woman to the neglect of the inner person. Let the light that is on the interior shine out so that your husband will see that.

He was not saying that it is wrong to get your hair done, or to fix yourself up. If the traditional religious interpretation were true, it would be wrong for women to wear clothes, because the last part of the verse says, **or of putting on of apparel.**

Let the Wife Reverence Her Husband

Ephesians 5:33 says, ... **and the wife see that she reverence her husband.** Now this word *reverence* does not mean to put her husband ahead of God, or to make him an idol and get into idolatry. It simply means "to respect him highly, to honor him." As I have been saying, if the husband's behavior is the way it ought to be, it makes it easy for the wife to *reverence* him. But if he is acting like a dog or an idiot, then he puts his wife into a very hard position.

On the other hand, there are some women who worship their husbands, and that is a big mistake. Man is not God, and things get bent out of shape when you worship a human.

But whether your husband is easy to reverence or not, the Bible says to respect him — so you need to do that.

It does not say, "If her husband is worthy, let her reverence him."

I simply said it makes her duty a lot easier if he is worthy. If he is not what he ought to be, she still has the responsibility to reverence him.

When she does that, it sets her free from some things. It will allow her to function in society as a fulfilled person, because she is doing what God said to do. She is being obedient. The bottom line is that God has spoken, and doing what He said is her responsibility.

Compliment your husband. Talk about how nice he looks, or what nice things he does. In nearly every husband, no matter how many things he does that you do not like, there are some things you can compliment.

It is not good to go around talking about what some other man looks like: "Oh, look at so-and-so on television." So-and-so on television is not buying his own clothes. Fashion experts buy them. Cosmetic experts make up his face and do his hair. There is no way you can make a fair comparison between your husband and television or movie stars.

You may need to help your husband with his clothes. Some men have no idea what looks good on them. If you want him to look a certain way, you have to help him. I know women who buy their husbands' clothes. They match up shirts and ties, or those men would wear one brown sock and one blue! There are a lot of men who could not care less about what they wear.

If you love him, help him. But you do not honor him when you talk about other men in front of him, whether it is about their looks, the way they treat their wives, or whatever. Now, I do not mean to lie to him. You can find truthful things to say about anyone. Show him that you appreciate him. A little kind word here and there goes a long way in a relationship.

Do not take your husband for granted. You have a duty to encourage, inspire, and commend him. Confess his faults to the Lord privately in prayer, and pray for those things to change. But confess his good points to him. A little soft word here and there will go a long way toward cementing a relationship, making it more fruitful.

Jesus commends us through His blessings, and we ought to learn to do that for our spouses. Tell him when he smells good, and tell him tactfully when he smells bad. Do not let him out of the house smelling bad!

Also, do not just be a receiver, letting your husband do everything for you, but never giving anything back. Learn to be a giver, also. If he waits on you, act like you appreciate it.

Women Who Have More Education

Some women have had the advantage of a good education, but they marry men who have not. They apparently love these men, or they would not marry them. But after they are married, they begin to feel superior because of their education.

If you fall into this category, perhaps you are not willing to receive revelation from him because he is not as educated as you. He does not have as much "book learning" as you do. But going to school and getting a degree does not necessarily make you "educated." You may have a lot of facts, but you may not know how to deal with the affairs of life. You may have knowledge, but he may have wisdom.

So be willing to listen and not think your degree means you are smarter. Which is more important: your education or your marriage? If he is a good provider, a good husband, a good father to the children, then what does the education matter? In addition, remember that you do not have to have a college degree to receive revelation knowledge from the Holy Spirit.

All I am saying is be careful and use wisdom so that you do not cheat yourself out of something good just because your husband has not been to college. If you look down your nose at him, it is not possible to honor or reverence him.

In line with this same subject are situations where the wives own the houses or make more money.

In my opinion, the husband is still the head of the house no matter who owns it or where the money comes from to keep the house going. God did not make the man *head* because he owned the property or made the money. He made man the head of the house because he was *man,* or masculine. Adam was created first, and man has the first rank.

God's ranking system has nothing to do with how much money you make or how much you know. It has to do with whether you are a man or a woman.

Once you marry, there is no more "his" and "hers." Everything becomes "ours." If you own property when you marry, then you need to come to some agreement about it beforehand.

If you make more money than your husband, if you are not careful, you may get the "big head" and think you have a right to be the head of the family. The ideal, Biblical way is for the wife to stay home and take care of the family, but in today's world that is not always possible. I have no problem with women working, but I do have a problem if it creates conflict in the marriage. If you want to work and have a happy, harmonious relationship with your husband at the same time, there will have to be some adjustments made. And they will have to start with you.

So if your husband does not make as much money, that does not mean anything in terms of your relationship or your rank in God's system.

Chapter 9

THE DUTIES OF A WIFE: AREAS OF POSSIBLE CONFLICT

If your husband is unsaved, there are two things you can do: pray, and live the best life you can as an example before him.

If your husband is not saved, make very sure that you are not the reason he has not come to Christ. Some women genuinely are born again and love the Lord, but they badger their husbands about going to church and getting saved, and so forth. Some of them also do not live very good examples before their husbands.

If he hears you telling lies on the phone or gossiping one minute, and the next you are on his back about going to church, he will think, "Why do I need to go to church? I can already lie like you. I don't need to be a hypocrite. I can tell my lies without going to church."

Be careful not to be one thing out in public and another thing at home. All your friends think you are just an angel holding onto something to keep from flying away. They think you are so holy, so super spiritual. But at home, you are something else! At home, you are not doing the things you are supposed to be doing.

If you have an unsaved husband, do the best you can. Be the best wife possible. Then cast the care on the Lord, because you cannot make your husband do anything. The Lord will not *make* him get saved, either, but He will do everything in His power to answer your prayers. Just be sure not to allow your husband to find in you a legitimate reason for rejecting Christ.

Husbands Who Do Not Always Walk in the Word

Suppose you have a saved husband, but he does not want to pay tithes. He does not want to give offerings.

He says, "I am not going to give that preacher any of my money."

That is the way some people are. It will not do any good to tell him the money is not being given to the preacher but to God. The harvest will come from the Lord, not any preacher. But there are some penny-pinching, tightwad, cheap, miserly husbands who will not give God anything, much less another person.

But as a wife, that has nothing to do with you. The Bible says to bring all the tithes into the storehouse (Mal. 3:10), and that applies to wives as well as husbands.

"Yes," you may say, "but he is the head of the house. My husband has all the money. He controls our finances."

Don't you think God knows that? Then just give what you can. Maybe you only have $10 a week allowance or money left over from groceries. Fine. Give a dollar out of that. Believe God for a hundredfold return on that dollar, then you can go ahead and keep on giving. You will not have to bother your husband at all.

The worst thing you can do is to keep telling him about tithing or giving. He has already heard it, and the Holy Spirit is going to bring any conviction to him — not you. If he is saved, the Holy Spirit will remind him on the inside. His conscience will remind him to give.

There is something in the "old nature" of human beings that makes them want to do the opposite when you nag them about doing the right thing. Put a sign on the lawn, "Do Not Walk on the Grass," and lots of people will immediately walk on the grass, when without the sign, they would not have. It is amazing!

Just be sure that you pay tithes whenever you can. Also, remember that paying tithes and giving offerings is for your benefit. It is not for God. He is not going out of business because you do not tithe. Tithing and giving offerings are so that God can bless us. He wants to bless us, and our giving opens up a legal way in the natural realm for him to give us those things we need and those things we desire.

I have seen women do something, however, that may seem right, but let me tell you emphatically *not* to do it. Do not take the money he gives you for groceries or to pay the rent or utilities and tithe off it. He will find out and be very emotional and upset. All that will do is close the door and keep him that much farther away from giving.

My wife and I were ministering in a place not far from Los Angeles once when a young girl came up after the meeting, and she was a shambles! Her husband had given her money to run the house on, and she had gotten carried away and given it all to the church. Now she did not know what to do. Betty ended up giving her the money and telling her what to do.

She would never have influenced her husband in a positive way doing that kind of thing. And you will not either. If your husband will not let you tithe, God knows that. He is not going to hold you responsible. He is not going to curse you so that your baby is born with two heads just because you are not tithing. Do not get into bondage thinking God is going to do something to you if you do not tithe. He knows your circumstances. He knows your husband will not give and will not let you give.

If your attitude toward your husband is not right, God does not receive it anyway. Without the right attitude, any offering is empty. You do not have to leave him if he will not pay the tithe. Pray for him and love him into it.

And if your husband will not go to church or read the Bible, leave him alone. Cast that care on the Lord. Pray for him, bind the powers of Satan over his mind that would hinder him, and just make sure that you *are* going to church and reading the Word. Your responsibility to pray and study the Bible is based upon the Lord's Word, not upon what your husband does or does not do.

What About Your Relatives?

We talked some about relatives in the last chapter, so I am not going into great detail here. Just remember, wives, be careful about letting your relatives occupy your time, efforts, energy, finances, and so forth to the neglect of your husband. That is not the better part of wisdom. If you cannot get him into agreement about what you believe you should do, or want to do, about your relatives, then you will have to believe God for the extra time or money, or for a way to work out this disagreement. You do not have any right to bring any relative into your home when your husband is not in favor of it.

My judgment is that a newly married couple does not need any one else living with them for the first five years, except their own children. As the Apostle Paul said, however, that is not the Lord speaking, but me. That is Fred Price's advice.

That is a general statement. Special circumstances may arise that mean it is impossible to do that. But as a general rule of thumb, it takes five years for a husband and wife to grow together and learn to know one another. Having a relative around can be a problem you do not need, because you are already in the process of making adjustments to one another. Now a third person has to be added to the mix.

When you married, lady, you married a husband, not your mother. Give your relationship time to grow. Some marriages take more time than others.

Another area of possible conflict is in mother-in-law problems. First, it takes two to tango. It takes two to argue, and it takes two to start a war. Your mother-in-law may not know how to walk in the Word, but as a Christian, you are supposed to. If you have a horrible mother-in-law, just pray and stay sweet. Try to say as little as possible.

Should your husband get involved? He had better take heed of Matthew 5:9: **Blessed are the peacemakers.** If a wife and a mother are in conflict, the husband is the one who is going to get the short end of the stick! He is the one in the middle. It is to his advantage to make peace. He needs to be a referee who uses the Word, the love of God, and counsel from the Holy Spirit.

Children of a Previous Marriage

If you have a child by a previous marriage or out of wedlock who is not living with you but that you visit and are helping support, then make sure your husband knows the situation before you marry. Of course, if the child or children live with you, then he obviously knows what is going on. But, as I said before, do not just spring something on him all of a sudden. He may not react the right way if he comes home one evening from work and finds three strange little girls in his house.

"Who are these little girls?"

"Oh, those are my children. They are going to live with us now."

"They are what" — question mark, exclamation points, and trouble.

That is a surprise no man would like. Let him know ahead of time, so he can make an objective decision about whether he wants to be involved in this kind of situation.

If opportunity and finances allow, then of course you should do something for your children. But it should be with the consent of your spouse.

A situation comes to my mind about being honest before marriage that really has nothing to do with relatives or other children, but it is a graphic example of why honesty is required of Christians.

A man and woman in my church were contemplating marriage, but one of them had been in an accident that affected the sexual organs. That person was believing God for healing and exercising faith. It was fine and good to believe for that condition to be corrected so this person could be normal. But it was not fine and good not to tell the other party, just in case the healing was not completed by the wedding night.

So they got married, and on the wedding night, the marriage act could not be consummated. The couple had been living according to the Word of God and abstaining from any sexual activity, so the other person had no warning that there was any problem and was totally and completely frustrated. Even months later, the situation had not been corrected. The marriage ended in annulment or divorce, when that could have been avoided.

Secrecy that amounted to dishonesty caused the problem to become worse, not better, and the other person involved suffered rejection, frustration, and disillusionment. What love they had could not last under those conditions.

Any secrets that will affect the other person should be talked about ahead of time so that the marriage can begin with consent and agreement.

Should Couples Pray Together?

There is an old adage, "The family that prays together stays together." But that is not true in every case. Just because you pray together is no guarantee that you will stay together. What you do not know how to pray about — or do not want to pray about — can still affect the relationship.

I think a wife has an obligation to pray with the children, but I think both parents should be in agreement about who is going to lead the child, especially a young child who is born again. The Bible does not say anything about this one way or the other.

My wife and I, for all practical purposes, never pray together because our habits are different. Now if there are things we need to agree on, things that both of us are concerned about, we make a project out of it. Then of course, we get together in agreement and pray. But in terms of a regular on-going devotional time, spending time together with the Lord, we never do that.

My wife takes time to wake up. She does not hit the floor wide awake. She is awake, but it seems to take some time for her brain and body to get synchronized. She likes to get out of bed, go in the kitchen, put on a pot of coffee, sit down at the table, drink her coffee and read the Word, then immediately after that, pray.

I am different. I wake up instantly. What I like to do is pray first, then get ready to leave the house. Just before I leave the house, I read the Word. So our times are different, our needs are different.

In the early days of my walk with the Lord, I thought posture was important. I tried to pray on my knees, and in the wintertime, my backside would be freezing. My mind would end up more on when I was going to get through so I could get warm than it was on praying. I tried putting blankets around me, but they would fall off onto the floor. And I was spending all my time trying to drape the blankets around the strategic areas. I decided that did not make good sense. What worked best for me was praying in bed for an hour and a half after I woke up.

Now that will not work for my wife. If she tries to pray in bed, she goes back to sleep — instantly. So she gets up, gets her coffee, and prays in the kitchen. The main thing is to pray.

111

Is your husband praying? Then do not make an issue out of praying together. But, again, this is something you need to agree on. If praying together works for you, then do it. If it does not, just pray separately, and do not get in conflict over it. What is important is that you both are praying. Your posture while praying, who you pray with, or when you pray, is not important.

If a family *can* pray together, like in a regular family altar time, then that is good. The point is, do not get under condemnation if that is not working perfectly. There are no scriptures that deal with family prayer.

You cannot make a rock-hard decision, "We're all going to pray every morning at 6." That kind of thing sometimes creates more conflict than praying together can solve.

What Do You Do About Infidelity?

Suppose you have a husband who is running around with other women: In the natural, there is nothing you can do, unless you shoot him. (And I am not suggesting that!) But usually there are a number of possible reasons why he is doing this. Of course, this is not true in every case. Some men are going to run around on their wives, no matter who she is or what she does.

If this is the case, you need to bind that spirit of lust off him, and pray for him. Maybe you can get him to go for counseling to your pastor or another Christian counselor.

The one thing you *can* do is make sure you are not the reason. Make sure he has no time or energy to run around. I am not talking about giving in to perverted activities to keep him at home, however. I am referring only to normal, natural sexual activities. Within those guidelines, be sure you are fulfilling him within reason.

If you are giving him the cold shoulder, it is still no excuse for his infidelity, but it certainly is a good explanation. You make it very hard for him not to give in to temptation when Sister Suzie comes along looking good and giving him the eye.

Another thing: He may not like you four or five sizes larger than when you married a few years ago. Then you were campus queen. Now you look like "Shamoo's sister." (I used that word "Shamoo" on a telecast, and a lady wrote me from Chicago and asked what that was. Well, "Shamoo" is the name of a whale. Do you get the picture?)

Some men are not able to tell you things like that. Maybe he is embarrassed when you go out together, but he does not want to hurt your feelings. You have not taken care of yourself, but he does not know what to do. So he is frustrated.

If things are not working, and your husband is the type who is not able to talk freely, ask him what is wrong. Tell him to write down his answer and put it under your pillow.

Ask him, "What would you like me to be?"

Then do your best to make yourself that, so that he has no excuse. He may be working some place where little Mary Jane out there is foot loose and fancy free, and she makes him an offer. He might not want to get involved in an adulterous situation, but he is human. And you have thrown him into that thing.

Make sure that you are giving him the very best you can. After that, you cannot do any more. So cast your care over on the Lord.

Chapter 10

THE DIVISION OF LABOR

Perhaps you are wondering why we have to talk about a division of labor in a marriage. As I was teaching the concepts in this book as a series in my church, the Holy Spirit showed me that marriage really is like a business partnership in many ways. The reason many marriages do not work is that some people's "business sense" is no good.

In a business, things have to be done a certain way, or it will come to a screeching halt. There has to be delegation of authority. Job roles have to be defined, and job responsibilities have to be handed out. Everyone has to pull his or her weight, or too much weight falls on others.

It is the same thing in a home. Things have to be done for the family to operate, and if someone abdicates his responsibility, the smooth flow of the rest of the family life suffers. There must be things the husband does, things the wife does, and things the children do. Also, there may be things the family pays someone to come in from outside to do.

I am convinced that a lot of the problems we are seeing in family relationships are because people are not carrying their weight. They are not pulling the load they are supposed to pull. I have seen couples fall out over little things — I mean, actually coming to blows over it!

I remember one couple some years back who I think ended up getting a divorce over something that seems minor to us — carrying out the trash. But it was very important to one of them, and they never did come to an agreement. They were in the office any number of times for counseling over it.

Something that is important to you may not be important to the other person, and vice versa. If you work on what is important to your spouse, then you can expect him or her to work on something that is important to you. If you are not communicating, or are not being honest with one another, you will not know how important that thing is to your spouse. You are going to feel "put upon" at being asked to do the thing in question, and somewhere along the line, there is going to be a breaking point.

To avoid such confrontations, it is much better to have a division of labor understood and worked out ahead of time.

Follow the Leader

In 1 Timothy 3, where Paul gave guidelines for the office of bishop, notice that one criteria is **one that ruleth well his own house** (1 Tim. 3:4a). The word *ruleth* in the original Greek, *proistemi,* carries a beautiful definition. What it means is "to stand before"[1] or "to stand in front of and lead."

So the husband ought to be able to stand in front of his wife and children and say, "Do like I do" — not "do like I say." That does not mean to *tell* his family what to do, but to stand in front of them and *show* them what to do. That means the husband should do it first.

---

[1] *Vine's Expository Dictionary of Old and New Testament Words,* Edit. by W. E. Vine and F. F. Bruce (New Jersey: Old Tappan, Fleming H. Revell Company, Copyright © 1981), p. 307.

When I was a kid, we used to play a game called "Follow the Leader." The object of the game was to do everything the guy in front did. Everybody watched the one in front. If he hopped along on his right foot, then we all hopped on the right foot — and so forth. If you did something different, you would be out of the game. Finally, there would be only one or two people left.

Every Christian ought to be able to follow the leader — Christ — and watch Him closely enough not to be counted out of the game of life. Following Christ, every man ought to, in turn, lead his family that way. That does not mean having your wife and children scared to death of you. It means living such a life before them that they *want* to follow you. Your lifestyle speaks louder to those watching you than any words you might say.

If your family sees the honesty of your life, the consistency of your attitude and behavior, that is more convincing than anything you can say. Seeing you the same in all situations gives a child a great sense of comfort and security. They know their parents are real.

I am not willing to accept what the world has to offer as my goal. That happens to too many Christians. Their lives are governed by the system of the world. Their "game plan" for life is based on worldly principles. The system of this world has them so programmed that they do not think they can make it any other way.

But just because "everybody is doing it" does not make it right, nor does it mean God ordained it. It certainly does not mean God approves of it! It is a matter of choices, of exercising your free will. If that is what you want to do, God will allow you to exercise your will — but you will reap the whirlwind if you are not doing what He wills for you to do based on His Word.

Keeper of the Home

Titus 2 talks about the wife's role:

> **But speak thou the things which become sound doctrine:**

> That the aged men be sober, grave, temperate, sound in faith, in charity, in patience.
>
> The aged women likewise, that they be in behaviour as becometh holiness, not false accusers, not given to much wine, teachers of good things;
>
> That they (the aged women) may teach the young women to be sober (or wise), to love their husbands, to love their children.
>
> Titus 2:1-4

We have made love an emotional thing, a feeling. The Word says for the older women to *teach* the young women "to love their husbands and children." You cannot *teach* a feeling. Feelings are experienced. So when the Holy Spirit said, **Teach the young women ... to love their husbands,** there is something more involved than feelings. What God calls *love* involves actions, not just words or feelings.

Aged, or older, women who have never married cannot teach the young women these things, so the context has to be older married women. Some older women in today's society could not teach younger women how to love their husbands and children, because they never learned how themselves. Younger wives, then, need to seek advice and counsel from older wives whose lives show the fruits of real love and wisdom.

Older women should be teaching the younger women instead of running around gossiping and spending time on habits or hobbies of the world.

I realize some of what is in this chapter may sound very hard, and I realize that our culture and economy today are not like those in which the books and letters of the New Testament were written. But we allow the world too often to dictate to us our values. We let the world tell us how to run our homes. Instead of letting God tell us, we let the system tell us. And, if you ever get locked into the system, it is exceedingly difficult to get out of it. You *can* get out of it, but it is going to cost you something. Once you get locked into it, your whole life is ordered on that system.

You cannot break away from it instantaneously because you do not get into it instantaneously.

The home has lost its Biblical place of importance in modern society. And America is reaping the whirlwind because of it. You can see the consequences in the numbers of illegitimate babies and abortions, drugs and alcohol addictions in even very young kids, in the crime rate of juveniles, and in the rising suicide rate among teens.

Out of the home comes the moral and spiritual values, the ability to appreciate the right things, and the ability to love. The reason society is out of control today is because people have been abdicating the responsibility of the home since World War II. Women have delegated or shunted the responsibility of raising their children onto nursery schools, preschools, or babysitters. As well-intentioned as the people who operate or work in those places may be, usually they are not spiritually equipped enough to substitute for the real mothers of those children.

All that schools are supposed to do is teach your children facts or information from the world's knowledge, and to teach technical skills enough to develop a job or a career. Unless it is a Christian school, they do not teach them spirituality. If public schools do get into religion and related subjects, they end up imparting or encouraging occultism or Eastern religions rather than Christianity.

Children learn morality at home. Either they learn Biblical morality, or they learn immorality. But their values are developed in the home, and today's younger generation has not learned moral values, by and large. That is why young people who may not be into the really bad things — like sex, drugs, or crime — still have no respect for authority, other people's rights, or other people's property. That is why we have a world that seems to have gone crazy.

I rode a New York subway not long ago. I had not been in the subway for a long time, and it was frightening! I am not very much afraid of anything, but man, this scene was frightening.

Kids had spray painted the subway car, the floors and seats, the inside and the outside of the windows, and all the supportive posts along the platform. It was absolutely frightening, because it looked like the work of insane people.

Those responsible for this graffiti are young people out of control, with no sense of moral values, no appreciation for things that belong to other people. These are the children of people who put the responsibility for raising them on someone else. In many cases, there was no one else to do it. So the kids are "bringing up" themselves, which means no real upbringing at all. They have no sense of security because they have had no tender loving care. The values that need to be instilled in children while they are in the protective cocoon of the home environment have never been instilled.

We are raising an entire generation of children with no sense of values. In a few years, one of that generation with no sense of values will be the one sitting on top of the red button that launches the ICBM missiles.

And he may just decide, "Today I am going to 'paint' somebody's house," and *boom*, the world is in trouble.

These are the children who are going to be our policemen, firemen, educators, doctors, congressmen, senators, and presidents.

Can you imagine the havoc and problems that could result from a man with no sense of values who is loose on the streets with a .357 Magnum in his hand, a pair of handcuffs, and legal authority? You have a dangerous person on your hands. We are raising up those kinds of children, and more people are planning to get married and raise the same kind of children, because "this is the system."

If you do not operate within the system, you will never get two cars in the garage. If you do not work in the system, world knowledge says you will never get that kind of split-level house you want, you will never have that big screen television set. Both parents have to work.

But that is natural, or sense knowledge, and according to God's Word, that knowledge is a lie. God's Word says you can make it by giving away ten percent of your income. God's principles of living look crazy to the world because we live in a satanic-influenced world system, and it is opposite to God's laws. However, you can look at world situations and problems and see that the world's wisdom is not working.

God's Law of Giving

Some of you know you can prosper by giving. When you first heard it, you did not think it was feasible, but you tried it.

You said, "Wait a minute. I have to think about this. I am not making it too well on what I am making now. If I give away ten percent, how am I going to make it at all?"

But you found out that once you got into God's law, God's order, and God's plan, you began to prosper. It may not happen overnight, but remember, it took time to get into financial problems. Working your way out is a progressive process. You have to take one step at a time on God's principles. Use them as stepping stones to walk out of the muck and the mire of the world's system.

We started with ten percent, then went to twelve and a half, fifteen, twenty, and now twenty-five percent tithes and offerings. We give away $.25 out of every dollar, and God meets our needs. God will take care of you, if you do things His way. Put enough seed out there, and after a while, you will have the house and things you want. God will give them to you, but He has to have a channel through which to work. And you have to be obedient.

I have a fourth of my income planted every day, and I confess over it that all my needs will be met, so that I have more to give away. *The bottom line is to have it to give.* The more you give, the more you can receive, then the more you can give — and the harvest continues to grow. After a while, your needs automatically get met. All of your desires that are consistent with a godly life get met. Then you do not have any more needs, and you can spend all your time giving.

Have you ever wanted to give to a worthy cause, but could not because you needed it all for yourself? Well, when you have that seed out there, God will honor you. That is God's highest and best way.

The harvest coming in to us now is not because I am a pastor. God's Word is not just for ministers. It is for all of His children. The harvest is coming in because I have been planting for more than sixteen years.

You *do* have to be willing to pay a price. The price is bucking the system. The price is to discipline yourself to do what the Bible says out of love for God and His Word. If you have the giving right, the getting will come. You do not have to give to get. You give because it is right, because the Word says to, and because you want to please your Heavenly Father. He is the one Who attaches the blessings to giving.

Handling the Money

Who should pay the bills? Who should write the checks? Some people are not qualified to take care of the check book. They are absent minded, or they have no head for figures. If the husband cannot handle the economic affairs of the home, then the wife ought to be doing it.

In a business, if you have a person in charge of purchasing who has no expertise or talent in that area, he could practically bankrupt the whole store by buying up everything in sight. He has no ability or discretion. Those are the things that cause businesses to fail, and these are the same things that cause marriages to fail.

The person who handles the finances ought to be the one who is best at it. In some cases, it is the husband. In other cases, it is the wife. It might even be both of them. If one of the couple has to do the chore and is not good at it, that one will be upset all the time. And if the other is an orderly person who likes things done in a systematic fashion, that one will be upset as well.

The devil will see to it that one forgets to do things, and the other gets upset. He will use that domestic chore to keep them at each other's throat.

Domestic Duties

Giving to God and the handling of money are the "big" things. Now let us look at the "little" things, the domestic duties that can become crucial points of conflict if not handled right.

You might wonder, "Man, why is he talking about things like that?"

The reason I am talking about these things is because these are what come up in counseling sessions. These are the questions that come up in letters and telephone calls. You may think they are "no big deal," but when they become a bone of contention, they become a "big deal."

Here are some of the questions I hear:

Who washes the dishes?

Who cleans the house?

Who empties the trash?

Who shops for groceries?

Who disciplines the children?

Right away, some of you are going to say, "Well, those things are 'women's work.'"

That is the world's thinking. Society has stereotyped "women's roles" and "men's roles" in the area of domestic duties. What is required is a little common sense. If the wife stays home, keeps the house, and takes care of the children, that requires one division of labor. If she works as many hours as her husband, thus dividing the responsibility of supporting the family, then he should accept his part of the division of labor within the home.

A lot of men do not like to wash dishes, but make no provision — such as a dishwasher — to help get them done. They shunt all the dirty work off on their wives, who work eight hours a day outside the home. A husband whose wife works but who expects her to bring home the check, then wash the dishes, take care of the house and the kids, cook the meals, and then be his play thing after 11:30 p.m. is not being fair. He is not loving his wife as Christ loved the Church. Not only is he not giving his life for his wife, he is not giving a fair share of his time and energy.

It should not be the woman doing everything, nor should it be the man doing everything. *It ought to be whoever does it the best, and whatever the couple is in agreement on.*

Someone does have to do the little menial things. But different people deal with this situation in different ways. I know a couple who eat out nearly every day. They agreed on that when they got married. Now that arrangement is not for me. I enjoy eating out some times, but not every day! But she is not my wife, and he is not Betty's husband. So whatever works for them in peace and harmony is the right thing for them. They are happy, and that is all that matters. How they arrange their division of labor and their domestic duties is no one's business but theirs.

Of course, a house has to be cleaned. Suppose the husband does not do it, the wife does not do it, and no one is paid to come in and do it. What is going to happen? You will not be able to get in the house for the roaches.

Again, it seems to me that the task should fall to whoever is good at it, and whatever the husband and wife agree on. If a clean house means a lot to one of them, that couple will have marital problems if the house does not get cleaned. And if all of the labor falls on one — unless that one has agreed to do it — they will have a problem. Someone is going to be frustrated.

The Song of Solomon 2:15 says the little foxes spoil the vines. That means the little things can spoil a relationship as quick, or quicker, than the big things.

The situation where the couple fought over who was going to empty the trash is a good case in point. Every time the husband wanted to put something in the trash can, he found it running over on the floor. But neither of them wanted to empty the trash. It seems like a little thing, but little things can be aggravations.

I do not know where all the trash in a house comes from. You may think that is funny, but take an inventory in your own home for a week. You will be surprised at the amount of trash that accumulates. I ended up getting a trash compactor for our house. Then no one had to empty the trash. But the trash not being emptied became such a big thing to the couple I mentioned that they got a divorce.

The person who does the grocery shopping ought to be the one best suited for it. A couple should divide up the labor and agree on who does what based on who does it best and who has the time. For the first ten years of our marriage, I did all the shopping. My wife did not drive, so I would go by the bank after getting my paycheck, and then stop by the grocery store on the way home. Besides, I can shop faster than she can. I am more organized. I can do in fifteen minutes what it takes her an hour.

What about the bills? Who pays the bills? Someone better pay them, or you will be sitting there one night, and all the lights are going to go out.

You say, "There must be a power failure in the neighborhood."

And you go outside and look, but all the neighbors' lights are on. There is even a cat walking down the street with a light on its collar, and that is lit. The only place on the street that is dark is your house.

Then you go back inside and say to your wife, "Honey, did you pay the electric bill?"

And she looks at you strangely and says, "I thought you were going to pay it."

"Oh, no, no. I definitely remember telling you to pay it."

"No, you did not," she says, "Don't raise your voice at me! I'll go home to Mama."

Then you have a big fight going over something that is ridiculous. It may sound funny just reading about it. But it is not funny when it happens to you. A whole lot of these kinds of things sound trivial, but if they are not dealt with, they are not trivial any longer. They become major problems.

Is disciplining the children the wife's job or the husband's? Somebody better discipline them. They cannot "grow themselves up" very well. Again, it must be resolved according to the specific situation.

If the wife works, she is as tired as her husband when she gets off. She picks up the children at nursery school or wherever and brings them home. Maybe they need some discipline. She is tired. Her nerves are frayed from dealing with "wild beasts" at work all day.

But her husband does not want to be bothered with it, so he shunts the responsibility off on his wife. She is trying to push it off on him. Then she gets mad because she has to work and cannot stay home and look after the children. But who is going to discipline and train them?

It is an awesome responsibility to raise children. If parents realized the fullness of being responsible for a human life, it could literally frighten them. You can destroy that life in the home, or you can establish that life in the home. Children need a father image of authority as well as a mother image of nurturing and love.

Imagine a woman coming home tired to a child who takes an hour and a half to do what could be done in fifteen minutes, and even then she has had to keep after him and keep after him. What happens? Usually, she will take the path of least resistance and let him have his own way. She does not feel like being bothered.

He keeps on having his own way and developing self-will, then society has to deal with a spoiled brat as an adult. There are many adults out there like that today. Even in the Church, there are people who have no concept of authority. A person who has never been trained to come under authority but always has done what he pleases is a real problem when you come along as his boss or his pastor and try to tell him something.

I have seen some women who know how to exercise authority. Their children hop, skip, and jump when she speaks, but other women allow the children to run right over them. So who decides who is to discipline? The husband and wife must get together on who does thus and so.

I believe that if a wife stays home during the child's formative years, then the father ought to give the orders or instructions before he leaves, and the wife ought to carry them out. The child ought to know that daddy is going to come home and find out if he, or she, did what mama said, because mama was operating under the direction of the father.

But suppose both of you work. You are going to have to get into agreement about who takes charge of the child. Otherwise, you will have bigger problems to deal with later on.

Also, what about children from previous marriages who live with you now? Many wives do not want their husbands disciplining a child from a previous marriage. They are *her* kids, and that is the way she refers to them.

"Don't you hit *my* boy."

I have had couples in the office like that, with the husband totally frustrated. Perhaps the wife is not speaking to the husband because he is trying to correct the child. Now, obviously, I am not talking about abuse or improper actions and attitudes. I am talking about proper and right discipline.

A man will say, "Pastor, what am I supposed to do? She lets the kid get away with murder. She is ruining him. He is mama's little boy, and he is acting like a jack. Every time I go to discipline him or correct him, she gets mad at me."

She needs to realize that when she married that new husband, "her" child became "our" child. When you marry someone with children, you take on those children, if they are living with the one you marry. You, husband, take that lady with everything she has, good or bad, or you are not giving her full value. And that is what you will get out of that relationship, less than full value.

You should talk about that before you get married. You should decide who is going to do what, and who is going to back it up. Children are very shrewd. They will play the mother against the father and vice versa, if the parents let them. When they find out that mama does not like what daddy said to the child, that child will "butter up" mama and work her around like a con man. Then the kid will lean over against the wall while mama and papa are pulling each other's hair out or breaking one another's noses. It is "let's you and him fight." I have seen this.

Children can be very, very slick in getting their own ways. When they grow up, you have *manipulative* adults. I have seen this. These people are dangerous. They will manipulate things and people to get their own ways. Sometimes that starts as a defense mechanism because the home life is so bad. But those who have learned as children to appeal to people's need areas in order to manipulate them are dangerous. They wreak havoc in other people's lives.

If you sit down and get in agreement on what discipline, how much, and who does it, then the child cannot play one against the other. Certainly, you ought not to disagree with each other and one of you take the child's part in front of him. Wait until later when you can talk privately to correct your husband or wife and talk things over. Do not do it in front of the child.

A similar issue involves *community property*.

Perhaps you came into a relationship already owning a house, a car, and furniture, or this and that. What about that? I believe the Bible says when you marry, you become one. That means that your house, and your car, and your furniture, and even your bank account all becomes "ours." Otherwise, you are already preparing for failure.

Chapter 11

SHOULD THE WIFE WORK?

I want to make it clear that what I am going to say in this chapter is not meant as a "put down" to any individual. All I am going to do is deal with this subject to the best of my knowledge and insight for the purpose of bringing the greatest degree of light and understanding to difficult circumstances.

Most of us do not live on the level of God's best. We live on the level of "barely get along." All Christians at some time or other came out of the world. What happens, however, is that we drag everything we learned in the world into Christian relationships without even realizing it.

Many Christians function and operate daily on certain principles, or "programs," that have nothing to do with the Word of God whatsoever. But they are locked into an habitual, "Pavlov's dog" syndrome of doing things because that is the way they have always done it. (Ivan P. Pavlov was a Russian scientist whose experiments with dogs almost a hundred years ago were the first studies done on mind conditioning. The end result in our day has been "brain washing.")

Probably, you have never stopped to examine yourself and find out if the way you do things is God's way. You just struggle along in the system. Many Christians' lives are guided by what the world says, not by what God says.

So let us look at something Paul wrote Timothy about marriage.

I will therefore that the younger women marry, bear children, guide the house, give none occasion to the adversary to speak reproachfully.

1 Timothy 5:14

I believe the Holy Spirit was speaking through Paul when he wrote that letter to Timothy, because God is not the author of confusion. I do not think He would have allowed Paul to say this if He did not support it. Otherwise, He would have had to come behind Paul and clean up a mess.

It Is Not Wrong for Women to Work

I do not believe this verse is telling us that it is wrong for a woman to work, because obviously there are many instances when it becomes necessary.

It is not wrong for a woman to work. It is simply not the best way. It is not *wrong* if I go out into a field and start plowing the ground with my bare hand. That is not wrong, but it surely is not the best way! I can dig some holes in the ground and plant seed, and if that is the only way I can plant seed, then I had better do it that way. But it is not the best, most profitable way.

Notice that Paul did not say younger women *have* to marry, simply that he would rather they did. Then he gives his reasons for feeling that way.

The first reason Paul gave for "willing" that the younger women marry was in order for them to have children and replenish the earth. If you get married young, you have a better chance to have children safely and in good health. You are better able to handle them and grow up with them. You have more stamina, and you can put up with a little more than you can when you are older.

The second reason he gave was to *guide the house.* Now that does not say *guide the business or the store,* but the *house.*

So it seems to me that the woman is delegated the authority and responsibility of taking care of the domestic aspects of the marriage relationship. If you are not careful, right away your mind will revert to the world's wisdom:

"In order to get ahead, the daddy's got to work, the mama's got to work, the dog, cat, and kids all have to work.

"If you are going to have two cars in the garage, two mopeds to ride, two pairs of jogging shoes, a color television in every room, and a split-level or ranch-style house with a swimming pool, both of you have to work."

If you operate in the world's system, that is how you have to live. Unless the husband is a professional person making an awful lot of money, both husband and wife have to work in order to have the things the world tells you are necessary for a happy home.

It seems to me that the Lord is saying the woman's part of the division of labor is to be in the home to take care of it.

What Is God's Best?

This chapter is for women who can stay home and look after their children. Some wives and mothers cannot do that, so do not be intimidated! My purpose is not condemnation but to help.

There are women in situations that are exceptions to the rule, and this advice is not for them. These women include:

1. *Working mothers.*

If you have to work, you know that, and God knows that. So do not let yourself be offended by this teaching. A mother whose husband has left her, or a divorcee who has custody of the children but is not supported by her ex-husband has no choice but to work. There are a lot of women working now who would come off the job and gladly stay home, if it were possible.

A woman who has to support her children usually does not want to go on welfare. She does not want a hand-out from her mother or relatives. If she went to high school, at least, and has some abilities, she wants to look after herself. I do not think that is right or wrong, only expedient. She is doing what she must to survive.

2. *Women with professional abilities and education.*

If you have trained yourself for a job, and your talents would be wasted if you do not use them, and if your husband and family agree and are taken care of, then holding a job is no problem for the family.

3. *Women in special circumstances.*

If you have money for live-in help, or a family that willingly pitches in to help, or arrangements otherwise acceptable to your husband and to the Lord, then your working is not out of order. If you do not have any children at home, and you and your husband keep the house nicely so that you have a lot of spare time, you could be using your abilities and talents out in the world.

Another "special circumstance" is a wife who is working while her husband is finishing college or getting a graduate degree in his profession. However, as soon as he begins to bring home a salary, if there are children, God's best provision would be for her to stay home and be with them.

Not everyone at every point in life is ready to operate in God's best. The people I am talking to are the ones who can receive this knowledge from the Word and are at a point where they can act on it.

If you get locked into the pattern of thinking that you have to work to have the world's things and meet the world's standards, as I discussed in the last chapter, your marriage and your children are going to suffer.

If you get locked into the system and allow your kids to grow up only seeing you a few hours in the afternoon, you are sowing the seeds of trouble. Perhaps even when you do see the children, you do not want to be bothered because your head is spinning from all that garbage going on all day. That kind of situation is not fair to the children and not fair to society. All you are going to do is perpetuate some more "Frankenstein monsters" with no sense of values. Then the world is really going to be in a mess.

All I am saying to women is: *Do not sacrifice your motherhood on the altar of the economic system.*

What I am saying to both men and women is *do not sacrifice your children on the altar of success.*

Personally, I am not opposed to women working. If you want to work, that is your business. But I believe God has a plan, and if you will follow that plan, you will be able to enjoy the fullness of life and have the things you need. You will raise children who will be a credit, and not a detriment, to society.

Can you see how cleverly Satan has blunted the sharp edge of God's Word and obscured God's will for marriages by forcing his world system over onto us? Do you see how subtly he has "programmed" even Christians into thinking that having a certain lifestyle is their right? And to achieve that lifestyle, it takes both father and mother working full time.

If you say, "We are in financial trouble if I quit working," that is only because you have structured your lifestyle that way. That is the way you built it.

Let me give you a personal illustration from my own life. I began to live a certain way even before I knew what the Word said about it. I did it out of hard experience.

A Personal Example

When I was younger, my father had married three times, and he was somewhat older than my mother. Now I am not putting my father down. He had things to deal with in his life just as everyone does. But he had a drinking problem.

Every time we would accumulate a little bit of this world's goods, he would get drunk, not go to work, and lose jobs. He had his own business, a janitorial business, and if he did not service his customers regularly and efficiently, he would lose them. Or maybe he would get drunk and wreck the car.

So my parents were always arguing, fussing, and fighting back and forth. My mother was trying to make a home, and my father was doing whatever he was doing, and there would not be any money. Then she would get upset. It was a bad scene.

Finally, she got to the point where she realized that she had to do something to survive. He might go out and kill himself, then she would be left with me to raise. She did not have any skills or training, but she began to develop her abilities so that she would be able to support herself and me if she had to.

But between my father "doing his thing" and my mother developing her work skills, I was left in a vacuum, so to speak. I was left to myself. Many days, I came home from junior high school to an empty house. Days on end, I had freedom to do whatever I wanted. It was like nobody really cared.

My mother was busy trying to survive, and my father was either oblivious or too drunk to know the difference. The only time he ever bought me anything was when he was drunk. Now please do not misunderstand. I do not hold any of that against him. I have no malice in my heart. I am only using my own life as an illustration. I believe my father did the best he could under his circumstances. He did not know how to do better. If he had known how to get delivered and out of that kind of mess, he would have done it.

However, if you do not know better, you end up perpetuating the same junk into the next generation. If you are ignorant, you are going to perpetuate ignorance — unless somebody somewhere down the line does something about it, unless someone stops the process.

I had more free time on my hands than any child should have. As a result, I got into all sorts of things — everything you could name. I got involved with girls. I had time, and the girls had time. You sit around with a lot of time on your hands, and you are going to start thinking and experimenting. The old saying is very true, "An idle mind is the devil's workshop." It is not just his workshop, it is automated, running three shifts!

There were times when I would wonder if I was really my parents' own child. There were times I cried myself to sleep. My bedroom was next to the kitchen, and I would put my ear against the wall and hear them after I went to bed. They would be in the kitchen fussing and talking, acting crazy and ugly and so forth. And I would cry myself to sleep many nights.

In fact, I wondered if I was living in a nightmare, and one day I would wake up and everything would be nice, just like in the movies I went to where the families were so nice and pretty and treated each other so good.

I was not all that crazy about marriage, but I made up my mind that if I got married my wife would never work. There would never be a time when one of my children came home to an empty house.

Betty and I have now been married thirty-three years, and she has never worked except for a couple of times when I absolutely could not find a job. We went through a lot of hell at first because of my immaturity, stupidity, hard headedness, and a whole lot of hard stuff! You could not tell me anything. I would not listen to anybody. So I learned a lot of things the hard way, and that is *not* the best way to learn. And she had to live through all of that mess. But thank God it came out fine in the end, and we "lived happily ever after."

As a result of my determination that my wife would not work, we struggled at first, because I was not operating on the Word of God but out of the flesh. So we struggled. Finances were the crux of every other problem we had. There was never enough money in the beginning. The children did not have shoes or enough clothes.

Now Betty helps in the ministry, but even yet, no child of mine comes home to an empty house. We pick up our youngest, Freddie, at school, so that he is home when we are home. The three older girls always had their mother home when they came in. If they came home with a bruise, Mama was there. Many times as a child, I came in with hurts, and there was no one there, no one to kiss the hurt or give me a hug, no one to tell me that everything was going to be all right.

Our two oldest daughers are married, and the third is a teenager, but we have never had one minute's trouble out of our children. I have never been to the police station to pick up my children. I have never had the school principal call me down to his office because of my rowdy children. When my daughters married, they were virgins. That is what they were taught in the home by precept and by example.

Thank God Betty and I got into the Word early enough for me to be able to be the kind of father and spiritual leader they needed. When we first married, it cost us to get into God's best, but we have lived in it now for many years. I can tell you it is joy unspeakable and full of glory!

My wife works now in the ministry by her own choice. I do not require her to work. I take care of her. All of the money she makes now is her own to spend on whatever she wants. I buy her clothes, take care of the house, and do everything else. She could flush her money down the toilet if she so desired.

With our little boy in school, our unmarried daughter working every day, and a housekeeper coming in three days a week, there is little for Betty to do at home. She would not be happy staying home and twiddling her thumbs, so today she falls in the "exception category" of women in special circumstances. But up until a few years ago, she was home every day with the house and the children.

She is not working out of necessity, nor because we will go under financially if she does not. I take good care of her. Anyone can ask her that. If she says I am wrong, it will not embarrass me. I want to know if I am missing it. I will improve. I will straighten up, because I intend to be the best husband on the planet, the best provider for my wife that I can be, and to give her the best tender loving care I am capable of. But if there are any shortcomings, I do not know it. She has not told me of any.

Seeking God's best in our marriage and family has paid handsome dividends in the texture of our relationships and the fabric of our union.

Morality Comes Out of the Home

The morality of this nation must come out of the home. People criticize the school system, but the public schools are not supposed to give children anything but hard, cold facts. They are supposed to teach children how to add two and two, what a verb is, where Columbus came from, and how to research material in the library.

Public schools are not supposed to teach children morality or spirituality. That ought to be taught in the home. I do not expect some teacher to instill respect for other people's lives and other people's property into my child. I am not looking for some teacher to teach my children to respect their parents. All school is for is to teach facts. Your children are supposed to see morality in your life and hear it out of your mouth.

How are they going to do that when their mothers are running the streets working just like the fathers do? If you are a working mother, you do not have enough time for the children. When you come home, you do not feel like being bothered. You want to sit down somewhere, kick off your shoes, and put a TV dinner in the microwave oven.

Some people have come into the knowledge of the Word, a knowledge of faith, and a knowledge of what God wants for them and has provided for them through Jesus and the New Covenant.

However, when they found all of this out, they already were embroiled in financial problems. They may have been living at a standard that required two salaries. Few of them were living on his salary and saving all of hers for a rainy day! If both husband and wife are working, it is almost guaranteed that they are in a financial position based on both of their wages. If the wife suddenly stopped working, there would be economic problems right away.

What I am saying is that before a man legitimately can start crowing about being the head of the house, he should be ready to take on the headship responsibility. If you are not doing that, you have not arrived at headship. And I can testify that God will bless you if you accept the responsibility.

Society is in a mess today because we have moved away from ordering our homes, our schools, and our governments according to God's best plans. Things are not functioning as God designed them to function. And I refuse to accept the garbage that says, "Well, you know that's the way it is." That is not the way it is in my house, and it does not have to be the way it is in your house.

If you never set your sights on the best, you will never get to that goal. You have to set God's best as your goal, then work towards it. That is what we did, and we went without a lot of things along the way. But we had love, concern, and caring in our home. Our children never came home to an empty house. I could not always pay the bills, but Betty and I got in agreement to work toward financial prosperity — which means having our needs met and enough left over to give anytime God says, "Give."

God has brought us into a wide pasture now. Every need is met, and every bill is paid because we learned to walk in His way.

If the only reason your wife is working is to get a bunch of things that you want, then you do not know how to trust God to meet your needs. God is not your source. Your jobs are your source. And if it takes two jobs to run your household, then your house has two heads.

Headship Involves Rank *and* Responsibility

Remember that headship is a matter of rank. If you are the head, responsibility goes along with it. The General's responsibility is greater than the private's. If a General messes up, he can refer things up to the President. But the "buck stops" at the President's office, as the late Harry Truman once said. So there is a responsibility with being "the" head.

Let me interject a word of advice here to wives: *Do not quit your job and say Fred Price told you to!* All I am doing is showing you God's best. It is up to you and your husband to judge your own situation and then get in agreement as to what to do about it.

I have women with small children working in my ministry. In fact, most of the women on staff are married, and some of them have children. If I were against women working per se, I would not hire those women. There are circumstances that prohibit a woman from staying home. All I am saying to you, husband, is that if you expect your wife to work to help support the family, if you expect her to share the responsibilities, then you need to also share the equality of headship.

But if any provide not for his own, and specially for those of his own house, he hath denied the faith, and is worse than an infidel.

1 Timothy 5:8

If you are in a situation where your salary could provide for your family, and you expect your wife to work just for extra things, you are not really qualified to be the head. If your economic situation is structured on your wife working, then she has as much right to make economic decisions as you do.

There is nothing wrong with having things and being comfortable. But there is God's way to do it and the world's way. The world's way involves two salaries, two heads, a lot of confusion of roles, and neglected children — at least to some degree.

Now, do not be foolish. Do not tell your wife to quit working immediately if you are not in an economic position to do so.

Marriage involves economics along with everything else. You may have the same desire I had for your wife to be home and take care of the children, but right now you do not know how to do that. Like we were in the beginning, perhaps you have set up your family according to the world's arrangement.

To get out of that pattern, you have to make an adjustment — and you cannot make that adjustment overnight. In the next chapter, I am going to tell you how you can make the adjustment from the world's way to God's way.

Chapter 12

HOW TO REACH GOD'S BEST
IN FINANCES

Reaching God's best in your relationship involves God's part and your part.

The Word says:

> **But my God shall supply all your need according to his riches in glory by Christ Jesus.**
> **Philippians 4:19**

Now that is God's part. On your part there must be faith developed to the point where you can believe God to supply all your need. Faith must be developed. You usually must begin by believing God for small things, then progressing to the larger. Along the way, you have to use some common sense.

For example, you may be on welfare, and I do not believe that is God's best. However, thank God for welfare to keep you from starving to death until you can find out how to live by faith.

Do not read this book and go off welfare immediately. That could be disastrous. Until you can live by faith, it is the better part of wisdom to keep on drawing that welfare check, and in the process of time, learn to believe that God is your source.

And, husbands, you need to follow the same principle if your wife works. You can get to a point where your wife does not have to work. It took time for you to get into the situation where both of you have to work, and it will take time to make your way out of that position.

In addition to believing God's Word, you need to put legs to your faith. **Faith without works is dead** (James 2:20). You need to begin to tithe.

> **And all the tithe of the land, whether of the seed of the land, or of the fruit of the tree, is the Lord's: it is holy unto the Lord.**
>
> Leviticus 27:30

> **Bring ye all the tithes into the storehouse, that there may be meat in mine house, and prove me now herewith, saith the Lord of hosts, if I will not open you the windows of heaven, and pour you out a blessing, that there shall not be room enough to receive it.**
>
> Malachi 3:10

> **But this I say, He which soweth sparingly shall reap also sparingly; and he which soweth bountifully shall reap also bountifully.**

> **Every man according as he purposeth in his heart, so let him give; not grudgingly, or of necessity: for God loveth a cheerful giver.**

> **And God is able to make all grace abound toward you; that ye, always having all sufficiency in all things, may abound to every good work:**

> **(As it is written, He hath dispersed abroad; he hath given to the poor: his righteousness remaineth for ever.**

Now he that ministereth seed to the sower both minister bread for your food, and multiply your seed sown, and
increase the fruits of your righteousness;)

Being enriched in every thing to all bountifulness,
which causeth through us thanksgiving to God.

For the administration of this service not only suppli-
eth the want of the saints, but is abundant also by many
thanksgivings unto God.

2 Corinthians 9:6-12

Most people who find out about tithing are not in a position to begin. First, they have to use self-control and self-discipline
to stop buying things, adding onto charge accounts, getting new
charge accounts, and buying a lot of things they just see and want.
They have to limit themselves to buying necessities in order to get
to the place where they have enough bills out of the way in order
to have enough money to tithe.

It costs something to do that. It costs time, effort, discipline, and self-denial. You do not get there overnight, but you
have to start somewhere. Begin giving what you can and make a
commitment to increase that amount as it becomes possible.
There is a price to pay, and you may not be ready and willing to
pay that price. But it works, and I am a living witness of it. It
works!

I am the head of my house. I provide for my wife and children. I did not always do the very best because I did not know the
best. As soon as I found out about God's best, however, I began to
move that way as quickly as I could.

Giving your way out of debt is God's principle and does not
make sense according to man. However, I can testify that it works.

Sharing Responsibilities

Until you can give your way out of debt and be able to live
on one income, you husbands with working wives need to share
her responsibilities. After all, she is sharing yours.

A lot of men want their wives to work. They take her pay-check from her, then kick their shoes off and park themselves in front of the television set when they come in from work. In the meantime, after working as many hours as the husband, the wife has to come home, stop by the day care center or the pre-school and pick up the kids, prepare dinner, get the kids settled and see that they say their prayers, wash the dishes and clean up the house, then perhaps she has to wash and roll her hair for the next day.

She has had a hard day, and she is ready to go to sleep. He has gotten rested up, however, and is ready to play games. So he gets all upset and wonders what is wrong with her when she goes to sleep as soon as her head hits the pillow.

If you want your wife to work, then you need to share the domestic duties. If you are like me, you will not want to do them yourself. Personally, I am not washing any dishes or cleaning up any house. I could do it, but I am not going to. Therefore, I make sure my wife is well provided for so that she can keep house as a full-time job, or I make sure she has outside help since she want-ed to work in the ministry.

It would not be fair for me to expect her to work, take her money for "our" expenses, then make her do all the domestic chores. I think men who do that are dogs.

As I said, my wife did not work outside the home. As soon as we were able, I hired someone to come in three days a week, so that she is free to do what she wants to do. When our youngest went to school, my desire was for her to just stay home and sleep in, to get up when she wanted to, and go have tea with her friends in the middle of the day. She is in that kind of position now.

But she wanted to work in the ministry with me. She asked to be a part of it, and I appreciate that. I can trust her absolutely. She is not working out of ambition. She does not do things to make "goodie points." Her money goes into a benevolent account. Most of the time, she gives it all away. I buy her clothes and her cars, and she does not need the money. But since she holds a job, she deserves the pay. So she uses her money for giving. She is always giving to somebody. If I did not watch her, she might give me away!

Betty has had five children and taken care of me for more than thirty years. She deserves the right to stay home if she wants to, or to work with me if that is what she wants.

I do help with certain things around the house, however, even today. For example, my wife likes the bed in our room made up. To me, that does not make sense. Nobody is home all day to see the bed. What difference does it make? Leave the dumb thing unmade. Who is going to see it but the angels? Now if we were having company, I could understand it. Naturally we want to show our best side and straighten up everything.

But we live there. Freddie goes to school, Stephanie goes to work, Betty and I go to the office, so who is there to know whether the bed is made up or not? But having the bed made means something to her. So I took that upon myself. On the days the housekeeper does not come in, I make our bed. I do it not because I want to, but because she wants it made. I do it to please my wife. I do it out of courtesy to her.

Another thing I do involves our son. Freddie can fool around and waste a lot of time! I would be in our room trying to pray, and here would be my wife running from the bathroom to Freddie's room to try to keep him doing what he was supposed to be doing. She would come through our room and back through our room, while I was trying to pray. I could hear her getting on him to get dressed for school, and she was trying to get dressed for work.

I pray from 5 to 6 a.m. in the Spirit. I was not going to quit praying, but prayer can be slower or faster. God can hear as fast as you can speak. So there is not any virtue in taking nine hours to say something to God that you can say in nine seconds.

So I said, "Here's what I am going to do. I am not going to quit praying, yet I have to get ready on time also. What I am going to do to free you up and give you a little more time in the morning is get Freddie up myself."

One of the things that had been a problem was getting his shoes on. We used to call them tennis shoes, but now they call them by whatever brand name is their favorite. With these shoes, kids wear bigger, thicker socks that you cannot tell where the heel is sometimes. With dress socks, you can lay them down and see the ankle part and the heel and the toe. It is easy to see the heel. But in some of these athletic socks, you can turn them all kinds of ways to find the heel. And Freddie would take a lot of time putting on his socks. He could never seem to get it figured out.

I am a systematic person, and Betty is not an organizer. She has no system of doing things. So I told her to lay out his clothes — his socks, shoes, pants, shirt, everything he is to wear. I told her to place his clothes on top of the toy chest, and I would get him dressed.

At 6 a.m., when I finish praying in the Spirit, I hop out of bed and wake Freddie up. Of course, it takes him a little time to come out of the sleep stage. He is halfway groggy and does not want to get up. So while he is in that stage, I roll him over and put his socks on. Then he cannot "cop out" with the socks. He can dress himself, but he would take forever with the socks! He would get frustrated at not being able to find the heel, and come into our room and bother her.

Once I get him started, I go back in our room and pray a little bit in English, then run back into his room and see how he is doing. As long as I am checking on him, it seems to keep him going. He knows I am coming, but he does not know when I will be popping through that door. That sort of intimidates him. He stays on the job and gets ready.

Of course, I do not have to do that. But that is a small price to pay to help her.

Wives Are Equal Partners

Your wife is an equal partner in the relationship, so it is not fair for her to do all the domestic chores and still work eight hours a day. You ought to split that domestic stuff right down the middle. If you do not want to wash dishes, fine, but then you ought to hire someone to wash them for her.

Do you think Jesus treats His bride the way some Christian men treat their wives?

Another thing: when you marry in the Lord you become "one flesh." That means your money becomes "one" also. Part of your paycheck belongs to her. As I said before, I know women married to guys that do not even know where their husbands work or how much money they make. The husbands give them allowances and tell them to run the house on that amount. When or if they get a raise their wives know nothing about it. That does not give a wife a real sense of belonging, a real solid sense of security! Boy, that is unfair. I know Jesus would not treat us that way.

If you want your wife to work, then your salaries ought to go into one pot — whether you make the most or whether she makes the most money. These folks who have separate checking accounts are operating in the world's wisdom.

She is thinking, "Well, what if he leaves me. My daddy was no good and left my mama without any support. That is never going to happen to me."

And he knows some woman who went off and left one of his friends and took all of their money with her.

So she has her own little checking account, and he has his. He does not sign on her account, and she does not sign on his. What that couple is doing is making provision for failure. They are putting faith in not making it, and the devil will come along and accommodate them, if they keep that kind of mess going.

The money that comes in to operate your family ought to be shared together. If you are afraid to have a joint account, you are married to the wrong person. You have a real problem to begin with. If you cannot trust her — or if she cannot trust you — then you have no business getting married anyway. Find it out before marriage, so that you can make adjustments to work things out, or find someone else to marry.

Now I realize that everyone is not married to a Christian, but as I said in the beginning, I am writing to Christian husbands and wives. I am talking about both husband and wife being in the Word. If one is not a Christian and the other is, you have yourself a circus. All I can say is just do the best you can. Pray and believe God for the situation to change. Everything is subject to change.

But I am writing about the very best in God. If you will shoot for the best, you can improve your present circumstances. If you try, you have to go beyond where you now are. But if you do not set some higher goals, you will just wallow in the same mud all your life. And Christians do not need that.

Husbands, treat your wives with respect. Treat them the way you want to be treated. Share with them about your problems. Share your money, and share the domestic responsibilities, if they work. That is God's best.

Women Who Want to Work

I realize that some women are not going to stay home, no matter what. You might as well forget it. They are not going to stay home, look after the house, and take care of babies. They want to be men. They want equality in rank, equality in headship, or even superiority in headship. They are going to go out into the job market and work.

Some of them have abdicated the responsibilities of womanhood or motherhood because it is a lot easier to punch a clock than to do women's work. Women's work, domestically speaking, never gets done. It never stops; it just goes on and on. It is amazing! Husbands should spend some time following their wives around the house and evaluating what they do.

There is always trash to take out, dishes to wash, clothes to wash, meals to cook, floors to mop, furniture to clean, and so forth. Windows get dirty again, the carpet needs vacuuming again, the beds need changing. It is a never-ending cycle.

Husbands whose wives do stay home need to make sure she gets some time off, some time to rest and relax. They would not want to do all the things she does! As I said, however, a lot of women are not going to do those things at all. They want to wear designer clothes and be in the office all day.

Some of them say, "You don't expect me to cook dinner, do you? I have been working just like you."

Some might even say they have worked harder than their husbands. There are women who want to take the man's role. The real problem is that they do not like themselves as women. So they have to compete, and not only compete, but set out to outdo men. They want to prove they are as good as men, to be equal.

But oranges are never equal with apples. An orange is an orange, and an apple is an apple. A woman is a woman, and a man is a man. Both are unique.

A commonly used Scripture on the role of a wife is Proverbs 31. Some people have used this in an application to women working. But they have not understood the context.

What Does Proverbs 31 Really Say?

Who can find a virtuous woman? for her price is far above rubies.

The heart of her husband doth safely trust in her, so that he shall have no need of spoil.

She will do him good and not evil all the days of her life.

She seeketh wool, and flax, and worketh willingly with her hands.

She is like the merchants' ships; she bringeth her food from afar.

She riseth also while it is yet night, and giveth meat to her household, and a portion to her maidens.

She considereth a field, and buyeth it: with the fruit of her hands she planteth a vineyard.

She girdeth her loins with strength, and strengtheneth her arms.

She perceiveth that her merchandise is good: her candle goeth not out by night.

She layeth her hands to the spindle, and her hands hold the distaff.

She stretcheth out her hand to the poor; yea, she reacheth forth her hands to the needy.

She is not afraid of the snow for her household: for all her household are clothed with scarlet.

She maketh herself coverings of tapestry; her clothing is silk and purple.

Her husband is known in the gates, when he sitteth among the elders of the land.

She maketh fine linen, and selleth it; and delivereth girdles unto the merchant.

Strength and honour are her clothing; and she shall rejoice in time to come.

She openeth her mouth with wisdom; and in her tongue is the law of kindness.

She looketh well to the ways of her household, and eateth not the bread of idleness.

Her children arise up, and call her blessed; her husband also, and he praiseth her.

Many daughters have done virtuously, but thou excellest them all.

Favour is deceitful, and beauty is vain: but a woman that feareth the Lord, she shall be praised.

Give her of the fruit of her hands; and let her own works praise her in the gates.

Proverbs 31:10-31

What has to be understood here is the time in which this was written. For an Israelite wife of a prosperous man in the community, the above verses were a standard way of life. But to use it as an illustration for a virtuous women today is taking it out of context. To use this chapter as a proof text that woman should go out and work forty hours a week in the marketplace is misuse of Scripture.

If you read those verses very carefully, you will see that she was taking care of her family. Everything she did was of a domestic nature. She was not leaving the children and her husband and going away from her home to work. The point of this passage about a "virtuous woman" is not that she worked outside the home, but that she had the best interests of her husband and family as her focus in life, and she became a blessing to her husband, bringing him honor. These verses are really an example of a woman who kept her home according to God's best plan for marriage and the family.

An Analogy With Healing

The denomination I was in as a young Christian did not preach that God's best for me involved every area of my life. All we knew about was salvation, how to have eternal life with God. We knew nothing about having His blessings in this life.

When I found out about divine healing, I was excited. I had not even known healing was available. When I found that the Bible says, **Himself took our infirmities, and bare our sicknesses** (Matt. 8:17), I was so enthralled. I found out that meant me as a member of the Body of Christ. If divine healing belonged to nobody else, it belonged to Fred Price. And I took it as belonging to me.

I was so happy about the fact that healing belonged to me that I waited for the devil to hit me with something. I was just hoping he would attack me with something so I could use my faith and stand against him.

Then one day I woke up and realized that divine healing was great — but it was not God's best. The best way God has for us is to walk in divine health. To stay well is better than getting sick and then believing to get healed!

Do you see the analogy here? Thank God for healing, but let it be a channel to His best: divine health. Thank God for companies that hire women. Thank God the system will let women work. Thank God for welfare. Thank God women can exercise their abilities, talents, and training.

But do not let that be the end, the sum total, the center of everything in your finances. Let that be a channel to His best.

Chapter 13

THE MARRIAGE BED

Many Christians do not want you to talk about sex. They do not want to hear about it. It is all right if Dr. Ruth talks about it. It is all right if the devil tells us about sexual things in movies, on television, and in the print media. But it is not okay for the minister or the Church to talk about sexual matters.

The devil has been glad to oblige this attitude, to make use of it. He has been controlling the sexual attitudes of Christians for years, because the Church has not dealt with the subject, and for whatever reasons, apparently is not going to deal with it.

So young people are left to learn about sex in back alleys, locker or shower rooms at school, or from others in bits and pieces that are distorted. Or worse, they learn about sex from the easily available pornographic magazines. Because we have no clearly defined teaching from the Word, the Church leaves young people to learn about sex on their own.

Let's face it. Every one of us — black, white, brown, red, yellow, male and female — got on this planet because of sex. You have to have something wrong not to be able to face that. So it is not like *sex* is some hideous monster of the devil; sex is God's plan to perpetuate life on earth.

God made males and females with striking physical differences. We came from the "factory" like that. We did not enter this world and go by the "auto shop" and pick up all kinds of accessories we thought we might like and just hang them on our bodies. No, we came from the "factory" just as we are. So sex is normal and natural.

But because the devil has caused it to be the source of many troubles — in marriage and out of it — we need to throw some light onto the subject. Already, in an earlier chapter, I mentioned Paul's teaching to the Corinthians concerning marital rights. But let's look at those verses again.

> **The wife hath not power of her own body, but the husband: and likewise also the husband hath not power of his own body, but the wife.**
>
> **Defraud ye not one the other, except it be with consent for a time, that ye may give yourselves to fasting and prayer; and come together again, that Satan tempt you not for your incontinency.**
>
> **1 Corinthians 7:4,5**

To paraphrase those verses, we might say:

"The wife has no authority (that is what the Greek word used in verse 4 means) over her own body, but the husband does. And likewise the husband does not have authority over his own body, but the wife does."

The Greek word translated *power* in the King James Bible is not *dunamis,* which really means "power," but *exousia,* which in its true meaning is "authority, right, or privilege." What was the apostle really saying here? He was saying that God created man, and then He created woman to be his "helpmate." So woman was made for man.

Eve was not made for herself, but because God said, **It is not good that the man should be alone** (Gen. 2:18). He took Eve out of the man and brought her to Adam.

Adam did not say, "Oh, look at her, ain't she pretty?"

He said, **She shall be called *Woman*, because she was taken out of Man** (Gen. 2:23).

Then in the next verse, God said a man would leave his parents and *cleave* unto his wife. *Cleave* means "to stick to," so man would stick to his wife, and the two would become one.

God sees us as *one* in the marriage relationship. Therefore, the two-in-one share everything equally — and that includes their bodies. Belonging to one another equally is what sex is all about, and the experience should be beautiful. But Satan has distorted the sexual relationship so much that he has made sex a Frankenstein monster to the point where people are afraid even to talk about it. Yet sex is the basis and foundation of humanity. Without sex, there would be no *homo sapiens* on this planet.

God created sex, therefore it cannot be wrong — but it can be prostituted (used in some way for personal gain, maybe not for money, but for pay in the coin of one's own lusts), and it can be perverted (twisted away from God's original creation and design). Unfortunately, sex can be distorted from something clean and natural into something unclean and unnatural.

But we do not have to follow Satan's pattern. Just because some guy held up a gas station last night and some other person killed somebody does not mean I have to go out and do the same thing. So just because some people under the influence of the devil have taken the subject of sex and made it "dirty and horrible," we do not have to do the same thing.

Marital Rights

What Paul was dealing with in 1 Corinthians 7:4,5 was the human body, so it is obvious that God is concerned, that He cares about your body as well as your spirit. The Holy Spirit was ministering through Paul about the very foundation of man's existence on this planet.

If you are prudish, I want you to notice that Paul was writing about the *B-O-D-Y,* body! Also, it is obvious from the context that Paul was writing about the sexual relationship within the framework of marriage. The wife does not need her husband's body while she is cooking dinner. So he could not be referring to the husband doing things around the house.

I did not write those verses, remember. The Holy Spirit inspired Paul to write those words. And Paul's instructions tell me that my body belongs to my wife, and her body belongs to me.

Wife, hopefully, you have a husband who is willing to walk by the Word so that you have a reasonable man on your hands. But if you do not, you had better pray and learn to walk by faith. I believe a man of God walking by the Word of God is a reasonable man. If your husband is unreasonable in these matters, like I said, you had better learn how to pray to change things, because you are going to have to deal with that unreasonable man.

On the other hand, because of their upbringing, wives sometimes have problems with the sexual part of their marriages. Wives have sometimes had distorted views of sex passed on from their mothers, because the mothers had unfortunate teachings or experiences. So these particular women treat sex as a necessary evil, as something they have to "submit to."

A lot of women have become frustrated because men did not know how to be loving and kind and fulfill their wives, therefore the mothers passed on their frustration and disillusionment to their daughters.

They have said, "Well, men are just animals, and you are going to have to endure this part of marriage. Just get it over with in order to have babies. He is going to hurt you in the beginning, but it won't last long."

Several generations of women in the Victorian Age were brought up feeling that if a woman enjoyed sex, she was not "nice." They were taught enjoyment of sex was wrong and sinful for a woman. But in reacting against that teaching, the generations since World War I have gone past gaining liberty from that teaching into sexual license in many instances. The world is permeated with misuse of the sex drive. So we need to find out what the Word says in order to gain a balance, to get God's best plan for the marital relationship.

Notice Paul's use of the term *body*. He was not talking about spiritual matters. The Holy Spirit was speaking through Paul about physical bodies of men and women.

According to the Word, I have no right to keep myself from my wife, and my wife has no right to keep herself from me. And yet, I see couples in counseling all the time where the husband or wife is defrauding their mate. It is not only unfortunate, it is sad.

For the Benefit of Man *and* Woman

When Paul wrote **defraud ye not one the other,** he was not talking about grocery shopping or cleaning the house, he was talking about the body.

The first thing a husband and wife need to do is the same thing they need to do in any area of marriage: Get in agreement. Sex ought to be something that is agreed upon. But you are not going to have an agreement if you have no communication. There ought to be understanding. There ought *not* to be unreasonableness and surprises.

It is not right or fair for a man to wake his wife up at 2:30 a.m. for sex when she has to get up at 5 a.m. to go to work. To be at God's best, the marital relationship should be planned so that husband and wife can be ready for each other.

The wife's body belongs to her husband, but he ought to know her well enough, and of course love her enough, to want to please her. And the wife should know the same things about her husband. However, some men need to learn how to control themselves. They need to learn that sex is not just the physical aspect. They need to learn not to force their wives.

Make Time for Each Other

Also, there may be times when it is the other way around. The wife may be more ready than the husband. A lot of men are cheating their wives, running around working four or five jobs trying to get rich overnight. And they are so tired and exhausted half the time they have no desire for their wives. She is waiting for him to come home, and he drags himself in the house and plops his body in bed to sleep.

That is not fair to her. You should include your wife in your schedule, and you should not be so busy that you do not have time for your wife. You owe her that. Your body belongs to her, not to those people out there on that moonlighting job you have. You are running around dissipating yourself working, but there is a limit. If you get home too tired for sex with your wife, there is something wrong.

Learn to take some time with her. Take a day off, or a vacation together. Put your time together on the calendar, and work other things around it.

There ought to be some understanding about the sexual side of your marriage. My wife and I have found out over the years that our relationship works better with a period of time in between coming together. We set certain days for our times together, and in between, we look forward with excitement and expectancy toward those days.

Of course, you have to be reasonable even in this. If the night we have set comes around, and we have had a particularly rough day (one or both of us), we have a mutual agreement to forget sex this time or to move the day forward. There have been rare times that we have moved the time forward two or three days.

The point I am making is not to put one another off indefinitely. Do not keep going on and on in your daily lives with no time for each other.

The Word plainly says that wives have no right and husbands have no right to abstain from sex with one another **except**

for a time and that with full consent from both parties and *for a certain purpose.*

With Consent for a Time

The only purpose listed by Paul for marital relations to cease is for *fasting and prayer* when both husband and wife agree to this. If you are not fasting and praying, you have no legal ground for withholding or defrauding your mate. If you are not fasting and praying, you are out of God's order in withholding sex from one another.

If you are a wife, suppose your husband comes home from work, and he is starving. He is hungry, and his hunger is hungry! He walks into the house expecting to find a meal on the table but nothing is there.

He says, "Where is dinner?"

And you answer, "Oh, we are fasting."

I expect he would say, "Yeah? You are 'fasting' right to the refrigerator to get me some food!"

You do not go on a fast without coming into agreement with your husband. That is something you should be deciding together. My wife and I never fast food unless we are in agreement, because eating involves the preparation of food. It makes it more difficult for her, if she is fasting and I am eating, to stand over the pots smelling all the food. She is trying to fast, but she has to feed me. So we make an attempt to do these things together and be in agreement so it does not put an undue strain on the other person. We get in agreement on fasting food, and we get in agreement on fasting sex.

There are times, of course, when sex is not appropriate. One or the other of you is out of town, or you go for a convention or seminar, or you are visiting relatives. When Betty and I go to seminars and crusades, I do not have any time for her, and she has no time for me. We work from sunrise to sunset. When the day is over, we are completely exhausted physically. We have to go to bed to get rested up for the next day. We are in agreement at these times to abstain from sex.

What I am talking about is the normal everyday weekly routine of life. In the Word, you have specific instructions from God that you are not supposed to be defrauding one another. You are not walking in the Word plus being unfair if you are defrauding your mate.

In abstaining, you should be in agreement, and you should together set a time limit. At that time, the Apostle Paul said to **come together again** so that one of you, or both, will not be tempted. Paul used that word *tempt,* not me. And notice who is doing the tempting — Satan. And he will tempt you. If things are not going well at home, all you are doing is throwing your husband or your wife open for more temptations.

Satan never gets tired, never takes a day off, never takes a vacation. He does not observe holidays, and he never goes on strike. He is after you all the time. With most men, even when things are going well with their wives, temptations still come.

I believe you will find that if you and your spouse work together, instead of at odds with one another, everything flows smoothly in this very delicate and precious, but so misunderstood, area of your relationship. Sex should be mutually fulfilling, mutually agreed upon. When all systems are running smoothly, sex can make everything else work very nicely. But if there is an area of unfulfillment there on either side, it can really cause problems.

For example, six months abstention is too long! I had a counseling session with one woman — and usually it is the woman who comes in for counseling in these cases. The hard-headed man will not come in, because *he* does not have any problems. He and his wife are not getting along, but he has no problems. And what does a preacher know about these things anyway? With that attitude, I cannot tell him anything, and God cannot tell him anything. That is obvious. You cannot tell someone something or help someone if that person will not let you.

What Frequency Is Normal?

Sometimes women come into the office and right away burst into tears. In this one case, I said, "How may I help you?"

She said, "My husband has not touched me in six months."

Now there is something wrong with that. It was obvious that she did not agree with this abstention on his part, because she was there. If she had agreed, there would have been no problem, and she would not have come for counseling. But her husband was doing exactly what God said not to do: He was defrauding his wife in that intimate relationship. He was depriving her.

I know there must have been reasons, but I am not dealing with reasons or excuses now. The point I am making is that a situation like that is intolerable, unhealthy, and unholy.

Marriage is for the benefit of man *and* woman. It was not to take away from you, to leave one of you frustrated and at the end of your wits, to leave you crushed and hopeless, lonely and unfulfilled. The purpose of marriage is for us to be better as a result of it. Without communication and without honesty, it cannot work.

Here was this guy defrauding his wife. Sure there were reasons, but he would not talk to her, and he would not come in and talk to me. So what was she supposed to do? She was frustrated.

In another situation, a beautiful young lady came to me and began to tell me all about a similar problem in her marriage. Something was happening in their relationship. They were not communicating. They were not talking. They were not being honest, and the husband was doing some crazy things. He would not "straighten up and fly right." The wife was put into a position of being tempted, and adultery was the result.

The whole thing was a shambles. It was a bad scene. She was crushed as a result of it. Their relationship was all messed up, but he threw her into that. No, she did not *have* to commit adultery. I am not condoning her actions. What I am saying is that if her husband had been operating according to the Apostle Paul's directions, she would not have been tempted with that sort of thing.

If her marriage had been right, she would have let the temptation go on by. She would have said, "I don't need that." But if you already are torn up, unfulfilled, and defrauded, it makes it easier to fall into something illicit.

It is not always the husband. Most of the time it is the wife, and a lot of the time, her problem has been caused by a lot of stupid, ignorant, prudish, non-sensical talking. I will not call it "teaching," because it is not.

Most of the information passed on about sexual things makes such a mystery in young people's minds — or in most cases not even a mystery but negative concepts — that women go into marriage with a very distorted view of what the physical relationship is all about. They think the idea is to endure the physical aspect of marriage, have children, and that is it. That is very unfortunate and very untrue.

If that is all God's purpose was, He could have made humans like animals with everything operating on instinct. We still could have procreated, reproduced, and perpetuated the human race. But God created us with the capacity to enjoy one another. Man and woman should be *giving* themselves to one another in the marriage relationship.

What is normal in the area of frequency of sex? "Normal" is whatever the two of you agree on, and the emphasis is on *agree*. Obviously the man who abstained for six months was not in agreement with his wife. But a husband and wife do have to agree on what is normal for them. As long as the frequency does not interfere with their health and allows them to carry on with the rest of their lives, then it is normal.

Stay in Shape

If you are a woman, you need to keep yourself in shape and looking nice for your husband. If your husband married the campus queen with the best legs in the school, and now fifteen years later, you look like Shamoo's sister, you are selling him short.

There are all kinds of things you can do to enhance what you have. Maybe after having children and several years have passed, you cannot look quite the same slim girl he married. But you can find out what he likes and make an effort to please him.

Some women come to me suspecting their husbands are stepping out on them. In the first place, they have to know for sure before making a move. They cannot operate on supposition. But what do they do?

They can pray and ask the Lord to show them what is wrong. They can bind the powers of darkness that are influencing the husbands to commit adultery. But then one of the most important things is to sit down and consider seriously why that husband might be going with some other women.

It may be because the wife is not doing what she is supposed to be doing. I do not know what is on someone else's mind, but I do know one thing: It is very difficult, for example, to eat any more food when I am full. No matter how delicious and delectable the food looks like, if I am bursting at the seams and someone offers me something, I say, "No, thank you." When someone is full and satisfied, it is difficult to eat anything else.

It is not always because the wife is defrauding her husband, of course, but that is one of the first things she needs to examine if she suspects her husband is running around. Sometimes she has not been making herself as available as Sister Susie has. Maybe she is always griping, complaining, and crying about everything, when Sister Susie is whispering in his ear.

If Susie is saying, "Oh, you are so handsome. You are my dream man," that guy has a hard thing to deal with. Then he comes home to a nagging woman with rollers in her hair. He has rollers for breakfast, rollers for lunch, rollers for dinner. I am not condoning his actions. I am just saying there may be a reason for his falling into the temptation to be unfaithful.

Wife, make sure you have taken care of all your options before you make a decision to leave. Be sure you have all your bases covered. Be sure that he is not running around because you are not worth staying home for. If I were in that wife's place, I would find out first if I had been discharging my duties. Have I been doing everything I know to make myself attractive and alluring to my husband?

Then if the dog goes out, you have other options open to you, but at least you know that you have done all you can do. But first find out what he likes. What is it about Sister Susie that he likes that you perhaps do not do. Before you make some drastic move with your relationship, be sure you have covered all of your options.

If you are a man, *you* need to stay in shape and looking nice for your wife. My body belongs to my wife, so I keep in shape. She did not marry a fat, pot-bellied, out-of-shape somebody, messed up and carrying all that extra weight. Also, my wife likes things to smell good, so I make certain my body odor does not offend her. I want our time together to be precious, beautiful, and satisfying to her.

If you let yourself get out of shape; you could have a coronary in the bedroom. When you are sexually involved, it affects your entire body system. And when your body is not up to par, you can fall out in the bedroom and have a stroke or a heart attack. Your body cannot stand the pressure. If you hyperventilate when you walk up a flight of stairs, you need to get back in shape. Give your wife the very best. That is what she deserves.

Some men do not want to shave just for their wives. To tell the truth, it would be a lot easier for me not to shave, a lot easier and a lot less painful. But what makes you think your wife wants a shrub next to her face? All that stubby hair scratching her is not pleasant, although she may be nice and try not to say anything about it. She is lying there, and you are rubbing her with one of those wire brushes. A lot of times, you do not think about her comfort, just about your own self and how much easier it is for you not to shave.

Go on out and find a goat somewhere with rough hair and rub your face against it, if you want to know how it feels. See? You never thought about that. Or go get a wire brush and rub it against your face. Yet you want to get into bed and make love to your wife with that against her face.

Children are transparent and without guile. Most men have picked up a little child and snuggled up against them, only to have them say, "Daddy (or Grandpa, or Uncle Whoever), that hurts! What is that on your face?"

All I am saying is that your body belongs to your wife. You ought to take time to find out what pleases her. What is she comfortable with? What turns her on? Then you ought to be that for her. If it takes shaving off what is on your face, then do it.

Sex During the Menstrual Cycle

A question that frequently comes up is, "Can I have intercourse with my wife while she is in her menstrual period?"

Many people sanction this by using the same verse about not defrauding one another. But if a man cannot restrain himself for five days or whatever, he needs that demon of lust cast out of him! That is not a biological need. That is just lust going somewhere to happen. He is a person out of control, totally undisciplined. That is just greed, especially when he knows his wife does not want him to do that.

A woman's body goes through a biological change every twenty-eight days. Some women experience a lot of discomfort and pain, even to the extent of having to go to bed. The cycle affects different women in different ways. There are medications, of course, but nevertheless, most women are very uncomfortable during that time, to say the least.

Plus, by having sex at that time, you open yourself up to a lot of germs. Bacteria grow well and like to feed on blood. You know you can get a little scratch on your arm, and get an infection in just that little amount of blood. Making love while she is having her period is not only unhygienic but unhealthy.

I am not going to tell you how to run your marriage. That is not my business, but I am charged with the duty of saying, "Thus saith the Lord," then you do whatever you choose with it.

The Lord did not call me to tell you what to do. He called me only to tell people what He said and to pass on revelation knowledge He gives me of the Word, but never to the extent of running your lives. All I am supposed to run is my own house. You are supposed to run your life with the help of God and not the help of Fred. But if you can learn something from Fred that will help you be able to hear God better, then well and good, that is a part of what this is all about.

Chapter 14

A FREQUENTLY ASKED, BUT DELICATE QUESTION

Another question concerning what is "normal" and "natural" is one that comes up frequently. I have been asked this question relative to the interpersonal relationship of a husband and wife more often than any other question, and it needs to be answered and dealt with.

The question is this: "Is oral sex permitted for Christians?"

All we are dealing with here is my personal answer. I do not do this very often, but I am going to give you my personal belief. Then I will go to the Word of God for something. I am doing this because I believe the statements I am going to make can simply help you to answer this question — because people are asking the question. Someone needs to answer it and answer it rightly.

You can give the wrong answer on anything and mess people up. You can give them the right answer and set them free. This is the kind of thing I cannot answer for you, because it is such a personal thing. But here is my belief.

I want to simply point up some way for you to have a guideline because there are a lot of things not in the Bible that we have to deal with. If God were to tell you how to live every single day of your life, twenty-four hours a day, the Bible could not contain it! You would have to have a book as big as the planet to do that.

What God has done is to give us some basic principles — some laws — and those principles can be applied to everything. For instance, two plus two equals four. It does not matter whether I am buying a dozen oranges or a dozen Boeing 747 jumbo jets, two plus two is still four. That is a principle that you can take and apply to anything in life.

If you ever learn one of God's principles, all you have to do is apply it. So I want to give you some illustrations that I think will help anyone who wants to be helped. It should enable you to evaluate situations and put a principle into operation in your own life.

You are under no obligation to accept it, but I am sharing it because I believe it is a way to get you pointed in a direction to answer questions in your own life about what is right and wrong in marital sexual relations.

Illustrations of a Principle

One person came to me with a question right in the doorway of the church back when we pastored a very small congregation before we started Crenshaw Christian Center. The church was so small I could talk to everybody and shake hands with them as they went out of the church on Sunday morning.

This person asked, "Is it all right for a Christian to smoke cigarettes?"

And I said, "Why do you ask me that? You already know the answer."

The person looked at me with a strange expression, but I said, "I don't need to tell you anything. You already know the answer."

He said, "I don't know what you are talking about."

I said, "You just told me the answer."

The man said, "No, I asked you a question. As a Christian, is it acceptable to God within the framework of the Christian life? Is it all right to smoke cigarettes?"

My answer again was, "You have already told me the answer. Why are we both wasting our time when you already know the answer? Let me say this to you. Why didn't you ask me if it was permissible, spiritual, godly, and acceptable to God to use deodorant? What is the difference between smoking a cigarette and using deordorant?"

My point was this: The only reason he asked that question was because something down on the inside of his spirit was telling him smoking was wrong. Otherwise, he would not have asked. He was not really asking about right or wrong. He was looking for my approval in order to cloud his conscience and be able to keep doing what his flesh wanted to do. He wanted to be able to keep puffing on those "cancer sticks" and not feel guilty.

Never in all my years in the ministry have I ever had someone come up and ask me if it is permissible for a Christian to use deodorant. I have never had anyone ask me if it is permissible to take a bath. Why do they not ask that, but then ask about smoking a cigarette? The answer, obviously, is because they already know smoking is wrong, but they want someone to agree with them that it is all right. They know it is wrong. That is why they are asking, "Is it right?"

If it *was* right, they would know it and would not have to ask! So if you are asking the question, it means you know it is wrong, but you want to do it anyway. However, to do it without your conscience bothering you, you have to have some cloud or cover over you. If you can get a so-called "godly man" to say that whatever you want to do is all right, then you are home free.

It is a good thing that man asked *me* about smoking, because many preachers at that time would have had one in their hand while they were talking!

Let's use another illustration: Not in all the years I have been in the ministry, in all the marriages I have performed, and in all the counseling I have done, not one single person has ever asked me if it is permissible for Christians to engage in sexual intercourse as husband and wife. Is that not strange? I wonder why?

Why do people have the hang up about cigarettes but do not ask about these other things? Because they already know the answer. Like I said, God already put the knowledge down inside your spirit. You already know what you should and should not do.

So I say to you, if you have to ask any question about any aspect of your life, then it is already questionable. The best thing is not to do it. If you cannot find it in the Word of God in principle, then do not do it. You will find principles in the Word that will permit you to do whatever is right. They may not say, "Don't do this," or "Do do that," but you will be able to draw conclusions.

The bottom line is that you want God's approval, not Fred Price's. Usually, the person is afraid to ask God about it because he knows in advance what God is going to say to him. But he does not want to hear, "No," so he finds some supposed "great man of faith and power" who will say it is all right. Then he feels he is home free.

He can say, "The preacher told me it was all right."

I have given you my philosophy, my belief on this matter. I believe it is based on God's Word even though there is no specific chapter and verse. Several times in the New Testament, the Apostle Paul says, "I think," or *"I* say so-and-so, the Lord did not say this." That is what I am doing. If my principle of conscience makes sense, then fine, but if it does not, you do not have to receive it.

The Principle of Conscience

That question about oral sex is coming up more frequently than ever, and it has always been the most frequently asked question. Society is so much more open today, and things such as this are talked of so much more openly that the subject should not offend anyone.

I have to deal with this question all of the time. Some of the letters I get! You could not have a worse situation if you combined a half dozen soap operas! I know of relationships that have been wrecked over this question because the individuals involved could not reconcile their beliefs — or they refused to reconcile them. A lot of people have been challenged by this question in their personal lives.

In fact, nearly every married couple who were out in the world before they came to Christ are going to have to deal with this question. The devil will use this kind of thing to create problems in your relationship if you let him.

You are a spirit, you have a soul, and you live in a body. In your spirit, you have a conscience, and in that conscience is the voice of your spirit. You have it whether you are saved or not. Even unsaved people who are not in fellowship with God are spirit beings. They have a conscience.

Your conscience — if you will learn to listen to it — can be your best guide, *but that is all your conscience can do.* It can sound an alarm that will guide you in life. Your conscience has no ability to impart to you the will power to keep from doing what the conscience is telling you not to do. It does not impart any ability to make you do what is right or wrong.

Your clock can sound the alarm in the morning, but it has no ability to get you up. All it can do is tell you it is time to get up. Your clock cannot reach in the bed, pull you out, and make you get up to go to work. Its purpose, its design, is simply to sound an alarm when you set it to do so. And that is all your conscience can do.

The red light at the corner cannot stop cars. All it does is tell you it is time to stop, that you ought to stop. If you do not stop, you can drive right through a red light — and I have done that, but not on purpose.

All of a sudden I looked up and said, "You know? I don't think I stopped at that corner!"

Have you ever had that happen? Then you look in the rear view mirror and see some other cars that were crossing the intersection back there, and people are making funny gestures at you with their hands.

Well, I did not mean to run the light, but the signal could not reach down there and stop me. All it had the power to do was tell me I ought to stop. That is the purpose of your conscience. But you can run over your conscience. You can "sear" your conscience as you do a piece of meat.

Don't Sear Your Conscience

If you cook a steak on a grill, it will start dripping juices. But if you throw it on there and leave it for a second or two on both sides, it will be "seared." That will keep the juices on the inside. They will not leak out.

So you can sear your conscience so that you do not hear its alarm any more. It is still giving the sound of an alarm, but you have become insensitive to it. That is dangerous. Then you have no more warnings.

I have a tender conscience because I have allowed it to develop. It is an horrendous conscience! Anytime I do something wrong, my conscience just tears me up on the inside. When I do something wrong, I know it!

This question on sex, on what is permissible to husbands and wives is wrecking homes. It brings a lot of consternation and conscience problems that affect the relationship in other areas.

Some husbands and wives get involved in this activity — and others just as questionable — against their consciences and their wills. They begin doing these things to please their mates. Finally, the situation ends up surfacing in some kind of behavioral pattern because the person operating in this against his or her will becomes so frustrated. That person has to strike out in some way as a form of protection because the conscience is being run over.

Some people have mates who insist on this, that, or the other. They are in a quandary: What shall I do? There are a number of different sexual techniques and habits that bring up some questions to the child of God. To the person in the world, they bring up few questions. That person's mind already is under the dominion of Satan. People in the world do not even know what they are doing, anyway.

But the child of God is different. Most of those with conscience problems brought these habits over from the world. They did not find them in the Bible. They did not get those things from the Holy Spirit. The Spirit of God did not inspire them to be involved the way they are sexually. Those things came out of the pit. They cannot be found in the pages of the Bible.

God Does Not Sanction Unnatural Acts

Hebrews 13:4, which says the marriage bed is undefiled, does not provide freedom to indulge in exotic, pornographic acts even with a mate. Marriage is *honorable,* but that does not mean you have a license for sexual perversions. That word does not mean that you can do some weird thing out of an imagination that has been programmed by Satan and have it be right simply because you are married.

I do not see where people interpret *undefiled* to mean "doing anything you want to do." Some people think that means they can do whatever they want to do in bed, as long as they are married. They think a marriage license makes any kind of sexual perversion or variety of sex act "indulged in by two consenting adults" *honorable.* But that is not the context of that verse at all.

The author of Hebrews is not dealing with sexual acts, only with *married* and *unmarried.* If you are unmarried, any kind of sexual relationship is *defiled.* If you are married, then the marriage bed is *undefiled* — but there is no blanket endorsement for *any* type of sexual act even in a marriage bed.

Some people have taken this verse as a proof text to be involved in actions such as the question we deal with in this chapter, along with a lot of other activities. But you have to be deaf, dumb, blind, or dishonest to see such permission in that verse! If you read carefully, you will see what the writer of Hebrews was talking about, and it had nothing to do with any kind of sexual perversion.

Marriage is the subject of the discussion, not Mickey Mouse or Brer Rabbit or sexual habits. This verse is dealing with the premise that *marriage is honorable,* and therefore — because marriage is honorable — the bed is undefiled. In plain, old American language, that means the husband and wife have a legal right before God to be involved in sexual intercourse.

But the rest of that verse says: But **whoremongers and adulterers God will judge.** *Whoremongers* includes everyone who is participating in fornication, and *adulterers* takes in everyone who is committing adultery. Now the bed on which fornication and adultery is committed is *not* undefiled.

You cannot use this verse honestly, however, as an excuse to satisfy perversions.

One man coerced his wife into performing oral sex against her will by refusing to talk to her if she did not. He would go a whole week and not talk to her, just treat her as if she did not exist. That was her punishment:

"If you do not play my game, I won't talk to you."

And she loved this guy. She almost idolized him, almost worshipped the ground he walked on. But she did not feel this sexual act was right. It made her feel dirty and unclean. She felt it was not Christian. Every time she committed this act, she was going against her conscience. Then she would feel condemned for the next three weeks and walk around with her head down. She was ashamed of it within herself.

Instead of trying to please a man with a warped, sadistic, perverted idea of sex that came directly from the devil, she should have been trying to please God.

Now they are divorced. She is living with some guy and not even married to him, and one of their children died an awful, horrible death. This couple knew too much about the Word of God. You cannot play around with the Word.

> **For unto whomsoever much is given, of him shall much be required.**
>
> Luke 12:48

They were exposed to too much knowledge of God, and paid a heavy price for going against that knowledge.

Another couple used to belong to my church. Supposedly he accepted Christ and was filled with the Spirit. He had a Bible with all the right colors in it. He had everything marked right, so I assumed he was a Christian.

But he had been out in the world, and everything big enough to do, he had done. And in the process, he had become a sex-o-holic. Sex can be as addictive as alcohol or drugs or anything else. And he was addicted to oral sex. He felt he could not live without it. How they came to terms with this addiction I do not know, but they are no longer in the church.

Oral sex is not organically normal. There is no biological need for it. It is a perversion of the mind.

Mortify the Flesh

How do you deal with unnatural sex drives? You deal with them as with any other sin: by mortifying the flesh.

> **Mortify therefore your members which are upon the earth; fornication, uncleanness, inordinate affection, evil concupiscence, and covetousness, which is idolatry:**
>
> **For which things' sake the wrath of God cometh on the children of disobedience:**
>
> **In the which ye also walked sometime, when ye lived in them.**
>
> Colossians 3:5-7

Now *fornication* and so forth are not members of the body, but they are committed with members. Paul dealt with the end result of what our members can be involved in. If you "put your body to death," you do not have to worry about sexual perversions.

Chapter 15

ADVICE FOR SINGLES

When I first taught this series on television, I received some letters complaining that "you didn't say anything about the singles." The reason is that the Bible does not say much about singles, not in the sense it does about husbands and wives, parents and children.

But the very fact that I was talking about the Christian family means singles were included. In this book, I want to make it plain that if you are a Christian, you are in the Church family. I have a couple of children not yet married, but would I say they were not in my family?

So whether you have never been married or are a single parent, you can glean things for your life out of what has been said about male and female relationships. You can find out how to act if you do get married again. You can see how to treat your brother or sister in Christ.

You have not been left out or ignored. We are not opposed to singles. But there is not much in the Bible pertaining to living as a single. I am well persuaded that the Word allows for persons to live single; however, I must tell you that I believe God's original intent was for every single man to have a wife and every single woman to have a husband.

Here is why I believe that: God created the very first humans as *two people,* a man and a woman set in a family relationship, not as singles. He did not make a man and a woman to live in the Garden of Eden as singles. He made them husband and wife. So naturally most of the information given in the Word relates to husbands and wives, because that is God's best plan.

If God's plan for mankind was to be single, he would have made us sexless. Singles are not going to have babies. Singles are not permitted in the Word to have sexual relations. Therefore, if God wanted us to be single, He probably would not have made us with sexual organs. Or perhaps the ones He intended to get married, He would have made with sex organs and the others sexless.

However, everything I have said is directed to those who are single as well as to husbands and wives. Even if you are not legally tied to a husband or wife, your Christian lifestyle should not be any different. You should not walk in any less holiness than a married person. And you should not be any lonelier than a married person.

Did Jesus not say He would never leave you nor forsake you? (Heb. 13:5.) If you are lonely, then you are not doing what He said, or you would not have time to be lonely. Loneliness comes from time spent doing nothing.

But there are some things that affect single people that I want to touch on.

What Should You Expect From a Fiance (Fiancee)

Now this is directed to two Christians, acting as Christians should, and living in separate houses:

What about friends of the opposite sex? Should the fiance still have female friends, and vice versa?

Is it selfish to think the right answer to the last question is no? Or is it selfish if either of the couple thinks the answer should be yes?

How much of their lives should be shared prior to marriage? Along the same line is this question — is it wrong for two Christians who are engaged to be living in the same house, although they are not doing anything morally wrong?

Is it wrong for a fiance to expect to know all about what his bride-to-be is doing? Should there still be things that are none of the other's business?

What is being trusting, and what is being foolish?

Many of those questions involve matters of opinion. Some of them must be adjusted in different circumstances and with different people. You cannot draw a black-and-white line that applies to every couple in some of these areas. You cannot find "chapter and verse" on them. At least, I have not been able to. So the best thing I can do is just give you my "best shot."

Notice, we are dealing with *fiances* and *fiancees*. In my humble opinion, being engaged is the next step to marriage. That is as close to being married without being married that you can be. It usually means that some token, such as a ring, has been given from one to the other that stands as a symbol for the fact that now the two people are *committed* to each other.

It seems to me then, that once you are engaged, that is the end as far as either of you talking intimately with others, seeing others on dates, and so forth. Whether that is selfish or not, I leave to your judgment.

On my own part, I always was a one-woman man. In other words, when I was dating Betty, I was committed to her. Some guys played the field with four or five girlfriends, like one in every little suburb. I could not do that for some reason, although I was not yet a Christian. I committed myself to Betty, and I expected her to commit herself to me.

Once we became engaged, once I put my ring on her finger, I did not want anyone else coming to visit her. She was mine, and I was hers. We were not married yet, but we were as close to getting married as possible before the actual ceremony. Once she accepted my ring, she accepted me as her future husband. There was no need to talk to anyone else because she already had her husband, and I already had my wife.

I did not want to hear about "Joe" calling her. That was it for Joe. He had his time at bat, and he had struck out. He was out, and I was in. I hit a home run.

When I called her after we were engaged, and we shared the happenings of the day, I did not want to hear about how George had called, Jim had been by her house, or Joe had taken her to lunch.

Again, every situation is not the same because people are not the same. You may disagree with me, but I believe that when you get to the engagement stage, that is it for other people.

Why would you want to see someone else, talk to someone else, have someone else over to your house, or go out to dinner with someone else, when you have accepted a man's ring — or when you have given a girl your ring? All engagement means is that you have set the date for the wedding, or you are planning to set a date. But you are committed.

I realize that you can still break it off standing in the doorway of the church before the ceremony, but by the same token, becoming engaged is a commitment. Even if you change your mind later, you do not compromise with the world at the engagement stage — in my opinion.

That is it! No more dating anyone else. If you still want to see other people, then do not get engaged or compromise.

Shun the Appearance of Evil

As far as living in the same house before marriage, the answer should be obvious.

One lady who wrote and asked me this question said, "We did not plan it this way, but his roommate threw him out and he had no where else to go. I did for him what I would do for any other Christian seeking my help. There is no "hanky-panky" going on between us. He respects me and my household and would not dare tempt me. But some people say I did the wrong thing. What do you say?"

I say she did the wrong thing. Now, I am not picking on this woman, but her question is a frequently asked one. It is a question that needs an answer for the sake of many people. First, let us say why it is wrong and find out from the Word why it is wrong.

A lot of people are "shacking up" today, just to put it bluntly. These are Christian people we are talking about — Bible-toting, tape-recorder-playing, red-green-yellow-orange-pen marking Christians!

I think that lady did something that was not wise. I think allowing her fiance to move in was a dumb thing to do. There is no way under Heaven she will ever be able to convince her friends who are not Christian that she is living in a house with a man and not, as she says, be involved in, as she put it, "hanky panky" — whatever "hanky panky" is. There is no way in the world anyone is going to believe that.

So what has happened? She has lost her testimony. She is living as if she was married, but was not. So she was promoting a lie. There is a Scripture in Thessalonians that deals with this kind of situation.

Abstain from all appearance of evil.
1 Thessalonians 5:22

Even if the lady and her fiance have separate bedrooms, I doubt if very many people would believe there was no immorality going on. The "appearance of evil" is present.

Now notice she said the man "respected" her and her household enough not to tempt her. I disagree. If he respected her and her household, he would not place her in such a compromising position. So her rationale in this situation is off base. Also, this is how people get trapped into temptation.

Then was Jesus led up of the spirit into the wilderness to be tempted of the devil.

And when he had fasted forty days and forty nights, he was afterward an hungred.

And when the tempter came to him ....
Matthew 4:1-3

These verses put her situation in the proper perspective. Perhaps the lady is right about her fiance "respecting" her. Perhaps he was just misguided as well. But he is not her problem — Satan is. Satan is the tempter, not that man living in her house. And I have news for all of you: Satan does *not* respect your household. He does not respect you, God, Jesus, or anyone else. He will speak through that man's heart, and the man may end up doing something the lady will be sorry for. It is not the man she should be concerned about, but Satan.

She said, "In fact, he is the one who is the first to be sure we don't put ourselves in a position to be tempted."

Then what is she doing in the same house with him? You cannot get much closer to temptation than that.

She goes on to say she is confused about "believing for a mate," and adds, "You see, I knew my fiance before we were saved. After we became saved, many things in our relationship changed. Some things are still being changed, all for the better and in line with God's Word. God is actively at work in our lives.

[Well, God certainly did not tell them to move in together.]

She went on to write, "I believe he is the man for me. I have even had a vision of us at the altar. I don't believe the timing is right now, but I am willing to wait until it is. While I agree with the singles who are believing for mates, what about the ones who came to Christ already with a mate, even if they were not yet married?

"If two unsaved married people came to Christ and began to act on the Word, God would not require them to get a divorce simply because He did not send them to each other. And I don't believe God would require me to give up my fiance [although He may not have put us together]. We are not 'unequally yoked' now."

I do not believe that He would necessarily make her give up that man either, but I surely do not think God is going to require or even endorse their living in the same house unmarried. We are not talking about giving up the fiance. We are talking about giving up *the appearance of evil.* That is all we are talking about. He

182

may be the one for that lady, but not living in the same house and not yet married.

Then she says, "I do believe God gave me enough common sense and discretion when it comes to choosing a mate."

At this point, I have to again take exception to her thinking. She does not have enough "common sense" to choose a mate. There is no one on this planet who has common sense enough to choose the *right* mate. You can choose a mate, and many of you have and are living in hell right now.

Perhaps a better way to put it is this: You cannot use common sense to pick a mate because all you can see is the exterior. You cannot see what is on the inside of people. You do not need common sense, you need the Spirit of God. The exteriors of people are facades. When you marry, you have to deal with the inner man or woman. The outside can change on a daily basis. "Common sense" is not going to tell you what is inside someone else's heart. You need the Spirit of God to do that.

Now you can see that even this lady's common sense is off as she continues:

"For those of us who have already chosen our mates, I am believing God will open our eyes, hearts, and minds during our engagements and help us change whatever needs changing prior to marriage so we can produce the God-kind of marriage, the kind God had in mind when He created Eve for Adam."

See how her common sense is off? Those statements from her letter are great. But while she is making them, she is living with someone to whom she is not married. That is "uncommon sense."

Owning a House Together

This same lady had one last question: "Do you believe that engaged couples should make long-term plans for their future, such as buying a house together prior to the wedding?"

NO!!!!!!! Absolutely not. Did I make that plain enough? You are *not* married, although you have made what should be a permanent commitment to one another. However, "engaged" is not the same as "married" where sexual relationships are concerned, and it is not the same where joint property ownership is concerned.

There is nothing legal in an engagement. It is only legal when you get married. To get engaged, you sign no papers. So do not get legally involved in any kind of agreement before marriage. I have seen people come right down to the wire for marriage and then dissolve the whole thing.

I am not putting this lady down or others like her. But I want to make it clear that being engaged is not a legal state. You cannot trust the human intellect. What you intend and what you think in the beginning of an engagement can change, and buying a house together could leave you in bondage to a legal agreement.

Intellect Is Incapable of Ordering Man's Course

Man without God is a garbage pit going somewhere to happen. We have more educational facilities available, more ways of getting education than ever before in the history of the human race, and more academic knowledge than ever before. We have learned more in the past fifty years than man has learned in all the history of the world. Yet we are still living in fear of one another.

War, arms races, terrorism, prejudice, hatred, and starvation are still prevalent in spite of man and all his vaunted knowledge. He does not even know how to come in out of the rain. Every day people are killing each other just through driving and drinking. Man does not even have enough sense not to mix alcohol and gasoline. Where is the common sense in that?

People are dying every day from drug addiction, while all over television, newspapers, and magazines, the message is finally being blazed forth: Don't fool with cocaine, don't fool with heroin. It will kill you "graveyard dead." But many, many young people are still doing drugs. Where is the common sense in that?

So do not make any long-term plans such as buying a house during your engagement. If you want to plan for buying one after the wedding, that is fine. Making plans and getting legally tied into something together before marriage are two different things. Because engaged is *not* married.

You have no business living in the same house together just because you are engaged. I do not care if he has put a ring on your finger with a diamond so big you cannot even lift your hand. You are still not married. I do not care what he whispered in your ear. I do not care how many times or in how many languages he has said, "I love you."

You have no business living in the same house, and you certainly have no business getting involved sexually before marriage. If you do that, you are opening yourself up to consequences that sometimes you cannot even imagine.

There are many women — Christian women — who have made this mistake, and if they had the nerve to stand up and witness to their experience, they would tell you they have "played the fool" like this. They lost everything that was sacred to them, and now they are sitting around hoping the guy will still want to marry them or that some other man will even after they have had three children and no husband.

Engagement means nothing legally. I understand the sanctity of an engagement, but people who get into these kinds of situations do not understand the consequences of engaging in things that belong only to marriage before that marriage is legal.

Engaged is not married. In fact, you are not even married when the preacher says, "I now pronounce you man and wife." You are not legally married until those papers go downtown and are recorded.

We are instructed by God to be governed by the laws of the land as long as those laws do not violate the clearly revealed Word of God. He said the laws of the land are ordained for our benefit and protection. God does not necessarily choose the people who are in the offices administering the law, but law and order are ordained of God.

I think the above discussion also answers the question, "What is being trusting, and what is being foolish."

Waiting for a Mate

Another area that seems to confuse singles, especially women, is what to do while waiting for God to bring a mate. They pray and believe God, but it seems to be very hard for them to deny the flesh and rest in Him and *truly* wait. Many of these women seem not to be able to resist helping God along, or at least putting themselves in a position where they can make mistakes.

They say, "We are seeking the Lord for a mate, but we are human. We need companionship in the meantime. Going out in groups is fine, but don't you have to spend some time with a man to know whether he is the one God intends for you?"

The Word says very clearly to:

Seek ye first the kingdom of God, and his righteousness, and all these other things shall be added unto you.
Matthew 6:33

If you are seeking the Kingdom, you do not have time for seeking him or her. And God will bring you that person, if you faint not in seeking the Kingdom.

You do not need to go out. If the Lord is going to bring you together, you do not need to go out. That is how many women have gotten messed up. They are married and miserable right now, because they began to help God out. A woman can see some guy who looks good, begin to talk to him and find out he sounds good, and be deceived by her mind or her flesh into thinking he is the one. Then they get married, and she finds out she cannot stand him.

I would advise singles not to take a chance on this kind of thing. It is so easy to be fooled. It is so easy to make plans and act on wishful thinking instead of believing God. What singles, both male and female, should be doing is allowing God to prepare them for the proper mate. Then when God puts them together, they will know it is the right one. They will not have to go out "shopping" all the time.

Some people have gone out with nineteen different people and did not end up marrying any of them. So what was all that for? That was wasted time. They could have been praying in the Spirit, reading the Word, and building themselves up. Single persons have a marvelous opportunity to spend time with God and develop their spiritual lives.

Most single people run around looking at faces and figures, but that is foolishness and deceptive. "Looks" is just the wrapping on a package. Besides, every time you think this is the prettiest or the handsomest person you have seen, along will come another one who looks a little better. You can go crazy that way. Turn loose of all that, and let God. Let God bring the man or the woman to you, and that way you will know that you are getting the one with whom you ultimately can be happy.

The exteriors, the looks, are not going to stay the same, anyway. When he, or she, gets to be forty or over, the hair may not be the same, the figure almost certainly will not be, and so forth. What are you going to do then? Also, beauty or handsomeness does not guarantee a good life.

If you are doing what God said and spending time with Him, you do not have time to get lonely. **Seek ye first the kingdom of God** because you are in a time of preparation. The person who is going to eventually be your spouse is in a time of preparation. They are not yet ready, or you are not. If both of you were, God would already have brought you together. You may think you are ready, but you are not.

Get down to the Lord's business, and before you know it, you will be prepared for the right one. And the right one will be prepared for you. Before you know it, the Lord will bring you together.

As soon as you see the person, you probably are not going to get married. You are not going to look up and say, "Oh, there he (or she) is," and the next second you are married. No, it does not work that way. You have to set a date. Both of you probably are involved in jobs or careers, and other affairs of life. So there will be some time between meeting and marrying.

During that time is when you get to know one another. But you will know while you are getting acquainted that this is the person you are going to marry. This is not just someone you are going to spend a lot of time with and spill your innermost thoughts to, and then not even marry them. And all that time was wasted, time when you could have been praying or building yourself up on your most holy faith.

Single people have a marvelous opportunity to get to know God. Take advantage of it. Thank the Lord you have that free time. Enjoy it while you can. Marriage is an entirely different arena than being single.

Some Good Advice

Another young lady wrote me with some very good advice for single women:

"Last Sunday, you read a letter from a single young lady whose mother had discouraged her from ever being married. My heart went out to her. Even though I have no idea who she is, my prayer for her is that she will continue to let the Word minister to her, and that she will keep her eyes only on the Lord.

"I know God will reveal to her the joy and happiness that can be shared when two people wait on Him. I remember her mentioning that when she was ready for a relationship, he would be a Christian man. That is the first step in the right direction. But that factor is not enough. Having a Christian man is not the only prerequisite needed to have a good marriage.

"After listening to some of the letters you have read from hurting, lonely, and mentally abused wives who are with 'Christian' men, I strongly urge the unmarried to take their time. I am still single and will be until the right person comes along. I may have high standards, but I expect a lot because I am willing to give a lot. Personally, I do not think I am asking for too much. I want someone to love, trust, appreciate, and support me as I will him.

"Most of all, I want someone who truly loves the Lord and lives it each day, not just on Sundays for everyone to see. I know that if he has honestly committed himself to being a doer of the Word [not just a hearer], then I will be treated the way I should be.

"I have made up my mind only to marry once. It is true that we do not know what may happen in life — but God knows, and God does not make mistakes. I decided long ago to wait on God. I refuse to marry for the sake of being married. I am not desperate. God has always supplied every need, and I know He will continue to do so.

"People try to make you feel strange because you are not married, but I have faith that God knows who is best for me and that when he comes, I will know it. I have [a few] last things to say to singles in Christ:

"1. *Don't be in a hurry.* Don't marry just because everyone else is getting married.

"2. *Don't think you are over the hill at 25.* [This is mostly for women.] Just appreciate the precious time you now have, and utilize it wisely. This is the perfect time to establish a solid relationship with the Lord. Don't compromise your standards because you feel you are running out of time. You will end up losing out on God's best when you settle for less than your heart's desire. Just because you're single doesn't exempt you from controlling your temper, eating habits, spending or anything else. Start taking control now because if you desire a good marriage, it will take hard work, good communication, and self-control."

Boy, that is good advice. That young lady knows what she is talking about.

Situations Open to Deception

Another letter we received shows the potential damage living together before marriage can cause. This couple did begin living together before either of them was saved, but it could happen with Christians. This lady was divorced, had two boys, but had gone back to college. In college, she met a man who said he loved her and wanted to marry her.

But he did not marry her, although they moved in together. Then she became born again. She wrote:

"I felt something was not right between us and had no idea what it was. He loved me, and I loved him, so why weren't we married? Then his job sent him away for six months. During that time, I spent my time studying God's Word and getting to know Him better.

"I decided I did not want to marry him, so I wrote him and let him know I had changed. I was not going to live with him any longer without being married. He accepted the fact that we were living a lie and agreed to leave. He saw the change in my life and that I had grown in faith as well as in God's Word. He accepted Christ as his personal Savior.

"Then after receiving Christ, the Holy Spirit began convicting him, and he told me the truth. All the time he had been living with me and asking me to marry him, he was already married and had been for seven years previously. Naturally I cried, but I went along with him. After all, we had spent several years building our relationship.

"Later, *we moved together again but refrained from sexual contact.* [Sound familiar?] We were going to wait on his divorce. Then one day, the Holy Spirit spoke to me that I had [to make a choice] to serve Him and let Him be my husband and provider. So I asked my mother and some of her friends to pray in agreement with me to move this man out of my life. I asked him to move, although I had no money, no job, and no car.

[Now, watch this. Mr. Tall, Dark, and Handsome was providing the money and the car. It was kind of hard to let that go.]

"I had really depended on this man for my blessings. But two days after he moved out, I had two job offers ... with one being close enough to get to on the bus. But the rent was more than I had ever paid alone, so I let this man come back again. My faith was not built up like I thought it was. However, several months later, he removed himself quietly from my life.

"My children and I live alone. I know what it takes to live as a Christian family and without a man in the house."

A lot of women have gotten caught in situations like that. While you are on the outside looking at someone else, you can see how pointless, non-productive, and even stupid those relationships are. But when you are in it, you think you cannot do anything else. Learn to trust in God. He will provide everything you need. You do not have to choose between living with someone outside of marriage and spending lonely nights. But the choice is yours. God cannot do anything for you while you are helping yourself.

Another tragic situation involved a single, middle-aged woman who had led a good moral life. Less than a year after receiving Jesus as her Savior and beginning to attend our church, she met a good-looking, well-dressed man who had been very active in the helps ministry here. (He had lied on the forms we require people to fill out to operate in the church.) She wrote, "I had prayed for a husband, but had not learned to wait on the Lord. I allowed my own emotions to lead me. I could hardly wait for this man to be mine. After all, I was nearing 50 years of age, and Satan kept saying to me, 'You don't want to grow old alone.'

"I had committed myself to live holy before God so what else was left but to marry him, so I could be in God's perfect will and live happily every after? Needless to say, it was a tragic mistake. The marriage only lasted fifteen months. I knew on the honeymoon when he started cursing that he was not the answer to my prayer.

"Later, I discovered that he was a 'closet' homosexual. When he knew I had found this out, he left me and the church and divorced me. If it had not been for the teaching ministry at the church, I would have gone under. I asked God to forgive me for not waiting for His answer, and I had to forgive my ex-husband for being deceptive with me. I started all over with Matthew 6:33.

"I now have joy unspeakable. To the middle-aged single woman who is believing for a husband, I would say, 'Do not be anxious, because many times in your anxiety, Satan will place someone in your path who will appear to be the answer to your prayer. If you yield to this, the outcome could be disastrous. God is no respecter of persons, and he will honor your heart's desire at any age. I am now 55 years of age and still believing for a husband. But now I am perfectly willing to wait for the Master's voice."

See, these are the things some people live through by not observing the Word.

Part II

THE FAMILY

Chapter 16

INTRODUCTION TO THE CHRISTIAN FAMILY

The whole plan of God for mankind is centered around the family structure. Remove it, and you remove the basic foundation ingredient of the purpose of God for establishing the human race. The family is the channel through which God works in the natural realm. And marriage is the center of the family relationship.

God established the home, He established the family, He established marriage, and His power works best through the relationship that is functioning the closest to the terms on which He designed it to function.

Even in the Church, however, there are unhappy Christian husbands, unhappy Christian wives, and unhappy homes. Too often we see in the lives of Christians very shoddy relationship situations. Yet they love the Lord. Many are filled with the Holy Spirit, but they are experiencing domestic problems that shake the very existence of their foundation.

And there is no real need for the unhappiness. It is not necessary at all. It is not in the plan of God. It is not in His will. If we do not know how to operate within the framework of His plan and purpose as revealed in His Word, then we are going to be the victims of the circumstances of life.

The Christian family is very important. As we talk about the family, that is an inclusive term. It means the husband, the wife, the children. It means the parents, the singles, the divorced persons. "The Christian family" means everyone who is a Christian within the framework of the family relationship. Whether you are male or female, young or old, does not make any difference. You are a part of the family.

I want to show you family life from a Biblical or a Christian perspective. Not as the world views it, but as the Heavenly Father reveals it to us in the written Word. There are two ways of looking at family life: one is from the world's way and the other from God's way.

The family is Satan's targeted area. If he could do away with the family, then he would pretty much have society in the palm of his hand.

This is not intended to be an exhaustive study in the sense that once I say everything I have to say, there is nothing else that can be said! But I want to deal with the things the Spirit of God would have me deal with. I want to be open not only to the Spirit of God but to the needs of people. It would take a lot of books to deal with every single possibility, but I do want to deal with some basic things.

There always are other things that someone else knows about which could broaden the individual subject matter, but in this book, I can only deal with each subject in a limited way. What I believe the Lord wants in this book is an overview, an outline of certain principles that can be applied in individual situations.

Thus Saith the Lord

The family is the cornerstone of God's creation. He created this planet for His children, His family. It was to be their dwelling place, their home. He created Adam and Eve, the first couple, and placed them in the Garden of Eden. He created them as a family. Ever since that time, there has been a concerted effort on the part of Satan and his demonic forces to destroy the sanctity of family life.

Satan hates God, but He cannot get back at Him directly. He has been whipped. Jesus whipped him. And the Christians who know their God and are doing exploits in the name of Jesus are constantly whipping up on him. So he has tried to thwart God's creation. Man is unique, the pinnacle of God's creation on Earth. He cannot get to God, so he tries to get to God's family.

Because He intended man to be His family, the family unit is very important to God. The first four books of the New Testament called "the Gospels" mirror the earthly life of the Lord Jesus Christ. It is interesting to note that whenever Jesus talked about God, it was not in any judicial way. He always talked about God as Father.

The idea of God as the great Father figure implies family of some sort. So God is interested in the family. Before we ever see any reference to the visible church, the family was instituted.

Being a Parent Is Not Easy

From the time when Adam and Eve had to leave the Garden of Eden and begin having children, parents have had the same problems. It is easy to make babies, but it is not easy to be a parent. But God only has one methodology to bring up children. In the world, they are always changing methods, trying to work out something new and better. When you have the best already, you do not have to change it. Men are experimenting because they do not know what they are doing.

If we followed God's plan in everything, His best, this would be a much more peaceful world. We would live in a sane society. But raising children by man's methodology is what most

Christians try to do, and that is playing Russian roulette. If you get a few winners, you are lucky, the world says. In God, there is no such thing as luck. And if you lose in child raising, it means the death or crippling of a life entrusted to your care.

Thousands of years ago, the Lord laid down His child-raising principles, which have never changed. However, you cannot teach His principles if you do not have them in your heart. That is one of the things that hinders parents: They cannot teach what they do not know or what they do not believe. It has to start with the parent. The things being taught to the children have to be *in* the parents' behavior as well as in their mouths.

You can never teach even what you know and believe with conviction if you do not live by it yourself. Children have an uncanny ability to see through a phony mother or father. Your children may see you saying "Praise the Lord" at church, saying "Amen" and dancing in the Spirit. But if there is no teaching or discipline at home, your Christian witness is not going to be worth anything.

Although each of us is a unique individual, and each family is a unique unit, we still have to live in the same societal framework. Therefore, we are all bombarded with the same basic temptations that everyone else is bombarded with. Satan is going to attack all of us in basically the same ways. There are some areas of temptation that affect fewer people than others, of course. But also there are those few general areas that everyone seems to be vulnerable to in one way or another. Four of them always seem to crop up on anyone's list.

In the next chapter, I am going to talk about two of these four main problem areas in marriage and family relationships, areas that are potential sore spots for everyone. Then in chapter 18, I am going to talk about the duties of a parent as they are found in the Word. Those duties involve loving, teaching, training, providing for the needs of children, disciplining, and correcting.

Parenting: The Greatest Single Occupation

Whether you realize it or not, the greatest single occupation that a human can have is to be a parent. That is more important than being president or prime minister. It is more important than being an earthly king. It is a high and exalted position and carries with it awesome responsibilities.

God is the great Father figure, and there is no estimate you can place on the value of a mother and a father. I believe it to be the highest privilege a person can have: to be the guardian of another human life from conception to adulthood.

Divine laws work whether you are aware of the laws or not. Even some non-Christian parents raise children in the way they should go without knowing about divine laws. If they did not, the world would be in even worse shape than it is. You can do the right thing without even knowing you are doing the right thing, and it will still produce results.

The beautiful thing is that when you become a child of God and know that you know that you know what the divine laws are and how to operate in them, you can get the full, maximum benefit out of God's plan.

Chapter 17

COMMUNICATION AND HONESTY

We have already talked about some things that involve the family: husbands and wives, marital relationships, tithing, and various aspects of family life. In all of my years of counseling and listening to other people's problems, four main problem areas show up on nearly everyone's list.

In addition to sex and the *division of labor* within the family structure, which already has been discussed, the other two "biggies" in family problems are *communication* and *honesty*. They show up in parent-child relationships as well as in marriages.

To be forewarned is to be forearmed, so that when the enemy comes in like a flood, you can raise up the standard of the Word of God concerning these areas and back him down in the name of Jesus. If you do not know how to deal with these areas, you are going under.

Problem Area Number One: Communication

I believe *communication* is the A-No.1 potential problem in relationships. I have talked to more people with problems that boil down to a lack of communication! In other words, if they had really been talking to one another, the problems would never have come up. The couples thought the problems were going to work out by themselves, I guess. They did not realize that way down the line Vesuvius would erupt.

I encourage couples who are just dating, or those who are engaged, to spend more time talking about other things than, "I love you. I love you so much. I have never loved anybody as much as you." That is typical of courting couples, and there is nothing wrong with it. If no one has ever told you he, or she, loves you, you have really missed something.

However, you cannot build a lasting marriage relationship on saying "I love you." You can build a courtship, yes, but not a marriage. When you say, "I do," you had better have more going for you than "I love you." That will get old fast. That does not mean you do not say it anymore, but it means you have to talk about other things.

Socrates, the father of philosophy, said once that in order for two intelligent people to discuss any matter, they first of all have to define their terms so that each knows what the other is talking about. So if I want to truly communicate with you, I have to define my terms. When I use a word, I want you to know what I mean by that word.

I have found that people have all kinds of meanings in their minds about words, varying shades of meanings. The world calls that *semantics*. Sometimes I have been talking to someone and spent forty-five minutes with him, wondering why I cannot get through to him. I wonder what in the world is going on. Then I find my interpretation of a word I have been using was "up" and his interpretation was "down." No wonder we never got together!

So let me define *communication*. Here is an example: Mary wants to talk to John about buying another dress. So she begins to talk about "Issue A." John listens. He is tempted to talk about "Issue B," which is his thing. But he loves Mary, so he listens to her. When she finishes, he talks — but he talks about her issue until the matter is settled, until he is sure he understands what she means.

Then John begins to talk about his issue, and Mary listens until he is finished. They talk about Issue B until they come to an agreement. When one talks, the other listens. Then the other responds.

This will take some time. It involves dialogue, speaking back and forth on the same subject. That is communication.

Most of the time, people do not communicate. They bounce words off one another's eardrums. Most of the time when one party is silent, he is not listening to what the other person is actually saying. He is just waiting for a chance to put his two cents in. He never even heard what the other person said. He was *listening* without *hearing*.

So those two people are not communicating with each other. What they are doing is talking at each other, not to each other. Husbands and wives go on day after day, week after week, and year after year. They live together for ten years and are more strangers than they were when they began.

It takes time to communicate and to get to know one another. But society today has us running back and forth trying to catch up with ourselves. Everything is "instant this," and "instant that." Pop it in the microwave oven. Instant-on TV. Television sets are partially on all the time now. All you have to do is press the button. A few years ago, you would have to wait a few minutes for the tubes to warm up.

Everything is instant, and we want communication to be that way — but it is not possible. It takes time to understand one another.

"What is this woman saying? What is this man saying?"

It works the same on both sides, because people are constantly going, especially when a husband and wife both work. They pass each other along the way, back and forth all day long.

The most important thing in any relationship is communication. I tell this same thing to those who come for counseling. I only have one plan: the one that works. I do not try to come up with anything new. If I find something that works, I am going to stay with it. My motto is: Don't fix anything that works. If something is working leave it alone. And real communication in marriages and in families *works*.

Establish lines of communication. Talk about everything, but make sure you know what the other person means by the words he, or she, uses. Take time to define your terms. That way there will never be any room for any doubt. You will never have to wonder what the other person is thinking. You will know because you have communicated.

What happens with people who do not like to talk? That is fine — outside the home. Don't talk to anyone if you don't want to. But the people whom you have to talk to if you are ever to have a wholesome, working relationship are your spouse and your children.

If you are an average person with some feelings or ideas of your own, you are going to have to take the time to develop a relationship of communication. You cannot know someone when you are just going together, kissing and hugging and so forth. You do not know that person, really. You are only going to start knowing that person when you wake up each morning and see that face on the pillow next to you!

When a man and woman go together, they show their best sides. They are on their best behavior. After they have been married for about six weeks, that old ugly nature comes out. She was so nice, and he thought she was the most docile person in the world. He thought she would make a good wife. Then she starts throwing her weight around, and he finds out she is not so docile after all! She would scratch his eyes out in a minute if he crossed her.

On the other hand, he always went to see her with his tie tied right and his hair and mustache trimmed. She is not going to

COMMUNICATION AND HONESTY

find out until she lives with him for a while how sloppy he is. As soon as he walks through the front door, he kicks his right shoe under the couch and his left on the chair, and begins dropping his jacket and things all over. She has to go behind him the next day and pick up all the dirty underwear and stuff.

All of that is only going to come out when you start living together. What are you going to do then? You cannot go by sign language or body language. It is a mistake to base your relationship on sign language. I know of more relationships where the biggest problem is the lack of communication. They may scream and yell at each other, but they are not talking.

The most important thing you can do is learn how to make other people understand what you mean. If you talk, and I take the time to listen carefully to make sure I understand what you mean, how can we have a misunderstanding?

Many people live together for years and never really talk to each other. They spend years talking at each other, but never really know one another. They end up — husbands and wives, parents and children — being strangers because they never really learned to communicate. They never learned to say what was inside of them.

You cannot operate a family on "body language" — a raised eyebrow or a supposition. A grunt here and a grunt there will not get it. You have to really communicate.

Many Christians in their relationships are not honest with one another. I do not mean overt lying, but remaining silent on some issues can be a lie. By remaining silent, you indicated approval when perhaps you did not mean it. You could have been against the issue totally. Also, establishing lines of communication is as important between parents and children as between husband and wife.

A Personal Example

Betty was one of a family of twelve, and both her parents had to work just to keep a roof over their heads and food on the table. The brothers and sisters talked to one another, but they hardly ever saw their parents who went to work early and came home late. So it was one of those kinds of things where it was assumed that your mother and father loved you because they were out working and providing a place for you to stay.

It was not that close, tender, touching, holding, and hugging one another parent-child relationship. When you have twelve children, how are you going to get around to hugging them all? So she grew up in an atmosphere of assumptions:

"I assume my parents love me. They are taking care of me. They are both here. My daddy did not run off and leave us with Mom to take care of twelve children by herself."

However, the result was that Betty never developed the habit of talking and communicating her views. When we were dating, we talked on the phone for hours. Of course, most of it was spent saying, "I love you." After you marry and do not have to say that so much to get one another — you already have one another — what are you going to talk about? Mostly, you sit and look at one another.

Betty was not a talker. I had to *work* to get her to talk. I had to initiate every conversation and just *make* her talk.

Then she is such a sweet, precious woman that she cannot bear to hurt anyone's feelings. So she feels that if she never says anything, she runs no risk of hurting anyone's feelings. If your feelings get hurt dealing with my wife, one thing you can know for sure: There has been some sort of tragic mistake. She is such a sweetheart that she would not hurt a fly intentionally. I have known this lady for more than thirty years, and she has no malice in her at all.

So her family environment and her own soft, sweet spirit combined to make it hard for her to tell me if she did not like something about me. I had to drag things out of her. She became pregnant as soon as we married — instantly it seemed! And everything made her sick in those months. We were newlyweds, but it seemed every time I got near her, she regurgitated. I almost went crazy trying to find out what was wrong. It turned out the stuff I put on my hair was nauseating her, and she did not want to hurt my feelings! The point, of course, is that I got hurt worse thinking she was rejecting me than if she had told me the truth.

Thank God, I had a little book on marriage that my mother had given me, and it said the most important thing was "communication." Without that book, I would not have known the importance of talking. I was not even a Christian, but I knew it was important to talk to one another.

It may sound odd, but I have never been much of a big talker. I was rather shy in my early years. But somehow I never had trouble expressing myself. In my teen years and just before Betty and I married, I could talk about everything with my "crime buddies." I did not have any problem talking to them about anything. I knew I needed to talk. However, in myself, I am the kind of person who feels if you do not want to talk to me, I do not want to talk to you.

What a mess that would have been! Two people living in a house and not talking. But a lot of people live like that. I kept on at Betty and finally got her to the point where she would talk. Even now, after thirty-three years, there are things she just does not like to talk about. But I know her now. I have her to the point that she will communicate. I know how to "worm" things out of her and get her to go ahead and talk about it.

But if I had not had that book that told me how important it was to communicate, we probably would not be together today. There probably would not be any Crenshaw Christian Center, either.

I have found that our problem was typical. In most relationships, you have one who will talk and one who will not, so they end up strangers living in the same house. If one runs off at the mouth all the time, that is not communication either. The other one wishes that person would shut up, and he or she will not shut up. So there has to be a balance. It cannot be one-sided.

The same thing can happen with children. What a difference it would have made to us if Betty had learned early to communicate with her parents, so that she would have been accustomed to sharing her thoughts.

Learn to Compromise

Some people think keeping silent keeps down disagreements, and in a way, it does. But is being passive and keeping silent worth having to live with a stranger the rest of your life? If you are communicating, you are going to have some things on which you have different points of view. But you can disagree without being disagreeable. In a case like that, you keep on discussing it in love and without anger until you can work out a compromise.

Compromise simply means yielding one to another, preferring one another. It does not mean keeping on at the other person until he gives in and lets you have your way. Nor does it mean you being a doormat and always letting him have his own way. Compromise means coming to a position where you both can function and be satisfied. It does not mean that you lower your standards and do something immoral.

For example, suppose you want a reddish-colored carpet in a room in your house, but your spouse wants a purple carpet. Who is right? Both of you are going to use the room, and both of you have a right to say what you want in it. The right thing to do is compromise: Pick a multi-colored carpet with both colors in it. That way, you are both getting what you want. Come to the place where you can both agree on things so that both of you are happy.

Most relationships do not work out that way, however. Take the guy who has a wife and three children and one car. When he buys the car, he does not discuss it with his wife. He never even talks to her about it. He comes home with it one day — a two-door souped-up vehicle that he needed like a hole in the head.

But he had always wanted that kind of car. Now everytime he takes the family somewhere, and they want to get out of the back seat, they have to lean forward, push the seat up, open the door, and try to squeeze out. A four-door car would have been much more practical. But he never even thought of discussing it with his wife.

In most relationships, there are only three people: me, myself, and I — just the three of us.

In another case, the man always wanted a motor home, so one day he comes home with this big monstrosity. Not only is his wife not happy, she is very upset. She does not want to ride in one, look at one, or have one on their property. But he never communicated with her about his wants.

If you do not talk but just go out and buy what you want, what is your family going to do? Women do the same thing. They go out and get hairdos and clothes without ever thinking to find out what their husbands like and do not like to see on them.

Do not assume! Share your heart, your dreams, with your mate. I cannot conceive of any problem that could ever arise that a Christian husband and wife, who are informed in the Word, walking in faith, filled with the Spirit, cannot deal with and iron out *if* they are in communication with one another.

The bottom line on communication is this:

> **Can two walk together, except they be agreed?**
>
> **Amos 3:3**

The answer is no, they cannot. How can you be agreed with your mate or with your children if you do not even know what to agree on? And how will you know what to agree on if you are not talking to one another? Keep talking until you agree. Finally, you will find that place where both of you can plug into a compromise.

Now, remember! I said, "Keep talking," not "Keep arguing."

Problem Area Number Two: Honesty

The second "biggie" that creates problems in family relationships is *honesty*. We have too many dishonest people today.

Too many dishonest husbands and wives who lie to one another on a continuing basis. Then they end up lying in all their other relationships: family, work, and the church. We have a lot of brothers and sisters in Christ lying to each other.

Lie not one to another, seeing that ye have put off the old man with his deeds.

Colossians 3:9

Now that is a commandment of God: *Lie not.* In modern English, we would say, "Don't lie to each other."

We attended the wedding of some friends of ours as guests, and the father of the bride wanted me to say something to the assembled guests. After the wedding, they had a beautiful reception with an orchestra to entertain, a master of ceremonies, and the whole works. And he asked me to make a little talk.

There did not seem to be any nice way to get out of it, although I do not like to do things like that. But I had no real excuse for not doing it. Unless I am to preach or teach, I would rather be seen and not heard. Ordinarily, I am a fairly quiet person. But I got up and spoke. He had asked me to give the bride and groom some words of encouragement. In the context of my little talk, I stressed *honesty*. I said to tell your husband and wife everything.

After I finished, the master of ceremonies came forward and went on with the program. He jokingly made a few remarks of his own. But the essence of what he said was, "Never tell your wife everything," which contradicted the remarks I had just made. But his opinion is the common consensus of opinion in the world's system. Men living in the world do not tell their wives everything, because they usually have a lot of things to hide. But a child of God should have nothing to hide.

I have been successfully married to the same person for thirty-three years, and I was saying to be totally honest. The dude who was acting as emcee had been married several times, and I think was divorced at the time he was giving the newlyweds his advice. But that is typical of the world's attitude. Relationships are based on subterfuge and dishonesty.

The world's philosophy is to tell everything that will keep you out of trouble. To most people, that is "truth." That is fine as long as it saves your neck. Just tell what will keep you out of hot water. Let me give you an example.

Defining a Lie

Suppose I am a businessman, and I call my wife one night to tell her associates from the East Coast have flown in unexpectedly. I tell her I may be about two and a half hours late, maybe even a little later. I tell her not to hold dinner up for me, but to go ahead and eat, and put the kids to bed. I will get a bite to eat on my way home. As soon as I hang up the phone, I head for the bar with the boys for the beer.

Everybody knows what that is. That is deception, a lie designed to deceive. My wife is going to think I am at the office working, when in fact, I am going to be somewhere else doing something else. Now that is an obvious lie. *That kind of lie is not the real trouble in most marriages.*

The kind of lie I am talking about is the subtle kind of untruth that has a cumulative effect over ten, fifteen, or twenty years together. I am talking about the insidious things where sometimes nothing is said, and saying nothing amounts to agreement in whatever happens. You hated every moment of something, but you did not want to hurt someone, or you did not know how to say it, or you did not want to rock the boat. So you did not say anything and left the impression that you endorsed whatever went down, when in reality, you did not even like it. To me, that is a lie.

Here is a good illustration: a couple's second anniversary is coming up, so the wife decides to take a personal business day off to make a special meal for her husband. She pulls out all the beautiful things they got for their wedding — lace tablecloth, silver, real china, the whole bit. So she works in the kitchen all day and has the table decorated with the candelabra out.

Her husband comes home, walks in the door, and realizes that it is sort of dark in the house. What happened to the lights? She meets him dressed in a beautiful gown. So he naturally asks what is the occasion.

"Well, dear," she says, "it is our anniversary. And last year we went out for dinner, but I thought we would have a quiet evening at home this year."

She flips on the music, and it is playing softly. He goes and washes up and comes back. She pulls his chair out and sits him down like a king on a throne. Then she starts serving the food. Finally, she gets to the vegetables. So she brings out this beautiful silver serving dish, takes the top off, and inside he sees green peas.

Now, he hates green peas. He detests green peas. He abhors green peas!

In fact, he used to say as a boy, "If I ever get out from under my mother's apron string, I will never eat a green pea again as long as I live."

But to make this a memorable meal, he does not want to discourage his wife. So he takes a few green peas, hating every mouthful. It is agony for him, but he does not want to rock the boat. He is not deliberately setting out to deceive his wife. He wants her to know he appreciated her efforts.

Afterwards, she asks him how he likes the meal, then specifically asks how he liked the peas. He compliments the meal, so she thinks he really liked the peas. Now on every special occasion, what is she going to fix him? Right! Green peas.

It may seem funny, but whenever you are put upon, whenever you have to take something that you do not really like, it is going to manifest out of you in some way, form, or fashion. It is going to eat away at your insides. You are going to get to the point where you feel someone is taking advantage of you. There has to be an outlet, an escape valve for all that emotion someway.

About six months later, this couple is invited over to some friends' house for dinner. The guys are sitting around talking about football or whatever. Then dinner is served. The guys are still talking across the table, when the hostess comes up to this man, takes the cover off the dish in her hand — and inside are green peas.

Spontaneously, he says, "Oh, no! No, thank you! I detest green peas. I have never liked them. In fact, I always said when I grew up, I would never eat any more as long as I lived. No, thank you."

His wife is sitting across the table, and while he was talking, Satan tip-toed up to her and said, "What else has that fool not been telling you?"

Suddenly the aura of suspicion rises in a dark cloud, "He has not been telling me the truth. He has been eating green peas all this time at home and not saying a word. What else has he not been telling me?"

This is the night they usually have set aside for making love. So when they get home, he goes to bed and waits for her — and waits and waits. Finally, she comes to bed with her hair in rollers and an old robe on. She slips into bed on her side and turns over. What is going on?

He says, "Honey?" and reaches over to touch her. And she pulls away. So he asks what is wrong, "What have I done?"

She says, "You said over at Janie's house that you never liked green peas. You lied to me. What else have you not been telling me?"

Now they have a great big argument going over nothing.

Multiply that by all of the things that could be involved besides green peas, and you can see how people get in such a mess sometimes. The only thing worse would have been for him to get offended when she turned over, not asked her what was wrong, and never get it straightened out. In that case, pretty soon you would have coldness, hardness, and an estranged relationship — and all over something as little as green peas.

He did not set out to deceive her with bad motives. His motives were good. They were to not hurt her feelings. But the simplest way to handle such a situation in honesty would have been to lovingly tell her that first night that green peas were not his favorite vegetable, but broccoli was. How about broccoli next time?

It may sound simple, but I have seen people have tragic misunderstandings based on things like that when plain honesty would have avoided all the trouble. Tell it like it is. Do not lie to one another. Be tactful and loving, but tell the truth.

In our early years, I did not always know how to be tactful. I had no finesse. I was blunt about being honest. I was like a bull in a china closet. If I did not like something, I said so without realizing that I might be hurting someone else. I was just trying to be honest. I realized, after I gained a little maturity, that there is a way to say you do not like something, a way to be honest without hurting someone's feelings.

I like to deal with people so that they do not have to wonder where I am coming from. If I do not like something, I will tell you right away, but I do it as nicely as I can. My wife always knows what I am thinking, all the time. If we go to a restaurant, and I do not like the food, I do not eat it.

All of God's children need to learn to be honest with one another. God is honest with us.

I even see ministers lie, exaggerate, try to impress one another. That is why I am such a fanatic about keeping records. I like to have something on record, so that if I mention something, it is not off the top of my head. My intention is to tell the truth. Stretching the truth is the same as lying.

I can feel it when the devil pulls on me to stretch the truth: "See? It will be more impressive if you say so-and-so."

It is a constant battle, and we all have to fight it to one degree or another. Even in the ministry, there is that temptation. It is easy to lie, if you are not careful. In fact, you do not even have to plan to lie. But just start talking, start running off at the mouth, and the first thing you know, you have stretched the truth and told a lie.

There are some people who thrive on lies. They have lied so much they do not even know it when they are telling the truth. They have cut corners so much that the truth to them is a lie, and a lie is the truth! They do not know the difference anymore. A person like that is dangerous. He can even beat a lie detector test. The body of a habitual or pathological liar does not respond to a lie one way or the other.

Sometimes husbands and wives get that way with one another. They have been living with each other for so long that one of them lies and the other puts up with it, or does not even recognize the lies. The one who habitually deceives, by commission or omission, gets to the point where the body language no longer shows deception.

I have to put up with it in the ministry, people who work for you, and supposedly for the Lord, but lie. Something can happen between two employees, and you know one of them did it. There was no one else there. Yet both of them say no when you ask, "Did you do this?" There have been situations in the ministry offices that are still not resolved.

Christians are people. You need to understand that. Few of us are perfected as yet. All of us have areas that God is working on, so if you see a brother or sister miss it, pray for him or her. Do not make the mistake of throwing out the baby with the bath water. Do not throw out Christianity because a Christian missed it Keep your eyes off men and women and on the only perfect man who ever walked the earth: Jesus.

I do not look for things wrong in a Christian, but anything anyone does never surprises me. I have seen so much, none of it takes me aback at all. Some folks get so surprised if they happen to run across a couple of Christians here on the church premises arguing, and they go away determined not to come back again.

"When I went to Crenshaw, I heard this usher arguing with a lady. I did not know Christians did that."

You didn't? Well, just hang around for a while. You might as well get initiated now. Folks sit in my church with Bibles in their hands and lie. Absolutely! Some Christians lie to each other, to themselves, and sometimes to God.

Do Not Lie to Your Children

Along this same line, let me admonish you: Do not lie to your children. We always tell our children the truth. We have never lied to them — never, never, never. If you lie to your children, they will lie to their children, and you perpetuate a lying spirit. At least, the temptation to lie will be greater for them than even for you because of the example lived out before them.

If you want someone to be honest with you, be honest with him. Telling the truth is a choice. It is something you have to decide to do. The truth may cost you, but in the long run, lies will cost you more. I have lost very valuable situations because I told the truth. I could have had a lot of jobs I did not get because I told the truth. Sometimes I was tempted to lie. But I always believed God would take care of me in some way. So I told the truth.

Live before your children the precepts you want them to grow up by. Just telling them is not enough. Don't say, "Do as I say," but "Do as I do." That is honesty.

Now, how are you going to tell the truth? How are you going to be honest with one another? Only by real communication. Do you see how the two "biggies" in family relationships dovetail? You cannot operate rightly in one area without operating rightly in the other area.

Now let us move on to another area of problems. In the next two chapters, I will discuss the duties, or responsibilities, of parents and children to one another. We have already touched on this in the chapters on duties of husbands and wives. But now I want to talk about parents and children.

Chapter 18

THE DUTIES OF PARENTS: TO LOVE, TEACH, AND TRAIN

Duty means "responsibility." And the first responsibility of parents is to love their children. The thing most people do not fully understand is that everyone has to be taught to love. We think of love as some sort of emotion that happens spontaneously, a feeling that comes out of nowhere like lightning and strikes you. But that is absolutely untrue.

God *is* love. The Word says so. (1 John 2:16.) Therefore, love is a characteristic, or a character development, a state of being. I know that sounds strange, because we are so conditioned through novels, movies, television, and so forth to think of love as an emotion that erupts within us.

Love is not an emotion; love is *expressed* through emotions. But it is much more than emotion. We have gotten the idea that if you do not have the emotion of love, then there is no obligation on your part to be involved with someone, even with your children, parents, mate, or other Christians. You do not really relate to other people, because you do not have any emotional feeling for them. Well, that is a fallacy.

The Bible shows us that love has to be taught, or has to be developed in children just as patience, or self-control. If you do not agree with this, you will have to argue with God, not me. He wrote the Word.

> **But speak thou the things which become sound doctrine:**
>
> **That the aged men be sober, grave, temperate, sound in faith, in charity, in patience.**
>
> **The aged women likewise, that they be in behaviour as becometh holiness, not false accusers, not given to much wine, teachers of good things;**
>
> **That they may teach the young women to be sober,** *to love their husbands, to love their children.*
>
> Titus 2:1-4

Now if everything were working according to God's plan, then the older women could fulfill this injunction. But if the older women have not been taught to love, how are they going to teach the younger women? And that is where the whole thing breaks down: the Church has not taught this. If you have been attending church any length of time, I will guarantee you that you hardly ever have heard a preacher tell you that the Word says "teach" your children to love.

Love is something you do.

Love Is Not an Emotion

So Christians go along with the idea of love as an emotion. What is spontaneous, however, is the capacity for love. Everyone is born with that capacity or potential. But the capacity has to be trained, taught, governed, controlled, and finally expressed. That is what is wrong with today's young people.

The word *sober* in verse 4 is from the Greek word *sophronizo*, which means "sober minded" or "to voluntarily place limitations on their own freedom," in other words, self-discipline or self-control.[1] The apostle was not talking about keeping them from getting drunk. He would have assumed that Christian women would not be out getting drunk.

Also, there must be a difference between loving your husband and loving your children. If there were no difference, it would not have been said that way. So there must be a difference between marital love and parental love. But the greatest example of teaching love children can have is what happens between their mothers and fathers in their own homes.

Children absorb into their own personalities the behavior learned in the home during the early years of their lives. Ninety-nine times out of a hundred, someone who is a wife beater or a child abuser will be the child of fathers or mothers who were wife beaters and/or child abusers.

If all they have is emotion, then love will never do them any personal good. Look at one of the most famous Scriptures of all, John 3:16: **For God so loved the world ...** Now if the verse had stopped there, what good would it have done us? God would have been sitting in Heaven saying, "I love you, I love you," while all of us went to Hell!

No, the verse goes on:

> **... that he gave his only begotten Son, that whosoever believeth on him should not perish, but have eternal life.**

That verse says that God did something, He *gave*. Giving of yourself in some way, shape, form, or fashion is what love is all about. Love is demonstrated in giving. It is not just a condition, but an action. And we are supposed to teach our children how to love.

How can you teach them if you do not love your husband, and he does not love you? If you are in conflict and strife all the

---

[1] *The Hebrew-Greek Key Study Bible, King James Version,* Spiros Zodhiates, compiler and editor (Grand Rapids: Baker Book House, Copyright © 1981 by Spiros Zodhiates and AMG International, Inc.), p. 1487.

time, and that is what the children see. That is what they end up thinking love is.

Romance and Love Are Not Synonymous

Romance and love are two different things that can function together. When you find someone you want to marry, you "fall" in love. There is this overwhelming feeling that everyone ought once in his or her lifetime to experience. It is a great time in life, and if you operate according to the Word through that time, everything comes out just beautiful.

It seems at the time as though you moved into an unreal world. You do things you never have done before and probably never will again! The reason is that there is this great volcanic emotional eruption going on inside of you that wants to express itself in deeds of tenderness and kindness for the object of your affection.

The same thing happens many times when people are first born again. That is why I have a policy of not allowing people to help in the church until after they have been here for a year. For the first six months, usually people act unnatural. They are at every Bible class and all three services on Sunday. Meeting God and meeting "Mr. Tall, Dark, and Handsome" or "Miss Pretty," seems to have somewhat the same effect on people.

The Bible said in Isaiah 40:31 to mount up with wings as eagles, to run and not be weary, and to walk and not faint. But that is an inverted progression. A big bird will begin walking, then start running, and finally take off. Airplanes operate the same way. That is normal.

So *walk, run, and fly*. You do not fly, run, and walk. The Bible does not say that we fly by faith or that we run by faith. The Word says that we are to *walk* by faith. (2 Cor. 5:7).

When I first got saved, I felt as if I was on eagles' wings. Everything in the church involved high emotion. It was wonderful. But if you do not know the difference between the romance stage, the first encounter stage, and Christian maturity, you will get into a problem just as I did. When I began to settle down into the everyday walk with Christ, I did not know I was settling down. I thought I was supposed to experience that high emotional state all the time.

You need to know that mature love goes much farther and way beyond that emotional stage with all the palpitations of the heart. That is not wrong, but it is not what a relationship should be based on. Otherwise, you will be in for a letdown. The human being was not created to walk in emotion all the time. That causes burnout.

If you do not know that emotions *express* feelings and attitudes *but are not the same as* feelings and attitudes, as soon as you get out of the emotional stage of being a Christian, you may begin to think you have backslidden. You may begin to wonder if you are "really" saved. In your marriage relationship, you may begin to think you made a mistake or that you do not love your spouse anymore.

For the first seventeen years of my Christian life, I spent most of my time wondering if I really was saved. But for the past sixteen years, since I learned that Christians are to walk by faith, I have not questioned my salvation. I do not walk by feelings any longer.

Actions, Attitudes Speak Louder Than Words

Another thing is: Do not belittle your children. That amounts to rejection. If you *say* you love them, but continually put them down, which will they believe? "Actions speak louder than words." So love must be expressed through actions. One way of showing children through your actions, attitudes, and behavior that you love one another and love them is to remember special occasions such as birthdays and anniversaries. Let them know they are special to you.

I know families where the kids were told, "You are no good. You are not worth a dime. You are not going to ever do anything."

Today, hardly any of those children are doing anything. Most of them really did turn out worthless. They were "programmed" by the beliefs of the parents. Only one of them rebelled against the attitude of unloving parents and went in the opposite direction, determined to prove those words were not true.

Also giving things to your children does not necessarily demonstrate love. When I was a child, a boy lived next door to me whose mother worked her fingers to the bone so that he could have nice things. She bought her children the best from the best stores. Man, I did not even go in those stores, much less own something from there! Poor folks did not go in those stores. Yet there was no real love in the home. What good did all those nice clothes do without love, tenderness, or togetherness?

The first, and perhaps most important, thing you can give your child is to let him know he is loved.

One last point: You should love all of your children equally. I love every one of my children the same way. They are all different, but I do not love one more than the other. I treat them all equal in every area, as far as love is concerned. If you do have some kind of feeling more for one than the other, you need to pray and ask the Lord to show you what is wrong. Then ask Him to change you or the child, or both!

The Best Way to Teach

The greatest way to teach is by example. I talked about teaching children love by showing them love. However, teaching our children involves more than just showing them how to love. We have a responsibility to teach them God's Word, for example.

> **And these words, which I command thee this day, shall be in thine heart:**
>
> **And thou shalt teach them diligently unto thy children, and shalt talk of them when thou sittest in thine house, and when thou walkest by the way, and when thou liest down, and when thou risest up.**
>
> **Deuteronomy 6:6,7**

From the above verses, you can see that God is talking about a total lifestyle. Christian parents have the responsibility to teach the mature Christian lifestyle from the Word. We are to teach our children "thus saith the Lord."

Everything we do should have a lesson in it for our children. In fact, everything we do does have a lesson in it, and they learn those lessons. Much of the time, the lesson is not from the Word but from the world. If you do not teach the Word to your children, you are sowing the wind, and you will reap the whirlwind. (Hos. 8:7.)

We see that all the time in today's society. Adults who were not taught love and morality are raising up another generation that is not taught.

The third responsibility of parents that I want to talk about is *training*. Whether you realize it or not, there is a difference between *teaching* and *training*. A lot of Christian parents are reaping the whirlwind. They are sitting around talking about how they do not understand how George could be doing the things he is doing. After all, he was raised in a Christian home.

What does that mean? If you were raised in a pigsty, that would not turn you into a pig. Just because you live in a garage does not make you a Cadillac. And simply because you were taught Christian living, that does not mean anything by and of itself. The Word deals with this problem and shows us that it is not enough for a child to be told or even shown. The child must be *trained* in the things he has been taught.

You can be taught the multiplication tables in school, but if you do not practice them, and if you are not required to do exercises in the use of them, you will not *learn* them. You will not be able to put them into practice. They will not become an automatic part of your everyday life.

Train Up a Child

God always tells the truth. He never makes a mistake. It is impossible for Him to lie. Look at what He said in the Word about child-rearing:

> Train up a child in the way he should go: and when he is old he will not depart from it.
>
> Proverbs 22:6

Recently some people delivered some merchandise to my home. As I was signing the delivery receipt, one of the men looked at me and said, "I have seen you somewhere before."

I said, "Maybe on television."

And he said, "Yeah! You're a preacher, aren't you? Once in a while, I flip across the channels, and I see you on. You are one of the few I listen to because you make sense. I'm not very religious, and a lot of these guys are just talking stuff that doesn't make sense to me.

"I am a [and he named a denomination], but I'm just raising my kids to let them do whatever they want. I believe that however they want to do, that is the way they should go."

He was talking about religion and about denominations, but the same principle is used across the board in the world — and you can look around you and see the result. Humans do not *know* which way to go. They have to be taught as children in order to grow up knowing which way to go.

Ask your child if he *wants* to go to church, and he will say no. My oldest daughter, Angela, got to a point in her life where she did not see why she had to go to church. We went around and around and around, and my temperature rose, my adrenal glands were working overtime, and the perspiration flowed. But she went to church.

Now, she is my executive vice president. She runs this ministry from the business standpoint, and she does a magnificent job of it. Where would she have been if I had allowed her to drop out of church because she did not *want* to go anymore?

Many people say, "Okay, Johnny, just watch television. Watch the cartoons."

That is because the world's wisdom says you should never make a child do anything against his will. You will warp his character. You will thwart his growth pattern. You will give him a psychological aberration of the brain. Never make a child do something he does not want to do.

I tell you what! If you want to keep your sanity as a parent and if you want your children to grow up healthy and well-adjusted, you had better make them do what the Word says. I am not talking about using undue force. I am not talking about breaking the child's will by overwhelming physical or emotional means. I am not talking about using guilt or shame to manipulate them into doing what you want. I am talking about patiently and consistently training the child to do what the Word says.

Training Requires Practice

Look at professional athletes. Would teams ever win any games if the coach came out to the football field and said:

"Now, fellows, it is such a beautiful day today. It sure would be nice to go to the beach. There is such a nice breeze, sunshine, and everything. Of course, you know we have a big game coming up next week, the most important game of the season, a championship game. I don't want to put any pressure on you or anything like that.

"But you need a little more practice, a little more exercise. If it is all right with you, maybe we could spend a couple of hours out here playing. Can I get a vote here? Are you fellows willing to do this?"

No, no, no. The coach does not ask you anything. He tells you what you are going to do, when you are going to do it, how you are going to do it, where you are going to do it, and how long you are going to do it. He will never lift a finger to touch you. He will not use force or manipulation. But if you do not do what he says, you will not play next week or any other time.

Are you following what I mean by *make*? He is in authority over that team, and the team respects him. If you get authority over your children when they are very young, they will respect you also.

The Book says to train them up in the way they should go, not the way they want to go. Everything they do in the natural is usually contrary to the right way to do it, according to the Word. Have you ever noticed how easy it is for you to do what is wrong, and how hard to do what is right?

The easiest thing in the world is to eat nine pieces of pie. But it takes blood, sweat, and tears to push away from the table and not eat even the second piece of pie. You open the refrigerator, and the ice cream is saying, "Eat me, eat me, eat me." I mean, you have to work hard at doing what is right in anything. But the younger you were when you learned, the easier it was.

You can tell the adults who were never trained. The man who comes in from work, drops his clothes wherever he is, leaving his wife to pick up behind him like his mother did, never was trained.

Training starts as a child. You can learn some things and change some patterns as an adult. But it is uphill work. It is like trying to swim upstream. It is a lot easier when you are floating downstream as a baby, and mama and papa are moving the boat in the direction it is supposed to go.

You had better have your kids brush their teeth, or they will not brush them as adults. You had better train them to wash behind their ears and the backs of their necks. You had better have them pick up their toys. Sometimes you have to tell them nineteen times, but if you do not give up, you win.

You have to make them go to bed, or they will stay up until they wear out, and wear you out in the process. Children do not ever go to bed on their own. I do not care if you try to be nice and give them an extra hour. They will still cry over that. You might as well put them to bed when you said you were to start with. They will take advantage of your mercy and whine and cry. Being firm and consistent will pay handsome dividends in the end.

Training Costs the Trainer Something

It will cost you something, however, especially if you have a strong-willed child. There will be trauma, your blood pressure will rise, your heartbeat is going to increase. But it is better to do it now than when the police station calls and tells you to come down, they have your child in custody.

All of my children have minds of their own. Plus I wanted them to have the freedom to say whatever they needed to say, to be able to come to us and get straight answers. So we always had an open forum. When we sit down to dinner, we talk about anything that comes up. We call a dog a dog. We do not say "something with four legs and a tail." So my children have wills and minds of their own.

Now when the Lord says to **train up a child in the way he should go,** He is presupposing that the one doing the training knows which way the child should go. And the way the child should go is the way the trainer should go. If the trainer does not know which way to go, then you are going to have a replica, a duplicate, of the trainer, which could end up being a second disaster.

The **way he should go** is from the perspective of the standards God has in mind, not from the world's system of doing things.

There is a way of training children without abusing them, without ever striking them to make them do what you want. But training means *making* them do whatever it is you are training them in. Trainers do not ask athletes if they want to practice. They tell them to practice. Your employer *makes* you go to work tomorrow. If you do not, you can find another job. And there are ways to make children do what they ought to do until they are trained in it. You have to use the wisdom of God, however.

Every child is different, and you will have to use different strategies with different children. With our own children, what will work on one will not work on the other. You can say one thing to Angela, and you will stop whatever she is doing. But Cheryl would just keep on going as if you had not said anything. With Stephanie, you do not know what will work. It depends on whatever is in question. And little Freddie, he is coming on, and he has his own thing.

The Way He Should Go Is Toward the Lord

As Christians you have the responsibility of training your children up in the things of God. You have to make them go to church, especially if your children have made a personal acceptance of Christ. If you have to physically pick them up and carry them piggyback, make them go to church. If you should not make them go to church, then you should not make them brush their teeth. Are you going to tell me their teeth are more important than their spirits?

In natural things, you have the child's natural will and desires against you. But in spiritual things, you have a supernatural opposition. A satanic influence is trying to stop you from training your children in the right way. Satan does not care if your children do homework or brush their teeth. He is not even dealing with that. Nevertheless, it usually is a chore to get kids to do their homework.

How much more of a fight are you going to have when it comes to spiritual things? You have an enemy standing there. Satan and his demon forces do not want you to learn anything about God. I made my girls go to church when they were young, and now they are in church on their own. God told us what to do, and we did it. It cost us something, too.

God said that if you train them up in the way they should go, they will not depart from it when they are old. He did not say there is a sixty-forty chance. He said they will not. If you do not do what God says to do, God is not involved in raising your kids. You are raising your children on strictly your own ability.

When you do not do it God's way, He cannot get involved. Mark 16:20 says that God worked *with* the disciples and confirmed

His Word with signs following. The disciples did it God's way, and He confirmed what they did.

I did not like those encounters with Angela. My heart raced and my respiration was at a higher rate. I would be just this side of hyperventilating. It was harder on me than it was on her. But I knew if I did not do what God told me to, He would not be involved in raising my child. And she was my oldest child, a pace-setter for the younger ones. If I let her get by, there was no way in the world I was going to get the younger ones to do anything.

A lot of ministers put the churches or their ministries ahead of their families, and they do not even realize it. But that is not right. That is not even Biblically right. Which came first in God's plan, the family or the church? The family. You can see it in Genesis. The family was instituted before the church was. God made the family before He made the church.

So if you do not have your priorities straight, minister, you will fool around with the church or the ministry and let your family go to pot. When you do that, you will also lose your church, at least from the standpoint of losing the influence you ought to have on it. The church may not say anything to you, but there will be people in your congregation who will sit right in the audience and laugh at you.

They will say, "Look at Mr. Preacher standing up there telling us how to live, and his own children are running wild. How come it is not working for you, Preacher?"

That is not going to happen with me. If I cannot get it to work in my house, I am not going to try to sell it to you. Although it is true, whether it works in my house or not. But I do not feel I have the credibility, the right, to stand up and teach you something that does not work for me.

And that is the way you should be with your children. Your loving them, teaching them, and training them will work if it has worked for you, if they cannot look at you and see that you are not operating on a double standard. You will not train a child in the way he should go by saying "do what I say" instead of "do what you see me do."

Chapter 19

THE DUTIES OF PARENTS: TO PROVIDE, CONTROL, AND CORRECT

Let's look at the fourth thing parents ought to do: provide for the children. If you do not want to provide for your children, you should not become a parent. Providing for them is your *responsibility*. It is not an option. It is a duty. You brought them here. You created them, whether it was planned or accidental. Those kids are still here, and you are responsible.

And the way out is not abortion.

The Apostle Paul wrote about this to the Corinthian church:

> **Behold, the third time I am ready to come to you; and I will not be burdensome to you: for I seek not yours, but you: for the children ought not to lay up for the parents, but the parents for the children.**
>
> **2 Corinthians 12:14**

Paul was writing to them from a spiritual standpoint, because he was sort of the spiritual parent of these different churches. He was the catalyst who the Holy Spirit had used to birth the people at Corinth into the family of God. So he considered them like his children. He loved them so much that he wanted them to get the whole truth.

As a pastor, I know the feeling. My congregation is made up of my spiritual children. I give them the whole truth. I would rather they get mad and not talk to me for four weeks than to withhold any truth that might change their destinies. Children are like that. I know because I was a child. Children get in a room and talk about their parents like dogs. They say all kinds of crazy things about their parents after they have been told something pretty hard about their behavior.

Some of my people react like children and say, "I don't care what Fred says, I'm not going to do that."

And they go out of church with their lips sticking out, just like Angela did when I made her go to church. But she went. And I love the people in my church enough to tell them things they need to hear whether they want to hear them or not.

I remember a man who was the nicest person you could ever hope to meet. He was so nice, in fact, that he never said anything worth hearing. You cannot say something that is worth anything without the potential of someone taking offense. What you say should not offend them, but they take offense anyway. Do you know why? Because they are being stubborn and rebellious, and they do not want to do whatever you are telling them.

That is the way children do. But Jesus said the truth will make you free. (John 8:32.) I have been bound, but now I am free. And free is better. I like being free, and you will too, although it may cost you something that you think right now is not worth the price. Once you get a taste of the freedom in Christ, you will be so glad you paid the price.

So we should provide material things for our children as well as the intangible things such as love and teaching.

An Open Forum Means an Understanding Heart

We ought to provide food, clothing, a roof over their heads, and protection in the form of as comfortable a home as possible. We ought to provide security, love, and a safe haven where they can express themselves and still be accepted — not a place to express rebellion, but a forum where their ideas and creative thoughts can be spoken forth without ridicule.

They have brains just like adults. They have ideas. They hear garbage and stuff at school. They ought to have a home where they can sit down and talk about anything they want to without worrying about being slapped down for saying something.

We always provided that for our children. We talk at home just as we do at church. I would rather have them talk to us than to some friend. You do not know what they are getting when they talk to their friends. Friends will lie to you sometimes for advantage, for all kinds of reasons. Everyone does not tell the truth. In fact, very few tell the truth — the whole truth, nothing but the truth, the unmitigated, unvarnished truth. Most people cannot deal with it.

So parents need to provide a place where children are not afraid to talk about anything. Otherwise, you force them to huddle up under the bleachers and talk to their friends about some things. Provide that listening ear and that understanding heart.

Lay Up for the Children

We have the duty also to "lay up" for our children. I am always thinking about my kids. They do not always know it, but I am always trying to figure ways to make their lives better. If I got hold of a million dollars, guess what I would do with the $750,000 left after I paid my tithes and offerings? I am not going to tell you, but it would not be spent on me! I want my children to have it better than I do, not easier so that it makes them lazy, but better.

We need to make provisions for our children, whatever that costs. We need to provide for their education in whatever way they want to go. Also, as parents, we need to be careful not to project on our kids the frustration we had because we could not do what we wanted to as a young person. In other words, suppose I always wanted to be a big league baseball player. Then when my son grows up, I move heaven and earth to make him a big league baseball player — whether he wants to or not.

Encourage the children. Give them an environment in which to do what they want, but let them find their own level. Do not try to have them do something because you wanted to and could not. You wanted to be a doctor but were not able. Now you are going to make your son a doctor. He may be the worst doctor in the whole world. If his own heart is not in it, he will not be worth a dime. He may make a lot of money, but inside he will be miserable and empty — unfulfilled.

Your children should be provided an environment in which they feel accepted and can develop a sense of self-worth. The worst thing you can do next to physical abuse is verbal abuse. Some people call it "reverse psychology" and think it will motivate a child to talk to them negatively. But it does not. All that does is damage a child's self-esteem and plant self-rejection.

Never call a child stupid, dumb, or ugly. Never say, "You'll never amount to anything." There may be times when you have to point out that what they did was thoughtless or careless or dumb. But do not confuse the child and his actions. Your child should still feel loved, even when he knows you did not like whatever he did.

Are you creating an environment in which your child can grow up and be an asset to society? You ought to let your child know he is worth to you exactly what you are worth to God. That child should know he is valuable and precious to you. You can tell him that, but you also can show it in many ways.

Children can tell from the atmosphere of the home whether they are loved and whether their parents truly are concerned about them. When they have no doubt about this, no one out there in the world can ever shake their sense of self-worth.

What About Nutrition?

Someone asked me if children should be made to eat food they do not like. Parents do have the responsibility to feed their children right. I imagine most parents have had the challenge of dealing with kids who did not want to eat certain foods. Well, thank the Lord He made a variety of foods with the same nutritional value. I do think you need to exercise wisdom.

The Bible does not say what kind of food to feed your children. I would go to a chapter and verse, but I have not found one. But wisdom would dictate that you do have to feed them and provide a good balanced diet. I do not think you should force a child to eat something if he does not like it. If you start out real early giving them certain things, they will develop a taste for them.

Personally, I did not make my children eat a particular thing they had a distaste for, because there are enough other green vegetables that can be substituted. Also, you know some times it is the preparation of the food. A child may not like green peas, but if you put green peas on vanilla ice cream, he probably will eat it.

There are things inherited from parents that could be involved, also. I am a very particular eater, so I could not have my kids eat something they did not like because I would not eat the things I did not like. But we made sure they got a balanced diet through substituting.

But parents can go to the extreme and allow the kids to eat *only* what they like. Some people had mothers who pampered them. They allowed them to eat anything they wanted, and those children developed lousy eating habits. They got fat as little pigs. People called them "chubby," and "fatty."

They developed an uncontrolled attitude towards food, and now there is no one to say, "Don't." Their mothers did not tell them don't, but gave them anything they wanted. It was so cute ... "She'll grow out of it. It is just baby fat." Now Baby is 35 years old and still has that "baby fat." If she was not taught self-control through being controlled, Baby is going to have a very rough time learning it as an adult.

Those people ended up hating themselves. Their mothers did not do them any favors. In addition to ruining their looks, fat ruins their health. It kills their hearts, their lungs, their respiratory systems, and the veins in their legs. They are destroying the temple of God, and wondering why all kinds of ailments and diseases are coming upon them.

So providing for your household must follow the guidelines of the wisdom of God. It is as bad to provide the wrong things as not to provide the right things.

Ruling Well His Own House

In 1 Timothy, Paul wrote about the requirements for bishops. But what is true for overseers is no less true for laymen.

> **One that ruleth well his own house, having his children in subjection with all gravity.**
>
> **Let the deacons be the husbands of one wife, ruling their children and their own houses well.**
>
> **1 Timothy 3:4,12**

Notice that he says **having his children in subjection** and **ruling their children.** That means you should have your children under control and not let your children control you. A lot of parents have abdicated their own responsibility. That is why society is so messed up. Folks are out of control, because out of control kids grow up to be out of control adults. The problem is that when they get to be adults, they can do more damage than when they were kids.

Now let me define the word *ruling*, because if you are not careful, you will get in your mind the idea of a dictatorship. The Greek word translated *ruling* actually means "to stand in front of and lead." Remember about love, about teaching the children to love by example? That is how you are supposed to rule — by example.

Ruling means to stand in front of your family and lead, not stand over them with a lead pipe. *Leading* means "to control by example." If a child is not controlled, he will grow up into an adult out of control.

Sex drives some adults crazy. They are out of control in that area. Drugs and alcohol are ruling others. Food is ruling others. They are nine sizes bigger than they should be, out of control. If you want your children to be disciplined in their lives, then show them by example. Do not let sex, alcohol, food, or anything else control your own life.

I have heard people say, "Well, to be fat runs in our family."

Most of the time that is because one generation shows the other how to be fat. They provide an example of undisciplined eating and no exercise. If adults cannot rule themselves, how can they rule their children? If we do not have some discipline and guidelines for our own lives, we cannot communicate it to others.

You only have the opportunity to stand in front of your children and lead them while they are under your roof. Once they are out from under your authority, you cannot stand in front of them and lead them anymore. You no longer have the kind of parental authority that you did when they were under your jurisdiction.

Once your daughters have husbands, they have a higher order of accountability than mama and papa. You have to love, teach, and train them while they are at home.

Remember, I am not talking to the world. You cannot expect sinners to do any more or less than they already are doing. They do not have any spiritual guidelines. But the Christian has no excuse. And Christians *can* make an impact by leading their own children well. Then those children will stand in front of theirs, and so forth.

Children Out of Control

Many Christians, however, allow their children to run out of control. The little brats are running around acting crazy. Mama

239

will not do anything, and papa will not do anything. In past years, there was a certain family that, when Betty told me they were coming over, I did not want them to visit. I told her not to let them come. I had been to their house and watched their little kids climb up on the coffee table, climb over the chair, get up next to the glass and put saliva all over it. And they thought it was cute.

I told her not to let them come, because I knew I would end up falling out with them. No little kid is going to walk on my couch. That couch came through blood, sweat, and tears. My own children were not allowed to tear up the furniture, and it would have been dishonest of me to allow a visitor's children to run wild.

When you come on my property, you are an invited guest. I am the law, the FBI, the CIA, the Green Berets, the Red Berets, and the Orange Berets. When you come to my house, you come under the dominion of the governorship of Fred Price. You are in my castle where we play by my rules, or I will put you on the street. It is just that simple.

All little kids will try to get away with stuff. They have to be controlled. For example, you hear all this noise above your head. You look up at the chandelier, but it is not moving, so it cannot be an earthquake. If it was an earthquake, the whole house would be moving. But you are hearing all this noise, and you wonder what in the world it is.

You go upstairs into the bedroom, and there is little Johnnie right in the middle of your brand new mattress and box springs, just jumping up and down. He does not know he could break his neck. He is very close to the ceiling bouncing on that thing. He could slip, fall down, and kill himself. Is he thinking about that? No way. Kids do not know about things like that. So they have to be controlled.

Freddie one time was running his little race cars from the front entry way and into the kitchen where the tile is real hard and slick. He got the wheels to going real fast, put them down on the floor, and boom! Right into the baseboard, chipping off the paint. He did not know any better, and he had to be controlled.

So I said, "Freddie, over here is where you play. You do it over here."

I controlled the destruction. Otherwise, we would not have a house left. If you do not give children some guidelines and stick to them, they will tear the whole house down. Give them one area, like their room, where they can be free. Just lock it when company comes!

You can watch some children in public and know there is no control at home. Go through a store and these little kids are pulling things down off the countertops and things like that. Then they grow up and get married, and they are out of control with their wife or husband. It starts in the home.

Paul said a Christian leader (and should laymen be any less accountable?) should have **his children in subjection with all gravity** (1 Tim. 3:4). *Gravity* means "with all honesty," and he was talking about having children under discipline. To do that, you have to start when they are very young — too young to talk back even.

If Paul said the deacon ought to *rule his house well,* what about the pastor? Or the usher? Or the soloist? Or the average church member? How should members of the church board or a trustee rule their houses? How should the church secretary rule her house? Are there different standards for Christians?

No! From the secretary to the pastor to the board member, all Christians should have their children under control. It is the same for everyone.

You can learn self-control after you are an adult, but it is hard. I did. I finally learned, but I went through hell. Every step of the way to self-control was torture for me. There were times in my life when I hated myself. I did not like me, because of the temper I had as a kid. No one really called me to account for it, and I would have a fit and slam my hand through a locker door at school. Or I would smash it through a window or door, or break up things.

Nobody really cared or took the time to do anything about it. I hated myself after I got to be an adult because of the way I acted. But I did not seem to have any control over my temper. I embarrassed myself, and I embarrassed my wife. Many times, I felt like five ounces of nothing.

Somebody needed to jerk the slack out of me. Somebody needed to beat my backside when I acted that way. I finally got control of myself, but man what a price I paid. I cannot count the wet pillows from crying tears, wondering, "What is wrong with me?"

I knew it was dumb and foolish, but it seemed as if something was controlling me. I would just blow up before I knew what I was doing. I would be sorry, but I had already said it. I had already done it, and it was already an embarrassment.

Thank God for my wife! The average woman would not stay with me. I mean, I would go completely berserk. It was frightening. It still frightens me when I look back on it. I was afraid of myself. I would go into a rage and hit anything in sight. It is a wonder my right arm still works. It is a wonder the board of education did not send me a bill after I graduated.

Even after I grew up, I acted like that. It was like a wheel in a rut — until I really got hold of the Word of God about sixteen years ago. I got filled with the Spirit and learned to walk by faith. That brought me under control. But I might have been much farther along if I had had some correction back there as a child.

I do not blame my parents. They had challenges in their own lives to deal with. They did the best they could, but all I am saying is that it was not enough to get me under control. I do not say that in any condemning way. That is just the way it was.

But I made up my mind my children were not going through that. And they have their first time to throw a fit. Children are like trees. When they are young, you can bend them the way they are supposed to grow. But when they get old and hardened in place, it is very difficult to change the pattern.

I see children in stores who want something, but when mama says no, they fall on the floor and have a fit. And she says,

"Come on, Johnnie, come on." She pulls at him, and he is screaming and crying. If that were my child, he would be getting up off the floor for real. That would be his first encounter and his last.

Despotism Is Not "Ruling Well"

But remember, as I said before, *rulership* is not "dictatorship." The word in the original meaning that Paul meant to convey was "to stand in front of and lead." It does not mean to stand over them with a lead pipe and smack them in the head every time they blink an eye. It also does not mean to get real loud with your children and rant and rave and slam the door and smack them in the mouth. If you do that, what you say will have no validity, because they will see *you* are out of control. What you say will go in one ear and out the other.

If you become a despot, your children will do a lot of things out of fear — but they will not learn and they will not be trained. They will wait for the day when they can get on their own. They are being forced, not controlled or disciplined.

Somewhere along the line, parents need to know they are responsible for controlling their children, but they need to know that control must be done with love and wisdom. I am not advocating child abuse. *I am totally and completely against abusing children.* God is not a child abuser, although He has been accused of being that.

I was driving to church one morning and passed a beautiful new motel, and the walls were all spray painted. That is terrible! That was done by youngsters who had not been raised properly. That was done by a child or children out of control. He probably started marking on the walls at home, and mama did not spank him.

She may even have said, "Isn't that cute? He is being so creative."

Now he is out of control. My children have never done that to anyone else's property. In fact, they have never done it to our property, because I would not allow it. The first time I would correct them verbally — after that came the spanking. My children are not perfect. None of us is perfect. But they are good kids. I have never had one ounce of trouble with them, and they never spray painted anybody's wall. They never have smoked or drank, used drugs, or run around before marriage.

The spankings they got did not warp their characters, and those spankings certainly did not constitute child abuse.

Speaking of spankings, let's move on to the last aspect of the duties of a parent. A parent has a responsibility to correct his children. In the context of this next section, I want to give you some words that mean different things to different people in different settings. Those words are punish, discipline, and chastisement.

Correction With a Rod

Some people believe, for instance, that *to chastise* means "to punish." Does it mean that? How does the Bible deal with it? The Word says that we have the responsibility to correct our children, to let them know this is wrong and that is right. Now, as I have said before, God's family plan began in Genesis, and He laid down guidelines for rearing children in Old Covenant days that are eternal, or universal, truths. Some of them are found in Proverbs. Let's look at one in particular.

> **He that spareth his rod hateth his son: but he that loveth him chasteneth him betimes.**
>
> **Proverbs 13:24**

That is from the *King James Version,* so we need to recognize that it is archaic English. So what does *betimes* mean? It simply means "early." That means to chasten your son before he gets bigger than you. When he gets to be six foot five and weighs close to three hundred pounds, it will be a little difficult for you to turn him over your knee and use a rod on him. That verse means to train children in the way they should go while they are young, and your children will not depart from the ways of the Lord.

244

You may think you are demonstrating love when you do not correct your child, when you let him get away with things.

You may say, "I don't believe in spanking. I don't believe in this, that, or the other."

Where did you learn that? From some dumb book in some school written by some guy who never had any children of his own. But he has a Ph.D. and a master's degree, so he must know. Honey, you cannot know anything about raising children until you live in the cage with some little monsters. Even taking someone else's child in your home for a while is not like raising your own children.

You are not going to learn things in anybody's library. There are no books written on some things. Some of it you have to make up as you go along. You have to be real creative as a parent. Children can come up with some stuff that makes you wonder where they got it. They can come up with some "off the wall" things. So you had better know how to deal with them from the Word.

In that verse in Proverbs, God was saying that if you really love your child, you will chasten him early while he is young.

Chasten Him While He Is Young

Another word I gave you to remember was *chastisement*. That translates "correction." It means to correct the child. Often we think of *chasten* as punishing, but that is not what it means. It does not always mean a spanking. And a spanking does not always mean punishment.

Child abuse is a horrible crime and should be stopped, but in this as in many other areas, society today overreacts. The end result is to let many genuine cases of child abuse slide by, while parents who are simply exercising authority over their children and correcting them are being penalized.

A child could fall down and get a bruise, and you have not even touched him. But under certain circumstances, the state could take that child, and you would have to go to court to try to explain and get him back.

Take my wife, for example. She is very "bruisable," if that is a word. If not, I just coined it. We have a long dressing table in our bathroom with a sink in each end. Then there are drawers on each side and cabinets underneath. She likes to leave her drawer open while she dresses, but I never do, because you can turn around and hit the dumb thing and get hurt — which she does. She will turn around and hit that drawer, and it makes a great big black and blue mark.

Someone who saw that might think I had beaten her, when I only touched her with tender, loving care. Well, it is the same way with a child. But they could take your child, and then you would have to go to court or go to the authorities and try to explain what really happened. It would waste a lot of time, cost a lot of money, and there is the tragic possibility that you might not be able to convince the court. Then you would stand unjustly condemned and lose your child.

Look at another proverb.

> **Withhold not correction from the child: for if thou beatest him with the rod, he shall not die.**
>
> **Proverbs 23:13**

Do you notice that God said the child is not going to die. If you correct the child in the right way, even with a switch, it will not hurt him permanently. He may think it is killing him at the time, but it will soon stop stinging — hopefully not until the lesson has sunk into his mind.

> **The rod and reproof give wisdom: but a child left to himself bringeth his mother to shame.**
>
> **Proverbs 29:15**

> **Foolishness is bound in the heart of a child; but the rod of correction shall drive it far from him.**
>
> **Proverbs 22:15**

The word *rod* in the *King James Version* is a very illuminating word. Do you know what it translates to in modern English? A stick, better known as a plain old-fashioned switch. Mama would go out back and get a branch off a tree, pull all the little leaves off that thing, and get in behind you. Man alive! You thought you were being killed, that is for sure. But you learned your lesson.

Chasten Him While There Is Hope

Chasten thy son while there is hope, and let not thy soul spare for his crying.

Proverbs 19:18

That verse does not make any sense at all *unless there is a possibility of running out of hope.* If hope is always possible, there was no need to say **while there is hope.** If there is always hope no matter how old the child gets, there is no need to qualify the statement. So that tells me that there is a time when it will become hopeless relative to chastening that child. You will run beyond the limits, and there will be no more opportunity for you to chasten that child. So do it while there is hope.

Thank God for His grace. Sometimes a child gets away from you and grows up, and it seems hopeless. But if he will finally come to a knowledge of Christ and gets into the Word, the Spirit of God through the Word will change him. You know he will change then.

But we are talking about the responsibility of the parent, not the responsibility of God.

The writer of this proverb said **let not thy soul spare for his crying,** and some of them seem to have earned a degree in crying! If somebody next door heard it, they would swear you were abusing that child. Children can cry and make you think they are going to die. Some of them will cry until they cannot get their breath.

The Holy Spirit inspired the writer to say, "Don't spare the rod for the crying."

God knew what He was doing when He wrote that. He can see beyond the exterior facade. He sees what is down inside. He knew kids would put on a show and make you think they were being killed when perhaps all you did was raise your voice. Someone outside listening would be ready to turn you into the authorities for child abuse, however.

What that verse means is, "Don't let tears intimidate you."

Tears from little Johnnie could cause you to back down. My kids, bless their darling little hearts, would sometimes start crying before I ever got to them, thinking that would fix things up and get them out of a spanking. They thought that would soften me up. They knew they had messed up by doing something after they had been told several times not to do it.

They would put that funny look on their faces and start to cry. But that did not fool me. I was oblivious to it. I have been a child and played all the games. That is something your children often forget: You also were once a child. Solomon said a long time ago that there is nothing new under the sun. (Eccl. 1:9.) They just put it in a different package today.

You have two choices: either the child cries or you cry. You are the one who has to make the decision. If the child makes the decision, it will be against you.

Chasten also means "to instruct," "to reform," "to reprove," and "to teach." That is a pretty versatile word. All of these different meanings are encompassed in that one word. In other words, *chasten* means "to do whatever it takes to get Johnnie doing what is right." That is what it means. It also can have the meaning "to correct with blows." Figuratively, it means to correct with words, and literally, it means to correct with blows.

Correct thy son, [and daughter, too] **and he** [or she] **shall give thee rest; yea, he shall give delight unto thy soul.**
Proverb 29:18

Do not correct him, and there will not be any rest. You will be spending too much time in court or down there in the principal's office. God is giving you some wisdom in this verse.

Now all of these proverbs have been God talking to you. They were written for all God's children in any generation who seek His wisdom. So you can do whatever you want. But I believe He knows more about raising children than anyone. The bottom line of all these verses is this:

If you do not do something to correct your children while they are young, they will grow up wild, and will bring you sorrow and pain, as well as ruin their own lives. But if you do correct them, your children will be a delight to you and will not depart from the ways of the Lord.

Chapter 20

THE DUTIES OF CHILDREN: TO HONOR AND TO OBEY

Do the children in a family have any duties? Are there any responsibilities that children have to their parents or to the home? And does the Bible specifically mention those?

Well, there is a little said in the Word about this area. There is not a great deal, but a little. But I think the little said is worth bringing forth. The Apostle Paul wrote more to the Church about family relationships than anyone, so look at what he did say about children's responsibilities.

> Children, obey your parents in the Lord: for this is right.
>
> Honour thy father and mother; (which is the first commandment with promise;)
>
> That it may be well with thee, and thou mayest live long on the earth.
>
> Ephesians 6:1-3

When Paul said, **Children, obey your parents in the Lord,** obviously that statement is a signal. It was spoken to alert Christians to a particular aspect of the family. But what does that verse actually mean?

Every Christian child does not have Christian parents. So was Paul saying children are to obey their parents regardless of whether they are Christian or not?

I believe Paul meant that no matter how young you are, from childhood to leaving home, you need to obey your parents *when what they tell you is consistent with God's Word.* You have no other alternative, if you are to remain in the perfect will of God.

But I believe Paul did not write the Ephesians a blanket admonition to obey parents, because some parents who were pagan were telling the children to do things contrary to the will of God. That would have been such things as worshipping idols, eating meat sacrificed to idols, and so forth. The child is not responsible to do something that is not godly. I remember something that is a good illustration of this problem operating in today's world.

When I was younger, a lady and her daughter were part of a group that I ran with. You never saw the woman with her husband on a consistent basis. We heard things about her, but we always saw her and her daughter together. Anytime you saw the mother, you saw the daughter. Later, we found out the mother was a prostitute, and she was training the daughter to be a prostitute. This was a known fact. Everyone knew about it later.

The Word and the Lord would be the only way out of that kind of life for that daughter. If she became born again, she would have to follow her conscience and God's will, and refuse to obey her mother. It would be a very hard situation for her, perhaps almost unbearable. But it would be a case where she would have to put God first, not her parents.

Other families teach their child to steal before the child ever has a chance to learn how to listen to his conscience. They send him into a store and make a game out of shoplifting. The child thinks it is fun. If that child became born again and got the revelation that what he was doing was sin, he would have to stop and not obey his parents. There probably would be hard repercussions, such as beatings, to endure. But his obligation is to God first. In such a case, hopefully, the child would have a pastor or a Christian friend to appeal to.

In a similar example to the first one, I went with a girl who I thought was really nice and sweet. Later, I came to find out her mother also was a prostitute who was training her daughter. I was just one of her test cases. And she was well trained, I tell you that! But I went with her as boyfriend and girlfriend. I really thought she cared about me, and that we had something special going. Then I found out that she and her mother were working a game.

Now if that girl had been Christian, she could not have afforded to obey her mother in that.

The principle involved is that children are only required to obey their parents **in the Lord.** We are talking about a Christian child with non-Christian parents or perhaps one Christian and one not.

There may be some things parents will tell you to do that are not Scripturally oriented in one way or another. There may be personal rules and regulations of the house. As long as these are not in clear violation of the Word of God, you are to obey.

The Bible does not tell you to brush your teeth. But if your parents insist that you brush your teeth, you have no right to disobey. If you do, you are in rebellion.

You cannot say, "The Bible does not tell me to brush my teeth, therefore I am not going to brush my teeth."

That would be disobedience. Doing that would really create some spiritual problems for you. So there are things not specifically itemized in the Word, things that are neither good nor bad, that are simply a matter of obedience.

Honor Is Not Obedience

Because one of the Ten Commandments is to honor your parents in order for your life to be long on the earth (Ex. 20:12), we might think Paul should have mentioned that first. But he did not, so we need to understand why. It is because *honor is not obedience*. Honoring is not obeying. You can honor something and not obey it. They are not the same thing.

In the context of the Ephesian church, children had to be taught obedience first. The concept of obedience to parents was not a universal principle in the pagan world. In the context of the Old Testament Israelites, however, obedience already had been taught. It was unusual not to obey your parents from the time of Abraham. What Israel was having a problem with was technical obedience on the outside and disrespect on the inside. So God through Moses dealt with the inner problem first. It is not enough to obey, there must also be respect (or honor).

Also, you can honor but not obey. They are not the same thing. You may be obedient out of fear. You may hate your parents every step of the way but have such fear of the consequences that you obey anyway.

If you have Christian parents who are taught in the Word, then your parents should not be putting anything off on you that is not godly in the first place. This is the same principle as wives submitting to husbands. A woman has no problem submitting, if her husband is treating her as Jesus does the Church.

Obedience in relationships is always related to how Jesus treats the Church. If you have godly parents who are dealing with you on a godly basis, and they are asking you to do godly things, you do not have a problem.

But what happens if you are in a situation where you are the Christian and your parents are not? Then you have a choice to make, because they may say things like:

"As long as you are under my roof eating my food, you will do what I tell you. Otherwise, you will have to leave."

That is something a Christian child may have to face. For example, those girls who were obeying their mothers to become prostitutes. I do not believe they had to do that. If they had become born again and refused to follow their mothers' instructions, I believe God would have honored their choices and found someone else to take care of them.

In situations like that, you can still *honor* your parents, because what you are honoring is the office. In another place, Paul said, "Give honor to whom honor is due." (Rom. 13:7.)

I give honor to leaders in the government because of their position. But that does not mean I agree with them, and I may not respect them very much as individuals. But I give honor and respect to them as representatives of this country. The person might be the worst official we have in terms of his own lifestyle, but as long as he is in that office, we are to treat him with the respect the office is due.

So a child can honor its mother and father, although the parents may not be doing all God would have them to do.

Now let's look at a Scripture in Colossians that, at first glance, would seem to be contradicting everything I have said.

> **Children, obey your parents in all things: for this is well pleasing unto the Lord.**
>
> **Colossians 3:20**

On the face of it, that would seem to be saying that even if your mama is telling you to be a prostitute, you have to obey her because she is your parent. In order to understand this verse, however, it has to be in context just as the first verse in Ephesians was seen in its context. So look at the things Paul is saying that lead up to the 20th verse.

> **Let the word of Christ dwell in you richly in all wisdom; teaching and admonishing one another in psalms and hymns and spiritual songs, singing with grace in your hearts to the Lord.**

> And whatsoever ye do in word or deed, do all in the name of the Lord Jesus, giving thanks to God and the father by him.
>
> Wives, submit yourselves unto your own husbands, as it is fit in the Lord,
>
> Husbands, love your wives, and be not bitter against them.
>
> Children, obey your parents in all things: for this is well pleasing unto the Lord.
>
> Colossians 3:16-20

Notice that verse 17 says **and whatsoever ye do in word or deed.** In other words, *whatever you do* do it in the name of Jesus.

From the other verses, we can see that the admonition is written, first of all, to Christian parents and children; and secondly, we can see that the context is about *what is pleasing to the Lord.*

Doing things unto the Lord or things that are pleasing to Him is the overriding thought here. Obviously, obeying parents in all things, such as prostitution and theft, is not *well pleasing* to the Lord.

There are even Christian parents who do ungodly things. Some of them are done out of ignorance of the Word and of how to live a life of holiness and sanctification. They end up yielding to the flesh, and become dominated, governed, and controlled by the flesh. Although they have accepted Christ as their personal Savior and Lord, they do not know how to live a godly kind of life.

Here is a very important concept to get hold of:

You are not a Christian because of the way you live. You ought to be living a godly life *because* you are a Christian. How you live ought to be the end result, or the working out, of the fact that you are a Christian. Your salvation is not based on how you live. It is based on accepting Jesus and being born again.

However, your enjoyment — your blessings — of the salvation you have received is going to be predicated in this world on how you live. Your effectiveness as a witness for Christ and your enjoyment of the covenant privileges and benefits bought and paid for by the blood of Christ will be affected by how you live.

Whether you are a Christian is based on whether you have been born again. John 3:16 does not read this way:

> **For God so loved the world, that he gave his only begotten son, that whosoever believeth in him** and liveth a godly life every single day, never committeth any sin, never lies, never cheats, never committeth adultery, never committeth fornication, liveth a perfect moral life, then that person **should not perish, but have everlasting life.**

The Word does not say that. We *ought* to live holy and godly lives. I believe in holiness. I believe in moral spotlessness. I believe in sanctification. I believe in it *but my salvation is not based on my living a sanctified life.* My salvation is based on faith in what Jesus did. My salvation is based on the blood of Jesus and on my having accepted Him as personal Lord and Savior. I am saved because of that acceptance, not because of how I live.

Colossians 3:17 said, **And whatsoever ye do in word or deed, do all in the name of the Lord Jesus.**

You cannot be a prostitute in the name of the Lord Jesus. You cannot peddle drugs in the name of the Lord Jesus. You cannot commit fornication in the name of the Lord Jesus, or adultery, or stealing, or gossiping and backbiting.

Even to children, Paul is saying, **do all in the name of the Lord Jesus.** That is the overriding principle and instruction. Under that covering, obey your parents in everything that does not conflict with the first principle, which is obedience to Jesus.

Parents do not have any business telling children something contrary to the Word. You can see that the main responsibility in the family reverts back to the parents, because they set the stage and the atmosphere for a child to grow up in. The child basically will be the product of what he, or she, is taught and the environment of the home.

Modifying Already Established Behavior

This problem may be more from the parents' viewpoint: How do you handle a child who has been allowed to run wild in the environment of an unsaved home when the parents get saved and begin to turn around?

The parents suddenly have changed their lives and the family's lifestyle. But the child's life has not yet been changed. Instead of being seen as a good thing and a blessing, most of the time, the parents' changes are seen as disruptive and traumatic. Although it is for the ultimate good, to the older child or teenager, it is like an earthquake is occurring. Everything he could count on is shaken. The ways he looked at his parents, the patterns he had formed for dealing with them, the standards in the home, suddenly all of those are turned upside down.

If the child does not also get saved, and sometimes even when he does, this can be a very disorienting time.

Now the parents want to live right, do everything by the Bible, and pray about things, but the child is still in the rebellious state. Perhaps he had been allowed to drink and smoke and so forth. Overnight, it seems, the parents want the child to stop. Well, it just does not work that way.

If the parents are not very careful, loving and kind, and do more praying than commanding, the child may run away or leave home for good. People run when they are in fear or danger, or are very unhappy, or feel threatened, or are in rebellion. They go looking for greener pastures.

My response to this situation is to make the children an offer they cannot refuse. Use the Word to the best of your knowledge. Pray for the child, bind the forces of Satan that cause rebellion, and set out to make home the kind of place where people want to stay. Make home a place where the child feels accepted, loved, secure, and fulfilled.

All I know is that the Word works. There is no question but that parents in this situation have a tiger by the tail, but if the child feels loved, that is half the battle. Suddenly feeling rejected and disapproved of can lead to rebellion and to thoughts of running away.

I ran away once. I thought home was bad until I was out there on the bricks. It did not take long for me to go home, and I stayed there until I was married!

Parents who have a rebellious child still living at home can, first of all, pray for him. They can lay hands on his pillow case and on his clothes and cast out rebellious spirits. Most people do not really want to be in rebellion. It does not feel good to be in rebellion. It is a situation of conflict all the time. But people are influenced and many times do not know why. There is satanic influence where thoughts are put in your mind, and you think they are yours.

Satan can con you into taking responsibility for the thought, then he will have you acting on it. You thought it was you, when it was really satanic influence to cause confusion and rebellion. And where there is confusion and rebellion, there is no peace. When there is no peace, God's Word is not prevailing. Satan is dominating the situation.

If you are the child who has been born again after having established rebellious behavior, then you need to ask the Lord to show you what things in your attitudes need to be changed — even if your parents have not yet changed. Again, you need to be aware that there is a price to be paid for being godly in an ungodly situation, whether it is home or school or work.

What About Abortion?

This is another area where choices have to be made sometimes between obeying parents and obeying God. Girls who are Christian sometimes get led astray and become pregnant, especially if the home environment has not been godly. Many parents today insist that the girls get abortions in order to save their own standing before friends, family, and even church members.

But let me tell you, teenager, abortion is worse than getting pregnant! Getting pregnant before marriage is wrong — fornication is wrong — but according to my standards — which I believe are Biblical — murder is worse than fornication. You should not do either of them, but if you have already committed one, do not compound the felony.

Abortion is premeditated, cold-blooded murder. It is not something done in the heat of passion. It is calculated. You have to make plans and preparations. You cannot have one without forethought. So for a Christian, it would be better to have the baby and let it be adopted, if you cannot take care of it. The hand of the Lord could be on a baby in that situation. Look at Moses. You can pray for the baby even if you do not know where it is.

The teenager should absolutely disobey the parents in this case. Again, there may be a price to be paid. Your parents may put you on the street. They may disown you. You may have to find a home that takes in girls in trouble, privately owned, church operated, or state run.

Whether or not you should try to keep the baby depends on circumstances, on how old you are, on whether you can get a job and adequate help with the baby.

What Do Adult Children Owe Their Parents?

One question that comes to me occasionally is:

"What do adult children owe their parents because of money, time, and efforts spent by the parents on the children? Or are children just responsible to take care of the parents in the twilight years?"

Personally, I believe that parents have the responsibility to provide for their children in every way possible, as we discussed in earlier chapters. The parents should not be raising children in order for the children to take care of them. From a legal standpoint or even a conscience standpoint, I do not believe adult children *owe* parents anything but honor, love, and respect.

However, if the children are brought up in the right way, they will help their parents if they need it. Most children nurtured in the love and admonition of the Lord would want to do everything possible if their parents got into a bind, or sickness, or lost a job.

I do think children have a responsibility to see that parents are taken care of when they get too sick or too old to do it themselves. If the child does not have the space or the money to do it personally, he or she can still investigate all the private and public possibilities and see that the parent or parents are in the best place possible.

I hope this book has been a help and a blessing to you. I have tried to deal with delicate and touchy situations under the guidance of the Holy Spirit as best I could. The Bible is a down to earth book with principles to cover every possible situation of life, if we will look for those principles, accept them, and live by them.

In the last chapters, I want to share some letters of praise or letters with questions (along with the answers I gave), that came in to Crenshaw Christian Center after I taught a series on "Marriage and the Family" which aired on my television program, *Ever Increasing Faith.*

These letters directly address specific situations with which you may be able to identify. When you read the answers to the questions, those answers may help you apply the principles in this book to your life.

Part III

QUESTIONS AND ANSWERS

Chapter 21

QUESTIONS AND ANSWERS ABOUT MARRIAGE

Prenuptial Agreements: Saving for a Rainy Day

"Greetings in the name of our Lord Jesus Christ:

"Pastor Price, my name is _____, and we have been studying with you the duties of the husband and wife. Last Sunday, you made a statement about community property, such as what belongs to the husband is also the wife's, and what belongs to her belongs to the husband.

"That opened up a can of worms in my household. I have been telling my husband that the law has changed to a certain degree now, that before marriage a couple can sign written contracts called prenuptial agreements. Please check this out for yourself. They are legal and binding in some cases, but can be overruled if not drawn up by a lawyer.

"This evening, my husband said, 'Did you hear what Fred said in church Sunday about community property?'·

"I have some friends who did this, and it is in my family legal advisor book. But when I tried again to explain my side to my husband, he took the remote control and turned the TV set up so high I had to scream — which was really dumb on my part because I know what the law says. But to him, your word on the subject was icing on the cake. And I wanted to hit him in the face with the whole cake — in love, mind you.

"After you have checked this information out for yourself, would you please read this letter so my husband can be set free from thoughts that this cannot be done? I thank God for using you to teach and correct us. Your wife is truly blessed to have a husband like you. Please don't get me wrong. I too have been blessed with an awfully good man, but sometimes I have to prove things to him.

"Love always,

"Your Sister in Christ"

Now I am not really sure what the gist of the letter is, but I assume one or the other of them had been talking about things they had before they were married. I thought this letter should be included, because I have seen things like this in people's relationships that really caused trouble.

I understand that people do have legal documents such as this drawn up nowadays, but as far as I personally am concerned, I think it is worldly, unspiritual, and dumb. I think such an agreement really sets the stage for the demise of the relationship.

Whatever you had when you came into the relationship and became one also became the property of your husband or wife. It all belongs to "one." If you want to keep your country estate, your blue Mercedes Benz, and all that furniture you had before you married, what are you getting married for? Is it just so that you do not have to get a prostitute? She is good enough to marry and carry your name, but she is not good enough to have half ownership in your estate or car?

Why do you want to have "his" stuff and "her" stuff? I had some things before I married Betty. If I wanted to keep them all to myself, I did not need to be married to her — unless it was for sex. Everything you have belongs to your mate. Why would you want a legal document to say, "This is mine, and that is yours?"

If you become one flesh, I think that principle covers everything. Why would you be one in the flesh, but separate in your personal items? Christians who do this are acting exactly like the world. That is what the world does: Come up with such contracts because they do not expect the marriage to work. So they want to have an out.

That is like talking about saving up for a rainy day. Keep on saving, and you are going to have some rain! You expect rain, or you would not be saving up for that day. I do not expect any rain. I am not saving up. I spend it all now.

That does not mean I do not invest so that I have more to spend and give. And it certainly does not mean I spend everything as fast as I get it. I take time to pray, and look at things wisely. But what I am saying is that I do not expect to have a "rainy day." We do not save special sheets in case someone gets sick and visitors come over. We do not plan on anyone getting sick, so we sleep on all the sheets we have right now.

Some younger people may not know about saving up "good" bedding and linens for such times, but you older folks will remember that. But we are going to use what linens we have now. Also, everything I have belongs to my wife. She has me and every thing that goes with me. I believe I have her and everything that goes with her.

We did not need any contract to divide our things. Our contract was "I do." My word is my bond. I would die before I would knowingly break my word. That is how much my word means to me. That is why I never make promises except on very, very rare occasions, because I know if I make it, I will have to keep it.

Divorce and Remarriage

"Dear Pastor Price,

"Praise God for your obedience to His word and direction in the ministry, especially in the teaching on 'The Christian Family' series. Both my husband and I have been members at Crenshaw Christian Center (CCC) for more than three years. During that time, we have grown in many areas of our lives. I wanted to share with you some of those areas.

"Seven years ago, we began watching *Ever Increasing Faith* on television. We are both ex-Catholics. We did not care for organized religion anymore, because we were hungry for something besides man's doctrines and feelings. We did not know what it was, but it was not being given to us. Both of us had been divorced for a number of years. In both instances, it was because of adultery by our mates.

"Our respective parish priests had told us, however, that we could never marry as long as our former spouses were alive. However, a Cardinal had gone to Greece to perform the marriage of Jackie Kennedy to Aristotle Onassis, a divorced man. We wondered why. I wrote you at that time explaining our feelings and our hope to become man and wife.

"You wrote us back such a beautiful letter using the Word of God to uplift us — which I still have — that it lifted a heavy burden from our lives. We were both in our forties when we met, and this was not a marriage of mad passion, although we do enjoy a very healthy sex life. But we loved and respected one another and wanted God's blessings on our marriage.

"You wrote exactly what you have been teaching, and we followed your advice and got married. Then we wanted to attend your church and see if you practiced what you preached. As often happens, people we talked to [told us a lot of rumors, and so forth]. They said:

"1. You cannot get into that church on Sunday unless you get there at 4:30 a.m.

"2. Those people are occult, always talking in tongues. They are 'headed straight for hell.'

"3. You have to take your pay check stubs to prove you are tithing.

"We lived fifty-five miles away, so we just kept watching you on television and hearing the Word of God. Faith comes. When you announced that a third service was being added, we decided that we were going to CCC at last! Until that day, we had watched and listened but had not truly accepted Jesus as our personal Lord and Savior.

"I really did not think my husband would, because he had so many negative things in his life: unforgiveness, anger, hurt, and so forth. But when you gave the invitation, I stood, and when you asked us to open our eyes and look at you for instructions, there stood my husband beside me!

"To make a long story short, we attended the New Members' Class, received water baptism, the baptism of the Holy Spirit, and the right hand of fellowship all within four months time. We attended every Sunday morning service and still traveled the same distance, but after attending "Papa" (Kenneth E.) Hagin's campmeeting in 1983, we began to believe that God would enable us to move closer in and attend other services and classes as well.

"Old Satan came at us in every possible way. After all, he had lost two good disciples, because our lives prior to meeting each other and coming to CCC were a mess — past wrongdoings and living beyond our means. We lost our home, our cars, a lot of money, went bankrupt, and almost lost one another because outside worldly influence and distrust had crept in. We did not know how to trust the Lord for our needs. We did not even know the promises that were ours according to His Word, but we overcame.

"When you began this current series, you touched on a number of things that had plagued our lives. I cannot tell you how my already changed and wonderful husband became a new and even better husband. I would like to believe I have become a new and better wife. We are even more loving to one another than we have ever been. My husband now:

"1. Cooks dinner when he gets home before I do.

"2. Washes dishes when I am doing the laundry.

"3. Has told me that when we move into our new home next month I can have a cleaning person once a week to help.

"4. Has been more free in his giving to the Gospel.

"5. Brings me flowers more often.

"6. Takes me out to dinner often, which we rarely did before you taught this series.

"7. Does not get uptight when I buy something new to wear. He says he wants me to look like his queen.

"We do not have any debts or use credit cards. What we have to spend is more than enough. He has even agreed to buy me a fur coat, which I had asked for a number of times before.

"8. He has a new and deeper love for our children, mine and his, which he never had expressed before. Our children are adults and have children of their own.

"I could go on and on, but it would take three or four teaching sessions just to give my praise report!

"I have said all of this to say that if anyone believes in and does God's Word, he or she cannot be defeated. Take it from a whipped, defeated, and depressed baby Christian, the Word works. And prayer can change everything when you have faith in God's Word and are a doer not just a hearer.

"Thank you for your obedience to your calling and to your attention to the Holy Spirit speaking through you. Keep on doing what you are doing because it is right.

"Your sister in Christ"

Isn't that a beautiful letter? Praise God! That is what it is all about, helping people.

Accusations and Possessiveness

"Dear Pastor Price,

"Question: What do you do about a Christian husband who acts in an unforgiving manner by accusing his Christian wife wrongfully and yet expects the Lord to bless him anyway?

"My husband and I did not get married 'shotgun style,' but we talked about marriage and planned it. We were single and friends for some years before even knowing that one day we would be married to each other, and we shared our past experiences with each other in conversations. He knew where I came from, and I knew where he came from.

"I work two jobs, one 9 to 5 and the other part time, not because I want to, but because it is necessary. My husband works a job, and we have agreed about me working the extra job and when I would quit. We are not at the point yet where the house is paid for and so forth. When I am not working, Monday through Friday, I am taking care of our home, i.e. washing clothes, cleaning house, shopping for food, and other household chores.

"It is a rare occasion when I talk on the telephone. I do not socialize with other people because I am always involved with my family, husband, and children. When I do socialize, it is with my husband visiting relatives or seeing a decent movie or something like that.

"But whenever my husband and I get into a debate, misunderstanding, or disagreement, he starts to accuse me of [seeing] other men, which has absolutely nothing to do with our marriage or the subject we are on.

"He will say, 'Do you want me to drop you off over at his house?'

"As a Christian woman, wife, and mother, I have no idea who 'he' is. Or if I am too sleepy or too tired to physically get involved with him at 2 or 3 a.m., he will do the same thing. He goes so far as to look for my underwear in the hamper and [inspect them for tell-tale signs of sexual intercourse].

"Then later on, he will act as if nothing happened and want to get physically involved with me after all that and wonder why I push him away. Prior to getting married, he was not like this. He was not accusative. But since we have been married, he does this on and off.

"We have talked about this, and he promises to stop wrongfully accusing me, admits that he is wrong for doing it, and asks for forgiveness. I have asked him why he does this. Why go over the same thing which creates strife? He never can tell me why, just says he is sorry — and does it again.

"I know the Lord tells us that all have sinned and come short of the glory of God. The Lord tells us that He remembers our sins no more. As far as the east is from the west, so far hath He removed our transgressions from us. I know who I am in Christ Jesus. But I don't want to hear a brother in the Lord example himself after the accuser of the brethren and not after Jesus.

"I know I am not perfect, and he is not, and we are all growing up spiritually. But I do not believe it is necessary or right, regardless of what we dispute, disagree, or whatever, for a Spirit-filled husband to ventilate his anger in this way.

"... [His] accusing me like this grieves my spirit and creates emotional and sexual uncomfortableness within me concerning my husband. I feel the things I confided in him he uses against me. I desire to and will continually serve the Lord wholeheartedly and with my husband.

"... I stand in agreement with my husband in prayer for many things, but when he does this sporadically, I feel betrayed, not respected, and spiritually unfulfilled. I know the prayers in which we have set ourselves in agreement are hindered because of his wrongful accusations. This may happen to Christian husbands as well, but I am a Christian wife confronted with this situation.

"As others who appreciate you in your stand in and for Christ Jesus, I also appreciate you."

Now I know we do not have any other husbands who treat their wives like this, do we? And I know we do not have any Christian wives who do their husbands like this, right? Accusing one another? But pastors hear this all the time.

As an only child, I learned something a long time ago — you can get very selfish about things. Every little thing that you want, it just has to be yours. You can transfer that attitude over to your husband or wife. You can be so possessive of them that you end up opening yourself up for distrust. Whenever they do something that annoys, aggravates, or hurts you, the devil will always feed thoughts to your mind that she is up to something, or he is up to something.

But I had to learn this, and let me give some fatherly advice to husbands or wives who are acting like the husband of the lady who wrote that letter:

Remember that he married you. If he had wanted Mary Jane, he could have had Mary Jane. But he married you. Or if you are the male, she married you. Trust your wife or husband.

If your mate is not trustworthy, and is living a clandestine lifestyle and committing adultery with someone else, you need to find that out as soon as possible so at least you have scriptural grounds for divorce.

The way you are going to find that out is not by hiring a detective. Let the Holy Spirit reveal it. If you are a child of God, walking by the Word, nobody can mistreat you for any length of time. God will vindicate you, if you will let Him handle it. However, if you are going to put your "little pinkies" in it, then you are going to mess it up, and God is not going to touch it.' While you are trying your own case in court, God is not going to send your chief negotiator, Jesus Christ, to intercede for you and be your kinsman redeemer. So you have to take your hands off the situation.

To that husband I would say: if your wife is running around, she is going to run around anyway. Your arguing with her, accusing her, and fussing about it is not going to change her running around. That is already in her. And you cannot be with her all the time. You will run yourself in the ground and kill your fool self, and the devil will have both of you.

He already has the person who is committing the adultery messed up. Now he is getting you messed up running around worrying about it, sick all the time over it, and messing around with your own life. You cannot be with your wife all the time. You have to either trust her or get out of the relationship. Otherwise you are going to be miserable.

If your mate is running around on you, you do not have to worry about it, God will vindicate you. If you are in line with the Word, your mate cannot keep this up in secret for very long.

However, do not let some crazy thing the devil puts in your mind cause you to accuse your wife or husband. You may end up destroying the best thing you ever had going for you in all your days. You may end up running off a good husband or wife. Are you following me?

If you are caught in a situation where unfounded jealousy rises up, there is no point arguing. Arguing is not going to change it. Trust the Lord to deal with this situation. Pray it through.

Learning to Forgive

"Dear Pastor Price,

"My husband and I were married in November of 1984 and separated in March, 1985, after we both accepted Christ as our personal Savior. We tried on several occasions getting back together, but we did not recognize Satan's tricks to keep us apart. We prayed and stood on God's Word. I asked the Lord to send a message through the church that would teach us how to yield to one another and how to love unselfishly.

"Then one Sunday, you began to teach on 'The Christian Family.' I knew then my marriage was healed. It was a confirmation of what was in my heart. I knew some of the things I should do because I read the Word, but the real revelation came when you talked about marriage and divorce. That confirmed that we had no grounds for divorce.

"I knew my husband would not listen to me, but he would listen to what the Holy Spirit was saying through you. Pastor Price, I used to think my husband was all wrong, that was why our marriage was not working. But I found out my faults and made a change in my life so that God could do the things He wanted to do for us.

"We learned how to forgive. We also learned how to be sensitive to one another and take our minds off self. Praise the Lord, Pastor Price, my husband and I are living in the same house again, and it is a real honeymoon. Our marriage has been renewed in every way.

"Thank you for being obedient to our Father for teaching His children the uncompromised Word. We love you and your family for showing us how we should live.

"P.S. I was not about to let this man go. He cooks, cleans, and irons — and is a great provider!"

Husbands and wives: Have you learned how to forgive? There are people who have been married for twenty years who are still holding grudges. That is like termites eating away at the foundation of your relationship. A wife is holding something dumb her husband did against him, even after he admitted it was dumb, foolish, and wrong. That was fifteen years ago, and she is still using sex as a weapon against him, determined that he will never enjoy himself with her because he ran around on her fifteen years ago.

No, it was not right, but what else can the man do? He blew it. He said, "I'm sorry, forgive me," but she is still holding it.

Husbands and wives: Are you sensitive to one another, or do you always have to have everything your own way? So many men are insensitive. Things just have to be your way, because you are the man, and the man is always right. No. God does not honor you because you are a man, He honors you because you are right. If you are a man *and* right, then God will honor you as the head of the house. But if you are a man and wrong, He will not.

Husbands and wives: Who is self? Have you ever run into Old Mr. Self? What I am saying is that when a marriage has problems, someone is selfish.

Anytime a marriage is reconciled, we ought to shout it from the house tops.

Standing for the Salvation of a Spouse

"Dear Dr. Price,

"Will you please touch on the area of mates who are standing for their mates? Please give some words, scriptures or encouragement, and some advice and teaching in this area. I have been standing for more than two years, and I will be standing until my marriage is healed in Jesus' name.

"Sincerely,

"Your daughter in Christ"

When I received this letter, I could have given some scriptures, but I remembered a woman who had successfully done this very thing. She had stood for her husband in the face of accusations and criticisms, even from some Christians. And I personally saw her husband come out of darkness into light. It is absolutely marvelous to see God's Word work in that kind of situation.

So I asked this lady to give me her game plan. I thought it would add a greater dimension of credibility to give the answer from someone who had actually lived it. What this woman did will work if you are willing to stand and pay the price, if you are willing to change. A lot of you want change, but you are not willing to change to get the change. That is not double talk: Change always requires change.

If you want a situation to change, you are going to have to change something in yourself, someway. Here are some "faith" scriptures this person gave me that she used to claim her husband's salvation:

First John 5:14,15; Mark 11:24; and Psalm 37:4,5.

The next set of verses are some that she used as obedience scriptures for herself. Sometimes people want their mates to change when they themselves are not doing what they are supposed to be doing. You cannot expect God to intervene in certain situations when you are not doing what you know is right to do. You can only claim God's best when you are doing His best. Otherwise, the other things will not work. She used these scriptures for personal obedience:

Exodus 14:14; 1 Peter 3:1; 1 Thessalonians 4:11; Proverbs 15:1; Psalm 37:4; and Philippians 4:6,7,11,13, and 19.

Then these are scriptures she confessed over her husband:

First Timothy 2:2; Colossians 1:9-15; Ephesians 5:25.

She pled the promises of God, bound Satan's power, and confessed these things over her husband.

Because her husband had told her, "I will never go to church," she confessed Psalm 35:18 and 111:1 over him. Apparently, he did a lot of arguing and cursing, so she confessed Psalm 19:14 over him.

She made Colossians 2:2, Psalm 138:8 and 19:14, and Philippians 2:2,3 and 13 blanket confessions over both of them.

Listen to what she said, "My husband told me that the single most important thing that turned his life around was the consistency of my lifestyle."

Isn't that amazing? He did not say the most important thing was that everytime he looked up she was reading the Bible; he did not say the single most important thing was hearing her speak with other tongues, yet you ought to read the Bible and pray in other tongues. But the consistency of her total lifestyle was what impressed him that there was something real to being a Christian.

Some of you want your mates to change, but you are inconsistent. You are inconsistent with your husband or wife and you are inconsistent with the church. You see, even while that mate is cursing, arguing, fussing, and fighting, he or she is watching you. Many people do not believe that anyone who says he is a Christian is for real. They do not believe it, and they have to watch for a protracted period of time to really test whether what you say is what you live.

They see you toting your Bible one day and talking about Jesus, then the next day they hear you telling or laughing at a dirty joke. You can put up a front only for so long. After that, you let your guard down and do not even realize you are doing it.

Who Chooses the Church to Attend?

"Dear Pastor Price,

"I really appreciate how you teach and say things straight out. We have not set the date yet, and I am still single, but my boyfriend and I got into a discussion. He said there would be a time when I won't always have the final choice. He said when we get married, we will become one, and I will have to go to his church because he is the man.

"I believe the man is the head of the household, but what about me? Don't I have any say-so as to where I want to go to church? I visited his church, and it is okay, but I love Crenshaw Christian Center and have been going here ten years. I have really grown mentally and spiritually, and the fellowship is so marvelous.

"He has visited my church and says it is nice, but he likes his better. We are both Christians, Spirit-filled, tithe, and read and mark the Bible together. He is the best thing that ever happened to me. He treats me with great respect. He caters to my needs and is always there when I need him. He is a very beautiful person inside and out.

"But we do not want this to be a big issue in our relationship. So I was wondering, can't he go to his church and I go to mine? We are both hearing the Word. But he said a wife should be by her husband's side. I agree, but when does the lady have the say and when does the man have the final say? I'm confused.

"Also, is there any scripture in the Bible about this subject? Or should I just pray and believe he will join CCC? But he is a Christian, so maybe he is praying that I will join his church. Maybe this question will also help other couples that might be going through this.

"Yours sincerely"

I think this question might be a challenge that many potential husbands and wives have to face.

The only scripture that I could use to deal with this would be in 2 Corinthians 6:14 where Paul wrote about being unequally yoked together. Of course, basically, that applies to a believer marrying a non-believer. But I also believe that it applies to a situation where, for example, one believes in tithing and one does not. They are not in agreement. One is going north, and one is going south.

If you believe in speaking in tongues, and your spouse does not, you are unequally yoked. Personally, I think you are going to have some challenges. How do you reconcile this?

I do know couples where the husband and wife attend different churches. I do not know how they do it, but they do, and from all outward appearances, they seem to be happy about it. I do not find any scripture that says you cannot do that. I would not want to, but I know people who do. I like to have my wife at my side, but I certainly would not force her to go. I would not want to intimidate her to go with me. I would want us to be in agreement about it.

As I have said before, I think before you marry, you should discuss every aspect of your lives together that is of any importance and come to an agreement on it. The young lady who wrote me that letter and her fiance are going to be in trouble unless they can work this thing out ahead of time. Somebody is going to be unhappy.

A very important truth was revealed in this letter: It is where she said, "We haven't set the date yet, but my boyfriend and I got into a discussion. *He said there would be a time when I won't always have the final choice."*

He is telling her something more important than where they go to church, if she just has ears to hear. He is telling her that he will be making most of the decisions. She might end up making *some* choices, but she will not have the final choice. When they get married, she will have to go to his church *because he is the man*. There was no room for discussion there.

The man did not even say, "You can go to your church, and I'll go to mine."

He said, "You're going to my church."

It sounds to me as if she does not have any choice. He is the man, and he is the head. Now that is fine, if that is what she wants. But I think she ought to be listening real carefully to what the dude is saying, because he is telling her that he is going to run the show. He is nice enough to tell her up front, if she is willing to "hear" what he is really saying.

I do not believe being the head of the house means that you tell your wife what color shoes to wear, how to fix her hair, and all of that. I do not believe in that. But what else is he going to have the final say in besides church?

"I am the man so we will live where I want to live. We are going to drive the kind of car I want to drive. We are going to have 18th century furniture in here even if you don't like it because I am the head of the house."

I do believe her boyfriend is sounding an alarm to her, and she had better listen.

Husbands Younger Than Their Wives

A number of queries came in on this subject, so I will just give my general answer and not print the different letters.

The Bible does not say anything about how old a person ought to be that you marry. And it does not matter whether the husband is older or whether the wife is older. It depends on the people involved and on circumstances.

Some young girls like men quite a bit older because they have a thing for a "father figure." That is fine if the two of them are happy. How old is "older" anyway? I do not know. The Bible does not address this, so if a guy wants to marry an older woman, that is his perogative. If he loves her, and she loves him, age has nothing to do with it.

God does not care how old your spouse is. If you love the person, love has no age. I mean, do you love God? How old is God? Jesus is at least 2,000 years old, dating from His earthly appearance. We still love Him, don't we? And we are still married to Him spiritually.

There is no right or wrong age. It is a matter of what you want to do. When a young girl marries a man obviously quite a bit older than she is, the first thing most people think is that she is after his money. But it really is none of our business. He may just be a good old man. So it does not matter. God is not concerned about it, so you should not be. It is not a matter of right or wrong.

Do not let it be a problem for you. If you are contemplating marrying someone, make sure you love him and he loves you. Be sure he is saved and filled with the Holy Spirit. Make sure you both want to go to the same church and read the same Bible. Be in agreement about the number of children you want and how you want to tithe. That way, you have a good thing started, and you have a good thing to build on.

The Greatest Husband in the World

"Dear Pastor Price,

"I have some good news that I thought you would be pleased to hear. I met a man from your church several years ago. His light was shining so brightly, and his lifestyle was so upright that he sparked an interest in me. I wanted what he had. He shared his knowledge of Jesus with me. I confessed Jesus as my Lord and Savior shortly after our meeting and several talks. He invited me to attend church with him, and I finally accepted.

"I must admit I was amazed at all the people in attendance, standing in line to go to church! That was new to me. After a few visits, however, I was convinced that Crenshaw Christian Center was to be my church home.

"To make a long story short, I am now married to this man. We have two daughters from previous relationships. I am saying all this to say that I have the greatest husband in the world. I have Jesus, this ministry, and you to thank, Fred.

"Let me tell you why he is the greatest husband. He helps me with everything. He washes clothes, vacuums, washes dishes, cooks, irons, mops the kitchen floor, goes grocery shopping, shops for clothes because he knows what looks best on me and our girls, makes the bed, helps train and supervise the girls, combs hair, helps with homework, doesn't sit around watching sports on the weekend, comes straight home after work. I never have to wonder where he is or what he is thinking. He sends me cards and brings me roses just because.

"You name it, and he does it. On top of all that, he is an excellent money manager. We have excellent communication. We can talk about anything and everything, and we do. He is very romantic, loving, extremely patient, kind, thoughtful, considerate, tall, dark, and handsome. He has a wonderful sense of humor. But most of all, he is my best friend.

"He is wonderful! He is everything God's Word says a husband and father should be. I consider myself extremely blessed to

QUESTIONS AND ANSWERS ABOUT MARRIAGE

be his wife. His number one goal is to be like Christ. Having a man like this makes it very easy for me to submit. His second goal is to make enough money so that I won't have to work.

"I currently work forty hours a week, plus go to school as a full-time student. He is looking forward to the day that I don't have to work, so that I can take over all the domestic duties. I can't say that I blame him. After all, he puts in fifty hours a week at work plus his share of the domestic duties.

"I can't say enough wonderful things about him. I am truly blessed. I would like all the ladies to know that all things are possible through Christ Jesus. Let your light shine and pray. You too can have a husband like mine, if you so desire.

"P.S. We have submitted our prayer request and are believing for a set of twins, a boy and a girl. We would like you to agree in prayer with us.

"Thank you"

Isn't that a wonderful letter? I wish all of them could be this kind of praise report. The next letter also is a praise report, almost better than this one.

God Can Do Miracles and Change Men

"Dear Pastor Price,

"My husband and I were married for twenty-seven years. I have to thank God, we did raise four lovely children who never really gave us any problems. But my husband was a very domineering man. He would never help with anything around the house. He was not gentle or patient. He was never thoughtful or considerate of my feelings.

"He felt a woman's place was in the kitchen, and I was supposed to keep my place as a woman and work too. My husband was one of those men who was in the world, and I mean literally in the world. There was very little he did not do.

"About four years ago, I looked up, and my children were all grown up. I felt I no longer had to put up with him and the things he did any longer. I won't mention some of the things he did. I do not want to embarrass him.

"I became a very bitter and resentful woman. I hated all men and detested marriage. I felt I had wasted a lot of years. All of my youth was gone, so I thought. So I left him. I stayed away for three months. I was still a very unhappy woman with even more pain and resentment.

"One day, a little over three years ago, our two daughters introduced us to your ministry separately. In other words, both daughters did, but on separate occasions apparently unknown to the other.

"My husband had very little teaching about God. Pastor Price, you should see and know him now! These past three and a half years have been a true blessing. Through your teaching, the Bible classes, and our faith and prayers, my whole life has changed.

"My husband is what I call a miracle. He is now a man of God. He is patient and gentle, thoughtful and considerate of my feelings. He even brings me flowers. I no longer come home from work to find him sitting down watching television or taking a nap, telling me to get his dinner. The dishes are clean, our bed is made, clothes are in the washer, and he tells me to sit down or take a nap for an hour or so.

"The only thing he doesn't help me do is cook. I prefer that he doesn't help me do that since he does not know how to cook. He is truly my helpmate. I am no longer a bitter or resentful woman. I am younger and happier, and I love and respect my husband more than I did when we were first married.

"I now have a marriage that you could say was made in Heaven, because without the Father, none of this would have come about. My staying with my husband turned out to be a true blessing after all these years.

"God can do miracles and change men. I know, Pastor Price, because my husband and I are one of those miracles. I hope in some way this letter has helped, or will help, someone who is having the same problems.

"I thank you, Pastor Price, for your honesty and truth. May God always bless you and your family. My utmost respect and blessings."

Isn't that beautiful? That is what ministry should be about: changed lives. Ministry should be the Word working mightily in the lives of people and making a difference.

"Marriage Has Always Scared Me"

"Dear Pastor Price,

"Your series on 'The Christian Family' has not only helped those who are married but has helped some of us who are still single — particularly me.

"My father walked out on my mother, brother, and me when I was a child. I don't ever remember him being a part of our family structure. My mother was left to tend for the three of us. Over the years while I was growing up, I saw my mother married three more times. One marriage was so bad and so filled with violence that it made a nervous wreck of me as a child, and the effects have carried over into my adult life.

"Over the years, I also have listened to my mother tell me what a bad thing it is to get married. As a matter of fact, to this day, if I even mention I am interested in getting married, she literally degrades me and marriage. She will ask didn't I learn anything from her experiences?

"Recently, I made a passing comment that I was interested in marriage just to see if her ranting and raving would still affect me. I honestly believe that if I decided to marry and invited her to attend the ceremony that she wouldn't come! Needless to say, I have had a very negative idea about marriage.

"Before listening to your series I *had not considered* the idea of getting married. Even after hearing your series, it still seems out of my reach. I still feel marriage and me is a lost cause, but I'm hoping to grow up in the Lord. At some point over the years, I promised myself I would never put up with what happened to my mother and that I would never be as unhappy as an adult as I was as a child.

"So far I have kept that promise to myself at the expense of not being able to form a solid and lasting relationship with anyone. What I wanted to tell you is how your series has helped me. I really was glad to hear that marriage was ordained of God. That fact might be trivial to someone else, but it was comforting for me to know that, if God says it is okay, then it is possible for me to get married and be happy.

"Now that you have explained the duties of a husband, I know what to look for in a Christian man. In my prayers, I thank God for a ministry like yours. You have helped me so much personally and in knowing God, and in knowing what He expects from me as His child and what I can expect from Him in return. You have helped me to realize that in God my life is okay, and I am okay. I have always found comfort in being in God's care, and I thank Jesus for making it all possible by His shed blood for me.

"Sincerely yours in Christ Jesus"

Again, I have to say it would be wonderful if all of the letters we receive could be like this. The majority, however, are from people who have continuing problems. This last letter on the topic of marriage concerns faith for finances.

Misunderstanding Faith

"Pastor Price, what if you don't have the provisions you need around the house, and all your husband says is 'Praise the Lord, we'll get it,' but you never see any action on his part toward doing something so we can succeed, and I can clean and keep house the way I should? Help!

"Desperate"

Now that is a real problem. I have seen husbands like that. Christians, period, just like that! But since this has to do with a husband, then I will just unload on husbands.

I have known instances where the guy is saying, "Well, I'm believing God. My God shall supply all my need," and then he lies out on the grass in the backyard and just waits for manna to fall from Heaven. But it does not work like that. *The duty of the husband is to provide for the family.*

Yes, God is your source of supply, but that supply is probably going to come through the hand of some human being, either an employer or through God having someone walk up and give it to you. That will not happen that often, however. The first way of meeting your needs is more common. Usually, God is going to work through a job or profession or something like that.

So you may be praying and believing God for your needs to be met, but if you are sitting on your backside, and you never go out and put in an application anywhere, God cannot bless you with all your needs being met. If you are not looking for a job, God is not going to rain money out of the sky. If He did things like that, I would already have found out about it, believe me!

I would have gotten all the blessing. There would be none left, for I would have gone into the basket-making business and put baskets everywhere to catch the blessings. But that does not work.

You cannot just sit around talking about, "Well, the Lord is going to bless us. The Lord is going to supply all our needs."

He is not going to, if you do not do something. He will not have a channel through which to bless you. He has no money in Heaven. When you are dealing with material things, God works through the earthly realm to meet your needs.

Suppose a man from my church comes up and says, "Fred, I have to go out of town on a business deal, and my backyard is overgrown. It is just like a jungle out there. There are all kinds of weeds and everything, and I will give you $50 if you go out there and clean all that stuff up for me while I'm gone."

Then suppose I say to him, "Wait a minute. I am God's great man of faith and power. God meets my needs. I believe all my needs are met."

What is going to happen? I am going to starve. God was *meeting* my need through this guy, and I refused it.

So if you are sitting around doing nothing and not treating your wife or family as a husband should, you need to make a change and begin doing something in order for God to be able to help you. If nothing else, you should have nine hundred applications in wherever it is you think you want to work and believe God to give you favor with the people at that place. Then they will give you that job, so God can use that as a channel to meet your needs.

Chapter 22

QUESTIONS AND ANSWERS ABOUT THE FAMILY

One question that keeps coming up is: At what age should parents put their children out of the house?

The Bible does not give an age as to when you should put your children out of the house. That would have to depend upon you, the child, and circumstances. I think it is a sad thing anyway when you have to put a child out of the house. I believe a child should go when he or she is ready to go, either to move to another state or city, or to go to college, or perhaps to get married.

Other than that, my children can stay at home as long as they want to. They have a home, and I am not in a hurry to put them out. They are going to be out in the world soon enough. So there is no hurry. I do not think there *is* a specific age at which they should leave.

Since the Bible does not address this, I just have to give my best judgment on it.

Following are questions from other letters that deal with a different aspect of this question.

Question One: "Are parents still responsible to provide a home, free of charge, and provide for most of the needs of adult children who are not yet married but earn an income?"

Question Two: "Wouldn't it be more important, especially for males, to encourage and require the adult child to save a portion of their present income for future marriage, such as a down payment on a house so money won't be wasted on renting?"

Question Three: "If rent is charged and paid, should this affect the division of labor and the overall authority of the parents over the adult child in the home?"

To the first question, I would say, absolutely not. Parents are not responsible in a case like that. However, there is no reason they should not, if they are able and want to — in other words, if all parties are in agreement. But the parents are not still responsible for the basic needs of an adult child who works.

Some parents might want to let the child live rent free on the condition he or she takes the money saved on rent and put it away for a nest egg. When Stephanie, our daughter who still lives at home, graduated from high school, I told her she had two choices: go to college or get a job.

I said, "You are not going to lie around here and let me take care of you. You have finished high school. Now if you want to go to college, fine. If you want to get a job, fine."

She did not want to go to college, and she did get a job. She buys her own clothes and takes care of her immediate needs. I provide her a place to live and her food. Also, I am encouraging her to save money for her own home later.

To the second question, I have to say, yes, you can and should *encourage* adult children who live at home to save money; but, no, you cannot *require* them to. How are you going to enforce that requirement? Threaten them with being put out on the street? But I certainly think you can encourage them to save money.

If you have the right children and the right parents, it is a joy to have adult children at home. Most parents want to help their children. For example, I do not want my children to go through the mess I went through to buy a house.

The third question sounded as if someone was saying, "If I pay rent, then I do not have any responsibilities in the home."

If an adult stays in a house, child or not, paying rent or not, there are some minimal things that person should do. Even if you rent an apartment, you have to leave that place the way you found it when you moved in — unless you do not mind losing a deposit and being charged for damages. So why should you do less at home?

However, again it depends on the family. If the child has been allowed to get away with murder all those years, the parents cannot suddenly begin to make him carry out the trash, or whatever. Our daughter helps her mother. She goes shopping for her and helps take the load off her mother in other ways. She washes the dishes sometimes and helps with Freddie — just little helpful things. She can stay the rest of her life as far as I am concerned. She pulls her weight.

Dealing With a Wayward Parent

"Dear Pastor Price:

"Greetings in the name of our Savior, Jesus Christ. I am writing you for some advice. I am a 20-year-old female, and my mother passed away three years ago.

"In September [a month after her death], my dad began seeing other women. What hurt me so bad was when he would have sex with them in the bed he shared with my mom. He has had about twenty different women here, and some of them have even stayed two or three nights in a row. Recently, one of them spent the night with her elementary age daughter, and all three of them slept in the same bed.

"Aside from his lewd sexual activity, my dad is an alcoholic. He used to beat my mom and brother and jumped on me three times. I am tired of his behavior. I have prayed and bound up demons. I don't blame God, Pastor Price. I love my Heavenly Father and thank Him every day for blessing me. But I even have thought about going to the authorities.

"Please respond."

"P. S. My sister and brother and I are saved and filled with the Holy Spirit. Supposedly my dad is saved, too. But he won't let my sister at age 16 date until she is 18. Yet he has sex with different women who sleep over at our house.

"P. P. S. You and your family are beautiful. I wish I had a dad like you."

What I told this young lady and her brother and sister is to get together and pray. They should not only pray over their father, but lay hands on his bed. Lay hands on his shirts. Lay hands on other things he wears, and bind the demons that are operating through him to cause that confusion.

What kind of example is that man giving his children? The Bible says to train up a child in the way he should go. The man claims to be a Christian, but what kind of an example is he training his children by? Number one, he is wrong about having sex before marriage, much less carrying on right there in the house. Fornication is wrong, and offending against the children and their consciences compounds the wrong. How he can do that as a Christian, I do not know!

If he is not saved, then he needs to get saved. Jesus loves him too and wants him saved. So I told this young lady to find out where he hides his bottles and lay hands on them. Bind the demons so that when he takes a drink of liquor, he will not even be able to drink it. Or he will drink it, and it will make him so sick, he will wish he had never seen that stuff.

Then if her father does not straighten up pretty soon, she is already 20. She needs to get a place for herself and her sister and brother to live together, and let their father stay by himself. Pray for him from afar.

This letter and response may help other people who have alcoholics in the family or have some sort of similar situation.

Bedtime, Eating, and Television

"Dr. Price, before you finish the series on Christian parenting and training up a child, would you discuss bedtime, eating, and TV-watching habits?

"I have kept children ranging from the ages of seven months to seven years. This age group reports watching television as late as 11 p.m. on week nights. Four-year-olds have told me in detail about adult pictures. I have had to stop children from getting with another child and literally acting out sexual intercourse scenes. I have seen very young children masturbating repeatedly. I have heard a three-year-old explain to another child the difference between kissing on the lips and with the tongue.

"I have had parents report that their children appear to transform from a human being to a demon. Many cartoons and movies are purely satanic, and the children watch them constantly.

"The majority of the children are junk food addicts. I have had children up to seven who have never been introduced to any kind of fruit or vegetable. Also, I have had a one-year-old who came with a cup of coffee.

"I keep children one to four, whose regular bedtime is 10 to 11 p.m. The parents report that they can't make the child go to bed.

"All of the children I keep have parents who are members of your church."

Let me address that last comment first. Do not think that because somebody comes to my church, or anybody's church, that they have sprouted wings and are heading immediately for Heaven. People go to church for all kinds of reasons, and their spiritual level of growth is at all different stages. Some come to church to "shop" for a husband or wife. Some come to "spy out the land" and report back somewhere else. Some come to find fault and criticize. Some come to learn but still have problems and patterns that God is working on.

I do not always know why certain people attend my church. I just have to assume that all of them are here for the Word of God, and I let them have it. If that is not their reason, that is between them and God. I lose no sleep over it, because there is nothing I can do about it. All other ministers are in the same boat. So just because people attend here, or any church, does not mean they are doing right and living right.

Now let's talk about bedtime.

Parents who cannot get their children to go to bed need to put them up for adoption. That may sound flippant or harsh, but I do not mean it that way. My point is that if you cannot do anything with them at four, you are headed for a disaster at fifteen and sixteen. You are sitting on an atomic bomb.

This lady who wrote me has an impeccable reputation, as far as I know, and I accept what she wrote as truth. But what she reported is certainly not the ways of raising children according to the Word.

However, what can you do when so many times you have children raising children? Many people may have adult bodies, but inside, they are still children. They need help, yet they are having babies and do not know what to do with them. They are the *parents*, yet they feel helpless to deal with children.

I never had any problems with my children going to bed. I told them, and they went to bed. It was just that simple. If you cannot deal with a four-year-old, you are in trouble. I am not saying children will go to bed on their own, because they will not.

You should fast and offer up offerings unto the Lord if you have a child who comes to you on a nightly basis and says, "Mommie, Daddy, I'm ready to go to bed."

You have a rare specimen on your hands. You should send that child to a university so maybe they can find out how to make up some pills to give to other people's children! Children will stay up as long as you let them. They will stay up until they fall out, until fatigue overtakes them.

But if you do not begin to train them early, you will have children who are going to be up all hours. The reason I never had any trouble with mine is that we began to train them early. I did not care whether they went to sleep or not, but they went to bed at a regular and reasonable hour. That is *training:* doing the same thing over and over for a period of time. For a while, Fred cried every time we put him to bed. But we kept on and kept on, and now he goes without fuss. He has found out crying, protesting, and fussing does no good. He is now trained to go to bed at 7:30 p.m. Now he goes without fuss and gets a good night's sleep.

The eating habits of an adult begins at home as a child. Nearly everyone will sneak a candy bar here and there outside, but that is not their major food supply. If kids are junk food eaters, they must not be eating at home, or junk food is all they are getting at home.

Parents have the responsibility to provide children with good nutritional meals. By and large, almost anybody should be able to provide an environment where the children do not become junk food "junkies."

And if kids are watching adult pictures, it is because certain channels are available on their television sets. That means Christian parents are watching movies they have no business watching in the first place. A Christian has no business having the Playboy channel coming into his house.

Should You Disregard Children's Opinions?

Here is another set of related questions:

Question One: "Are parents always justified in feeling that their child knows nothing and children's opinions and feelings are of no substance?"

Question Two: "Should parents always take the word of another adult as opposed to that of their child?"

No, I do not believe those attitudes are justified in either letter.

Children know a lot more than you think. I believe God even speaks to children or through children sometimes when they do not even know what they are talking about. God may speak through the child because the parents are not listening to each other.

I have heard God speak through my children so clearly that it shamed me sometimes. I realized that I was as wrong as a $3 dollar bill, and that God had used that child to get my attention.

You ought always to listen to your children's opinions. You certainly do not always have to, or even need to, take that opinion. But at least listen. You may have a genius on your hands, but you will never know it, if you do not listen. I do not think a parent ever should feel that a child does not know anything. Give a child opportunity for expression.

Withdrawn children often are shaped that way by parents who do not let them talk. How can husbands and wives communicate if they never learned as a child? It is very hard to become a communicator after you are an adult, as we discussed earlier in this book.

At home, we always had a sort of roundtable discussion at dinner time. We protected that family time by taking the telephone off the hook when we sat down to eat, so that everyone could eat and express himself or herself freely — within the bounds of wisdom — without being interrupted.

You will be surprised at the things that come out of your children's mouths. I learned to listen to my kids over the years, and I learned a lot of things. They even, as you might say, prophesied about some things.

They would say, "Now, Daddy, you just watch so-and-so," and sure enough, it has come to pass. So you would do well to listen. As I said, you do not have to take their advice if it is not right, but do not conclude that they do not know anything.

I hope you know that I am not talking about letting a child run off at the mouth, or be rude and opinionated, or attempt to tell adults what to do. I am talking about allowing your child to express an honest opinion in the proper place and at the proper time.

The person who wrote about parents taking the word of adults over children said:

"When I was a child, my parents believed that the adult was the one telling the truth, and the child would be lying. I personally experienced an adult lying to my mother, and she believed the adult over me."

The first thing I would say to parents is, "You ought to know your own children. Did you raise them? How did you provide an example in front of them? What did they see in you?"

I do not think adults are always right or will always tell the truth. Whether they tell the truth depends on their early training more often than not. I detest, hate, and cannot stand a liar. And I raised my children that way. I let them know early on, "You do not lie to me." So my children told me the truth, and I trusted and believed them. I never lied to them. I tell the truth if it hurts. It is not that I am so good or so spiritual. The decision to always tell the truth is a choice that I made.

I found out early that lying keeps you in a box. You tell a lie today and get away with it, then tell another tomorrow and get away with it. You might tell a lie the third month and get away with it. But somewhere along the line, you are going to have to compound your lies to keep that first one going. After a while, your lies will catch up with you. I have watched it. I have seen folks start out lying and go for years telling lies, but down the line, the lies caught up with them.

I would never just take an adult's word over a child's. I would interrogate both of them. But I know my children, and I have taught them by word and by example never to lie. So I would believe them over an adult.

I never lied to my children about the fat cat in the red suit coming down the chimney at Christmas. I did not lie to them about some reindeer flying through the sky. I did not lie to them about any of that, and the truth did not hurt their enthusiasm for Christmas and their excitement and expectancy in receiving and opening gifts. We have a great time at Christmas.

I know kids who were lied to about Santa Claus, then when they grew up enough to find out it was not true, they put Jesus right in the same box and thought He was a legend. One particular person who comes to my mind still had not budged off that opinion the last time I talked to him. I guess he had put his confidence so much in Santa Claus and had been so disillusioned that he was not going to believe in anyone else he could not see.

God does not like lying either. In fact, He said all liars will have their part in the lake, and He did not mean Tahoe. He meant the one that burns with fire and brimstone. The Word says it is impossible for God to lie. God's nature is one of truth, so He refuses to lie. It is impossible based on His nature.

If you have not raised your child to honesty, then he or she may lie to you, especially if it looks like an imminent judgment situation. But I would not accept the word of an adult over a child simply because he was an adult. I think each case would have to be decided on its own merits.

Here is a third letter with a similar question:

"Dear Pastor Price,

"My family and I have been born again and Spirit filled members of your church for about six years. When we first began to attend, you would have thought my father was Jesus. But over the years things have changed. Now you would think he is a demon.

"I have a few questions for you. Number one, do you think it is fair that a child does not have the right to speak his mind? For example, if something is said about my brothers, sisters, or myself that is untrue, my dad would believe it and not give us a chance to speak or to tell the truth. [In the answer above, I already dealt with this question.]

"Number two, my dad says he is saved. But I do not think a born again, tongue talking, active member of CCC should use profanity. For example, when he is mad at us, he [uses four-letter words and some very rough language.]"

Her third question was, "Do you think the right way of disciplining a seventeen- or eighteen-year-old girl is to slap her in the face?"

This is a *Christian* father? I agree with her. I do not think a born again member of any church should be using profanity, much less talking to his children in this way. No Christian, married or unmarried, father, mother, or child should be using language like that. That is foul, satanic, worldly speaking. It is not Christian language at all.

About being slapped in the face, I would have to say that is absolutely not the right way of disciplining anyone, whether six or seven to ninety. However, again, it would depend on the circumstances. You might have to slap someone to get their attention, to snap them out of hysterics or whatever. Also, it would depend on how hard you slap. But as an ordinary means of discipline, certainly not.

The Consequences of Negative Speech

"Dear Pastor Price,

"Your series on the family has been such a blessing. When you started the parent/child segment, I felt compelled to write. Hopefully, there are some parents out there who will listen.

"I came from a so-called nice Christian family. As a matter of fact, God's love was one of the things I was told would be taken from me because I was so terrible. The problem was that I could never do anything right. I was 'ugly, stupid, and lazy.'

"I realize raising children is difficult, but growing up is difficult also. I did not drink, use drugs, or sleep around with boys. Yet I never received one word of encouragement or one, 'I love you.' Instead, I was told how unlike them — my parents — I was. And how happy they would be when I got out of their house. I had no self-esteem. I could not even look someone in the eye and say, 'Hello.' I knew that if my parents hated me, everyone else must also.

"I never knew how to please them, so finally I gave up. As a young adult, I began to look for love in men, but fortunately, I realized early that was the wrong route to take.

"I had accepted Christ as a child, but He had always seemed so distant to me. At times, I even imagined He wanted nothing to do with me also. However, I knew in my heart that was ridiculous.

"I am finally learning to put the past behind me and allow God to heal the scars. I have had to sever contact with my family. I do not know if it was the right thing to do, but it was the only thing I knew to do to try to build some self-confidence.

"The sad thing is that I have talked to so many people whose parents treated them the same way. I guess a lot of people don't realize there is more to parenting than supplying room and board. I'm sure your children know how blessed they are to have parents who truly love them. God bless you and thank you for being an inspiration to so many people."

As I wrote in the section on the duties of a parent, the responsibility to provide includes providing an environment in which a child feels accepted. You should not downgrade your children in order to try to motivate them. You will never make them do the right thing by calling them stupid, dumb, and ugly, and saying, "You'll never amount to anything."

Faith comes by hearing, and you are programming negative faith into them. Destroying a child's self-esteem and sense of self-worth is a form of abuse. It certainly is not wisdom.

As a parent, ask yourself, "What kind of environment am I creating for my child or children? Is it one in which they can grow up and contribute to society?"

The way this woman was treated is certainly not love, and is emphatically not the way a Christian parent should treat a child. Children need to know they are of value to you and of value to God. You can show them that they are valuable and precious in a multitude of ways. They will know they are loved by the kind of environment you give them to live in. They will not have any doubt, and no one out there in the world can ever do anything to shake that when it is planted and grounded in them while they are young.

Eating Habits

"Dear Pastor Price,

"Although I have a long way to go before I arrive, at last I can see where I have come from. I wanted to write you in regards to the duties of parents.

"I am 26 years old, and before I started walking in the Word, I was very overweight. From the time I was a child, my parents trained me to always eat everything on my plate. If I said I was full, it did not seem to matter. Also, if I ever said I was hungry — watch out! I had more food than I knew what to do with.

"The fact that I was continuously growing larger and larger did not seem to matter. Don't get me wrong, Pastor Price, my parents are not entirely to blame. But I believe that if I had decent and orderly eating habits instilled in me as a child, that would have been half the battle.

"But praise God for His mercy and for the power of His Holy Spirit. I only have fifty pounds to go, and I will reach my goal. Also, God has blessed me with a fiance who cheers me on every step of the way.

"Please say something about this. I know from personal experience, it can be a big problem."

I watch my weight, and I am not overweight. But I never deliberately preach a sermon on being overweight, because I know that is a touchy area for some people. Whenever I mention it, I honestly believe it is the Spirit of God Who directs me. Some people have been helped, but others get upset.

However, the lady who wrote that letter has a very good point. Parents, it is as important to teach your child not to gorge and overeat as it is to provide enough of the right food to eat. A good start as a child helps a person be able to use self-discipline over food the rest of his life.

The Problem of Incest

"Hello, Dr. Price,

"I would like to share with you a blessing or one of the blessings that has taken place in my life.

"A lot of horrible things happened to me as far as sex is concerned starting at age three. You know when you are brought up a certain way, you tend to think a lot of kids are brought up the same. But at age five through eleven, I wised up. Then I knew better.

"As I write this letter, I can remember so clearly everything that took place. I must admit my daddy was and is today a very sick man. Dr. Price, I love my father. I always have and always will. I never ever, and God is my witness, held this against him, although I never knew why.

"At the age of five, my mother sent us to church. She was very sick at that time, but she wanted her children in a church. During that time, I memorized two scriptures. One was the Lord's Prayer, the second was the 23rd Psalm. Whenever my daddy made me do something, I would say inside of me, 'Lord, where are you? I need you. Now please help me. Somebody, someone, help me.'

"In the church my mother sent us to, I can't remember them ever talking about the name of Jesus. But at the ages of five, seven, and nine, I kept the faith.

"In my dreams then, there would be a man standing in a mist, and there would be a bright light upon His face. I didn't know then, but I know now that was Jesus. Every time I had this dream, He would talk to me and comfort me, and it would happen after Daddy sexually abused me.

"In the Word, He said He would not leave me nor forsake me. I know now without Jesus, I could not have made it on my own.

"Dr. Price, one more thing — if there is anyone else who has had the same experience and never forgiven the person, let me end my letter with this:

"Christ died for all of us. He was rejected, abused, spit upon, and nailed on the cross by man. Can you imagine being nailed in your hands and feet, pierced in the side, and after all that, forgiving them all? So how would I dare to hold anything against my father? He needs help."

That is surely not part of the duties of a parent to train your child like that. This young lady could have unforgiveness in her heart, and many people would think it justified. But she knows it is not right.

This may be an alert to some parent reading this. If you are abusing your child like that, you need to stop. That is not right. You are sowing seeds of destruction, not only to your child, but to yourself. That is a horrible way for a child to have to live.

But more horrible than to live with the memories is to live with unforgiveness. Bitterness, resentment, and hatred would compound the hurtful memories. Forgiveness allows Jesus to remove the hurt and heal the wounds.

Some of the things we have talked about in this book are not the most pleasant subjects to read about. But perhaps if someone had talked about these things when that father was young, he would not have abused his child. If somebody had talked about it — maybe. It certainly is time the Church started addressing the modern problems of life and stopped walking around them pretending they do not exist or that they do not happen to Christians.

In this book, we have seen the two institutions of marriage and family from God's viewpoint. Living by what our "guidebook," the Bible, says will result in the greatest degree of blessing, the greatest degree of love, and the greatest degree of fulfillment.

Part IV

INSIGHT ON FAMILY LIVING

by

Dr. Betty Ruth Price

Chapter 23

INSIGHT ON FAMILY LIVING

On the following pages, Dr. Betty Ruth Price, who has been married to Dr. Fred Price for more than 40 years, shares her personal insight on Christian family living. Because she genuinely believes in the power of prayer, she also shares the scriptures she has used over the years to secure and sustain a strong family unit.

Dr. Betty Price was ordained to the ministry of the Gospel in January, 1994. In addition to traveling worldwide with her husband as he ministers the Word of Faith, she is also often in demand as a speaker, particularly for women's conventions and seminars, on areas of concern for pastors' wives and women in general. She serves as a pastoral assistant at Crenshaw Christian Center, where her husband pastors.

"Behind every good man is a good woman," so the saying goes. For more than 40 years, the saying has held true for the wife of Fred Price. Dr. Betty Ruth Price has been the loving, devoted, supportive wife to her husband whose ministry has touched and affected thousands of lives in a positive way the world over.

As a married Christian couple, she and Fred exemplify for thousands the traits of marriage and family living that most deem worthy of emulation.

Wife, mother, in-law, grandparent, Betty Price has a wealth of Bible knowledge, coupled with experiential knowledge that has served her family well throughout the good times and the bad. She openly shares with others that same valuable knowledge she has learned throughout the years. Through the following questions placed to her, she provides wise counsel for successful Christian family living:

Question: What do you do when your husband refuses to listen to you concerning your business and family matters?

Dr. Betty: Once you have told him your concerns about the family and the other matters, then you have to leave it with God and trust God to speak to him. That is where prayer comes in. If you believe in prayer, then you will not worry about the situation; you will simply go about your business, confident that God will take care of your husband.

First of all, however, you have to be convinced that you are in a right relationship with God. You have to be convinced that you are important to God, and that He loves you. Once you have established a good relationship with the Father, you won't be concerned about your husband, your friends, or anybody or anything else.

You are going to have to believe God once you have spoken to your husband. Then just give that situation to the Lord. Now, that is the hardest part to do, because we tend to want to pick the problem up instead of letting it remain with the Lord. Too often we want God to solve the issue a certain way, and we want our husbands to act a certain way. But if we have truly given the situation to the Lord, we should be at peace. If we trust our lives to the Lord, we can trust our husbands to the Lord.

My advice, simply, is to be what you are supposed to be as a Christian, and God will take care of everything around you. I have learned that from personal experience. I began learning that very early in my marriage when I was quite young. I wanted my marriage to work, and I said, "If it doesn't work, I don't want to be the cause of it."

When two people come together, they are different people, often with different opinions. And if a problem arises, somebody has to yield. After all, how can two walk together unless they agree? The Bible tells us that. So, if one person does not yield, then you have to trust that person to the Lord. The Lord is going to confirm the person who is right. So, do what you are supposed to do, then trust the rest to the Lord.

Some people might say all of that is easier said than done. But how do you know whether or not it will work unless you do it. Just do what you are supposed to do, and I know from experience the Lord will work things out. I have personally experienced this. There were times when my husband thought he was right about a certain matter, and I disagreed. But during those times, I told him I was not spending all of my life fussing and arguing with anybody. I don't think that is what marriage is about. So, what I did in those times is simply tell him what I thought, and then I would go on with my life and let God speak to him.

Sometimes I would be right—but not always. But when I was right, God would speak to him, and he would come back and confess that he had been wrong.

Question: What if my husband is not seeking God's guidance? What should I do?

Dr. Betty: If you believe that God loves you, and God wants what is best for you, then God will work on your husband IF you are what you are supposed to be. If you are truly hearing from God and you are obedient to the Word, your husband will get in line. But this is where faith comes in.

Many times, things get messed up in a relationship because women want their way so badly that they end up fussing, complaining, and nagging. Your husband cannot even hear God speaking to him, because all your husband can hear is you nagging him. If you would be quiet, God could speak and your husband could hear!

Let God take charge and stop saying that your husband does not know what he is doing. Do not make that kind of confession. Just be prayerful. I always pray for my husband, that he will have wisdom and knowledge in everything that he does. God will be there on the scene, if you will only trust Him. Don't be so dependent upon your husband to give you the answers, trust God for all your answers. Trust God and God will work through your husband.

God ordained marriage and He wants it to be peaceful. And there is a way that it can be peaceful, but you will have to grow up in your marriage. The best way to do that is to create a oneness with Jesus Christ. Once you know who you are in Jesus Christ, then you can handle anything. But you have to grow. And you will grow if both of you desire that Jesus be the center of your life.

That is how Fred and I have made it through these more-than-42 years—by putting Jesus at the center. If you do that, you won't mistreat one another, and you won't do anything to the other person that Jesus wouldn't do.

In short, pray for your husband, if you believe he is wrong in some way. Then wait patiently. The Bible says to be not weary in well doing, for you will reap in due season if you faint not. But if you faint, you may never reap.

Question: My husband is in the five-fold ministry. He feels that in the beginning, when he begins traveling for ministry purposes, that I do not need to go because we have a family. But my feeling is that I should go as he goes. I was raised in a Baptist church, and I am leery about not traveling with my husband, because of some negative things I saw at conventions where many preachers came there looking for women. My husband and I agree that you and Fred are such wonderful examples, and he says that in the early part of Fred's ministry you stayed home.

Dr. Betty: I stayed home for only a very brief time. A lot of people wonder why Fred wants me to go with him all the time. He says it is for protection, in a way, because if the people see me there, they won't be so inclined to come up and hang around him. That's the way trouble starts. It's not that he thinks he will fall or yield, but he says it is very lonely out there. It is not a matter that he needs a bed partner as such, either, because when we are traveling, there's no time for bed! It's all work. But as his mate, I do think you need to be there with your husband.

Even though your husband believes he is called into a traveling ministry, God has to be the one to really get that in motion. Continue to pray about it. If God is in any decision either of you make, there will not be any unrest. It is something that both of you need to re-think and talk about, because you do not need anything like that to cause a breach in your marriage.

Question: I love my fiance, but there are some things he does that I do not like, and I do not want to compromise who I am in Christ.

Dr. Betty: You have to take a stand for what you believe. Too many women are afraid to take a stand on an important matter because they are afraid of losing a man. Well, I say let him go, if it means you will have to live apart from God in order to keep him.

When Fred and I first got married, he did not want to go to church on Sundays. He wanted to play baseball. But God was very real to me. I had a reverence for Him from the time I was a child, and I was not going to give up going to church just because Fred did not want to go.

I decided that he could go and do what he wanted, but God is more important to me than any man, so I was going to church. Anyway, Fred ended up following me to a revival meeting—mainly because we had just gotten married and he did not want me too far out of his sight. There was a little jealousy there. But when he followed me to that revival meeting, he received Christ that night. So, I can say because of my example Fred received Christ.

Question: My husband is in charge of the family budget, but how do I get the proper tithes released without being pushy? I have a budget of my own, so should I tithe from my allowance?

Dr. Betty: If your husband is not a Christian and he does not want you to tithe, it is not right for you to try to tithe out of the family finances. But you can tithe out of whatever money belongs to you— whatever he gives you. Surely the family will be blessed if you tithe out of all of the money, but your husband has to tithe out of his heart. No blessing will come if the tithe is not given from the heart. So, the best thing to do is to pray for your husband if he is a Christian and he does not want to tithe. In the meantime, you continue to be the wife that you ought to be and God will work with your husband. You can go ahead and give out of what comes into your hands personally and God will bless you for that.

Question: What does the Bible say about older women marrying younger men?

Dr. Betty: I have not read anything in the Bible about how old a person has to be in order to marry. But I believe wisdom would dictate some things. You have a brain, and some things you can think about for yourself.

First of all, if you marry a younger man, are you going to be able to keep up? That is, if he is quite a bit younger. Now if you can get a young man to agree with you about the important issues of life, and you can keep up with him then go ahead and do what you have to do. But there is no scripture that says, "Thou shalt not marry a younger man." God does not care. He only cares that the man be a Believer, and if he is walking in line with the Word.

Question: How do you make yourself available to your husband intimately all the time? I have been married 2-1/2 years and I am tired! Sometimes I just want to sleep. I am tired of the 4 AM wake-up calls.

Dr. Betty: I know the feeling. But you will live through it! When a couple first gets married, the husbands think they need sex every day. When I was young, I did not always respond every day. I am not going to lie and say that I did. I do not know if that was good; I did not always do the right thing when I was young, and I did not always really know how to pray.

As I got older, I began to know my husband, so I began to know the best time to be intimate. What I have done over the last 20 years or so is to set the time of our coming together. That way, my husband will be fulfilled and he won't feel left out. That way, those intimate times will be at *my* time, because I don't want to be awakened at 4 AM! Your body, at least my body, is still asleep at that hour! But for some people, early hours are good for them. So, really, it's an individual thing.

If your husband is a Christian, the two of you have to agree. Somebody has to yield when the time is right. There is this glamorous fantasy that some people have where lovemaking is always spontaneous. But I believe you do need to make plans, and it is no less fun than the spontaneous moments. But when you make plans, it is at *your* time, and you're rested.

If you have an overbearing husband, you will have to pray. Somebody must yield. No two persons are alike, and husbands and wives have different desires. There are all kinds of things that the partners need to agree on, including such things as techniques. You have to talk about those matters with one another.

There will be times when each of you will have to yield. That is why communication is so important. Your intimate times should be beautiful times. The reality, however, is that sometimes you are tired! And you might have to say, "Not tonight! I'm tired. But what about tomorrow?"

That is why I have learned to have a schedule. And whether I feel like it or not, I go on and yield to our time together—unless I am experiencing something so awful or unexpected that our schedule cannot be kept.

But I have found that even on those times when I did not feel like it, I have always enjoyed our time together. This is one of the greatest areas in which you can use your faith. You can walk by what you believe—walking by faith—not by how you feel. Simply because you do not feel like having sex does not mean you cannot do it; by faith, you can. So, on some of those occasions, I start out by faith—I start out with *no* feelings! That is the truth. But before it is over, I always enjoy it. You can do the same, by faith.

Question: What is a submissive woman?

Dr. Betty: Submission means to yield. Married people need to yield to each other. You are two personalities coming together and you have different viewpoints.

Question: I was married for about six years and have been divorced for seven years. I was a Christian and he was not, and I was trying to get him to receive the Lord. But he wouldn't. He was also mentally and physically violent to me. So, I finally made the decision to leave and get a divorce. I am doing fine, but I am being challenged about this now because he is now saved and he wants me back. But I still say "no." How can I deal with this now?

Dr. Betty: Unless God brings you back together, stick by your decision. If you have had no real occasions to be around him often, you still do not know if he is a Christian and if he has changed his ways. You do not have to take him back. After all, there is no law that says you do.

Don't let the devil put you into bondage concerning your divorce. Go on and live your life as unto the Lord—unless the Lord brings him back into your life, saved and walking in line with the Word of God.

Question: It is important for couples to take time away on vacations to renew and refresh their relationship. With your busy schedule, how do you and Fred have time for vacations?

Dr. Betty: We make sure that we have private times for ourselves, away from our day-to-day functions. Three times a year Fred and I take what we call mini-vacations. We just rest and relax. During the summer we take a two-week vacation. One week is spent with our children.

Question: Do you ever feel as though you are walking in the shadow of Dr. Price?

Dr. Betty: No. I am his helpmate. We complement one another. That is how I see it. It does not matter how big he looks to the public, or how famous he becomes, because we are one. When they are looking at him, they are looking at me. I do not feel left out at all.

Question: What is the key to your marital success since you have been married more than 40 years?

Dr. Betty: I believe the main thing in having a successful marriage is having a forgiving spirit. You have to allow your partner, your husband to make mistakes. Then you have to be forgiving and help him grow up and become what God wants him to be.

My Daily Prayer
for My Family
— Dr. Betty Ruth Price

"Father God, I thank You for a godly home, a godly husband, and godly children. I thank You that because we have made You, Father God, the Most High, our habitation, no evil shall befall us and no plague shall come nigh our dwelling, because you give your angels charge over us to keep us in all our ways. Your angels encamp round and about us to deliver us from any destruction.

"We are blessed because we fear you and delight greatly in your commandments. Therefore, our seed shall be mighty upon earth and they shall be blessed. Wealth and riches shall be in our house and our righteousness endureth forever. I thank You that we have the wisdom to make every decision that we need to make today in our homes, our marriages, with our children and on our jobs. Also, that our young ones are blessed in whatever decisions they need to make; such as their relationship to their peers, their teachers and their school work, etc. I thank You that they have sensitive spirits and alert minds and they will live for You all the days of their lives until Jesus comes.

"And I thank you for continued protection and provisions. I thank You for protecting Fred from any voice or spirit that is not from You, but surround him with those who are from You to help him fulfill the ministry that You have called him to.

"Continue to expose, reveal or remove any one or anything that is not right in the ministry or in our own personal lives that we might always be blameless in Your presence. Continue to give us an understanding heart to discern between the good and the bad for 'how can we judge this thy so great a people' (1 Kings 3:9). I commit this day to You Father that all that I do today will be done to the praise and glory and honor of Your name and to the exaltation of the name of Jesus. In His precious name I pray. Amen."

My Prayer Scriptures:

Because thou hast made the Lord, which is my refuge, even the most High, thy habitation;

There shall no evil befall thee, neither shall any plague come nigh thy dwelling.

For he shall give his angels charge over thee, to keep thee in all thy ways.

Psalm 91:9-11

The angel of the Lord encampeth round about them that fear him, and delivereth them.

Psalm 34:7

Praise ye the Lord. Blessed is the man that feareth the Lord, that delighteth greatly in his commandments.

His seed shall be mighty upon earth: the generation of the upright shall be blessed.

Wealth and riches shall be in his house: and his righteousness endureth for ever.

Unto the upright there ariseth light in the darkness: he is gracious, and full of compassion, and righteous.

A good man sheweth favour, and lendeth: he will guide his affairs with discretion.

Surely he shall not be moved for ever: the righteous shall be in everlasting remembrance.

He shall not be afraid of evil tidings: his heart is fixed, trusting in the Lord.

His heart is established, he shall not be afraid, until he see his desire upon his enemies.

He hath dispersed, he hath given to the poor; his righteousness endureth for ever; his horn shall be exalted with honour.

The wicked shall see it, and be grieved; he shall gnash with his teeth, and melt away: the desire of the wicked shall perish.

Psalm 112

That the God of our Lord Jesus Christ, the Father of glory, may give unto you the spirit of wisdom and revelation in the knowledge of him.

Ephesians 1:17

But my God shall supply all your need according to his riches in glory by Christ Jesus.

Philippians 4:19

BOOKS BY FREDERICK K.C. PRICE, PH.D.

HIGH FINANCE
God's Financial Plan: Tithes and Offerings

HOW FAITH WORKS
(In English and Spanish)

IS HEALING FOR ALL?

HOW TO OBTAIN STRONG FAITH
Six Principles

NOW FAITH IS

THE HOLY SPIRIT —
The Missing Ingredient

FAITH, FOOLISHNESS, OR PRESUMPTION?

THANK GOD FOR EVERYTHING?

HOW TO BELIEVE GOD FOR A MATE

MARRIAGE AND THE FAMILY
Practical Insight For Family Living

LIVING IN THE REALM OF THE SPIRIT

THE ORIGIN OF SATAN

CONCERNING THEM WHICH ARE ASLEEP

HOMOSEXUALITY
State of Birth or State of Mind?

PROSPERITY ON GOD'S TERMS

WALKING IN GOD'S WORD
Through His Promises

PRACTICAL SUGGESTIONS FOR SUCCESSFUL MINISTRY

NAME IT AND CLAIM IT!
The Power of Positive Confession

THE VICTORIOUS, OVERCOMING LIFE
(A Verse-by-Verse Study of the Book of Colossians)

A NEW LAW FOR A NEW PEOPLE

THE FAITHFULNESS OF GOD

THE PROMISED LAND
(A New Era for the Body of Christ)

THREE KEYS TO POSITIVE CONFESSION

(continued on next page)

BOOKS BY FREDERICK K.C. PRICE, PH.D.
(*continued*)

THE WAY, THE WALK,
AND THE WARFARE OF THE BELIEVER
(A Verse-by-Verse Study of the Book of Ephesians)

BEWARE! THE LIES OF SATAN

TESTING THE SPIRITS

THE CHASTENING OF THE LORD

IDENTIFIED WITH CHRIST:
A Complete Cycle From Defeat to Victory

THE CHRISTIAN FAMILY
Practical Insight for Family Living

THE HOLY SPIRIT:
THE HELPER WE ALL NEED

FIVE LITTLE FOXES OF FAITH

Available from your local bookstore

For a complete list of books and tapes by
Dr. Frederick K.C. Price, or to receive his publication,
Ever Increasing Faith Messenger, write

Dr. Fred Price
Crenshaw Christian Center
P.O. Box 90000
Los Angeles CA 90009